1989

CULTURAL AWARENESS IN THE HUMAN SERVICES

JAMES W. GREEN

University of Washington

With contributions by

Joseph Gallegos
Hideki A. Ishisaka
James W. Leigh
Nancy B. Miller
Calvin Y. Takagi
Theresa A. Valdez

Prentice-Hall, Inc., Englewood Cliffs, New Jersey 07632

Library of Congress Cataloging in Publication Data

Green, James W.
    Cultural awareness in the human services.

    (Prentice-Hall series in social work practice)
    Bibliography.
    Includes index.
    1. Social work with minorities.   I. Title.
II. Series.
HV3176.G73   362.8'4   81-15869
ISBN 0-13-195362-1   AACR2

Prentice-Hall Series in Social Work Practice
Neil Gilbert and Harry Specht, editors

In the country of the blind,
who are not as unobservant as they look,
the one-eyed is not king, he is spectator.

Clifford Geertz

Printed in the United States of America

10   9   8   7   6   5   4   3   2   1

Editorial/production supervision: Maureen Connelly
Cover design: Lee Cohen
Manufacturing buyer: John Hall

ISBN 0-13-195362-1

Prentice-Hall International, Inc., *London*
Prentice-Hall of Australia Pty. Limited, *Sydney*
Prentice-Hall of Canada, Ltd., *Toronto*
Prentice-Hall of India Private Limited, *New Delhi*
Prentice-Hall of Japan, Inc., *Tokyo*
Prentice-Hall of Southeast Asia Pte. Ltd., *Singapore*
Whitehall Books Limited, *Wellington, New Zealand*

CONTENTS

362.84
G751

132,923

iii

FOREWORD

This welcome addition to the social work literature reflects a commitment to promote a multiethnic perspective in the delivery of human services. As a society, we have begun to move from the perspective of cultural blindness associated with the melting-pot theory to a perspective of recognition and awareness based on a pluralistic view of recognition and awareness based on a pluralistic view of our society. Cultural awareness is a first step in equipping human service workers to engage more effectively with clients from communities that are culturally different from their own.

This book addresses two major needs: (1) the need for agencies to develop and deliver culturally relevant services, and (2) the need for college and university programs to develop and implement culturally relevant curricula. In human service agencies, there is an increasing recognition of the importance of cultural awareness in the development and maintenance of worker-client relationships. While it is frequently noted that white workers need to acquire an awareness of the different cultures of both clients and co-workers, it is equally important for minority workers to become knowledgeable about the backgrounds of other cultural groups (for example, black workers delivering services to Native American communities or Hispanic workers delivering services to Asian communities).

In addition to acquiring cultural awareness of others, whether they be clients or co-workers, it is also important that workers acquire greater awareness of their own cultural backgrounds. This process involves searching for and understanding one's own roots, whether one is a black American, an Irish American, a Polish American, or a Native American. One of the basic tenets of social work practice is the effective use of self. This proposition needs to be supplemented with the concept of effectively using one's cultural self as well.

It is also useful for social workers to gain a cultural awareness of their own profession as a special group. The social work profession is similar in some respects to an ethnic group. It has its own culture, tradition, beliefs, and socializing processes. There is almost as much cultural variation within the profession (for example, behaviorists, psychodynamically-oriented therapists, grass-roots organizers, and agency planners) as one might find, for instance, in the Asian community (for example, Japanese, Chinese, Koreans, Pilipinos, and Vietnamese).

In addition to the need for cultural awareness in agency practice, there is an equal need for cultural awareness training on the campuses of our universities, where future social workers are being educated. The cultural perspective has usually been a part of course offerings related to human behavior and the social environment. Yet there remains a need for cultural awareness education in casework and direct service method courses. Traditionally, the teaching of interventive practice has assumed that a fully understood and implemented counseling or casework approach has universal application to all clients. This assumption, as this book makes clear, is in need of constant reassessment, as social workers deal with clients from different ethnic backgrounds.

The increase in minority students and minority faculty members on our campuses over the past decade has heightened the sensitivity of educators to the need for additional courses which feature the special knowledge and skills that are relevant to minority communities. Many of the recently developed courses emphasize the role of the family and the degree to which family concerns in many different minority communities take precedence over individualistic concerns. The arrival of minorities in schools of social work and the emergence of new courses culminated in 1972 in the passage by the the Council on Social Work Education of a new accreditation standard (1234a), which states: "A school is expected to demonstrate the special efforts it is making to enrich its program by providing racial and cultural diversity in its student body, faculty, and staff."

As a result of increase enrollments of minority students and the recruitment of minority faculty members, many new courses related to specific minority communities have been developed. Out of this experience a need has emerged for a multiethnic perspective, which would give as much attention to the commonalities across ethnic groups as to the differences.

This search for commonalities provided the foundation for the development of this book, a search which involved interested minority and nonminority faculty members at the University of Washington School of Social Work in the winter of 1977. A discussion process based on sharing personal experiences began under the able leadership of Professor Calvin Takagi. By the spring of 1977, general consensus had been reached that a Curriculum Development Project proposal should be submitted to the State of Washington Title XX Agency, for the purpose of identifying both cultural commonalities and the unique differences with which all students of social work should be familiar. A Curriculum Development Project was begun in July of 1977 and concluded in the summer of 1979. The conceptual leadership required for this search for commonalities was provided by Professor James Green, a cultural anthropologist with experience in the social services, assisted by Collin Tong. A training manual, along with companion video training tapes, resulted from the Curriculum Development Project. This book is a subsequent revision and elaboration of certain ideas and themes identified during that project. It has benefited from and is the result of many hours of discussion, especially the insights about direct service practice with minorities supplied by Professor James Leigh and Professor Anthony Ishisaka, as well as the insights about community practice provided by Professor Theresa Valdez and Professor Joseph Gallegos.

While this book represents an important beginning, there are still many tasks that lie ahead. A future agenda for training and research in the area of minority content might include companion texts related to social work practice in each of the four minority communities identified in this book. In addition, it would be helpful for future students of social work to be exposed to a text that addresses the uniqueness of white ethnic groups (for example, Irish Americans, German Americans, or Polish Americans). There is also a need for a companion text that deals with cultural awareness in the arena of planning, administration, and social policy. And finally, it would be useful to see an in-depth text that addresses the issues of social work research in minority communities. Each of these text obviously would enhance existing courses in both undergraduate and graduate social work education.

The development of this text was made possible by the collaborative efforts of the Center for Social Welfare Research and the Multi-Ethnic Training Project at the University of Washington School of Social Work. It is being published as a result of a collaborative agreement between the authors, the School of Social Work, and Prentice-Hall, with the assistance of Dean Scott Briar and the Prentice-Hall Series Editors, Neil Gilbert and Harry Specht. This agreement includes the donation of all author royalties to a minority student scholarship fund at the University of Washington School of Social Work.

This book represents a milestone in faculty collaboration, commitment, and hard work. The substantial dedication of the authors to the issues of minority communities is reflected in every chapter. Much pleasure and satisfaction was derived from playing a role that facilitated the development and completion of this important book.

Michael J. Austin, Director
Center for Social Welfare Research
School of Social Work
University of Washington
May 1981

PREFACE

This book is the consequence of a concern, shared by all the authors, that the interests of clients, particularly minority clients, are poorly represented in the curricula of schools of social work and in the day-to-day practices of many social service organizations. There are many reasons for this, but two that must be cited are the lack of a satisfactory conceptual basis for guiding research and practice as they pertain to minority communities, and the inadequacy of existing training for those who work with minority clients. During a two-year curriculum development project, the authors systematically examined the literature of social work and discovered a striking gap between what is known about cultural diversity in the social sciences, particularly in anthropology, and what is said and done about it in social work. This book, then, represents an effort to draw out some of the implications of a cross-cultural perspective for social services.

Those familiar with anthropology will recognize the intellectual sources on which various portions of the book depend. Frederik Barth's conceptualization of ethnic group relations provides the general framework for the discussion of cross-cultural encounters. To explicate some of the complexities of those encounters, I have used an adaptation of the health-seeking behavior model developed by Arthur Kleinman. His approach seems to me to be suitable for describing a wide range of service encounters. It has the added value of having been tested cross-culturally and represents a significant advance in efforts to understand how people behave when confronted with crises. James Spradley's work on ethnosemantics and ethnographic interviewing was the impetus for the discussion on language and data collection procedures. I have found his approach to be particularly useful in classroom teaching and in training workshops. Of course, all of these authors have developed their ideas in far more detail than has been presented here. But I do not believe I have done violence to them. Rather, I have tried to convey something of the importance of what they have said to those who would provide culturally responsive and responsible social services.

It is important to note at the very beginning, however, that there is no way by which cross-cultural sensitivity can be easily acquired. Those who believe that the task can be accomplished in short-term workshops or by indulgence in a few training exercises will be disappointed. The ability to move smoothly and effectively between contrasting cultural worlds is the result of intensive training and persistent effort, but especially commitment over a long period of time. Margaret Mead (1978) once referred to anthropological fieldwork as "displined subjectivity" and that seems an apt description for culturally responsive social work as well. Cultural awareness is not an ornamental adjunct to other social service skills, but has features that are distinctively its own. It emphasizes the pre-eminence of the perspective of members of specific cultures, the wholistic nature of all cultures as complex and comprehensive designs for living, and the power of the comparative method for generating insight into the variety of human needs and concerns. Each of the chapters of this book elaborate on these themes in various ways.

Chapter 1 considers what it is we mean by ethnicity, particularly as it is expressed by clients in encounters with social workers. This is a necessary first step since popular, stereotypic, and even prejudical opinions of the nature of cultural variations are as common among students as they are in the population at large. We distinguish between the older but more familiar categorical conception of ethnicity and a newer, more useful transactional approach, one which permits us to focus on both the content and context of cross-cultural encounters.

Chapter 2 examines the notion of help-seeking behavior and explicates the component parts of the worker-client relationship in cultural terms. Each component is illustrated with examples taken from the ethnographic and social service literature. Help seeking as a process of utilizing specific cultural resources is the critical idea for understanding the significance of cultural differences in service relationships.

Chapter 3 on cross-cultural social work examines ways the worker can begin to acquire cultural awareness. The discussion centers on the idea of "ethnic competence," a term suggested to me by James Leigh, co-author of the black community paper in this book. The chapter describes ways that workers can examine their relationship to help seeking as it occurs among their clients.

Chapter 4 discusses the critical matter of language, the worker's most important tool. It suggests an interviewing approach that can be used to facilitate learning about the cultural background of others. I do not propose it as a substitute for other interviewing styles common to social work, although as a technique it may have therapeutic as well as information-gathering potential.

The chapters on the various ethnic groups explore ways the social services have (and have not) met the needs of minority clients and minority communities. Each of the authors of those chapters suggests something of the importance of knowing about specific cultural traditions in relation to social services. A short introduction to the chapters links them to the conceptual issues introduced earlier in the book and briefly considers the critical issue of "individualizing the client." An appendix contains a number of cross-cultural learning activities to be used in conjunction with the text.

Something must be said about the scope and limitations of this effort. As authors, we have tried to suggest something of the potential in viewing the field of social services from an ethnographic or anthropological perspective. No claim is made for comprehensiveness, since the literature of both disciplines is extensive. Only a detailed, heavily documented monograph could have cited every issue of substance and every article of relevance. The choice of theoretical perspective, while not arbitrary, represents only one of many ways that the linkage between anthropology and social services could be developed. But as a choice, the help-seeking approach seems to make sense, since it is directly applicable to the educational and training needs of social workers and suggests as well some of the concerns of a nascent applied anthropology. The entire argument, however, should be understood as one large and tentative formulation concerning the relationship between a people's culture, their personal and collective problems, and the institutions and programs of organized benevolence established by the larger society.

Of course, there can be no assurance that cultural awareness training and research alone will lead to improved services for minority or ethnic group clients. Much in the quality of services is a matter of good will as well as technique. Our concern as authors has been to identify some of the ideas and skills that we believe will be necessary in order to act on that will. Good intentions are not good enough. They must be tempered by knowledge and matched by capability.

I wish to acknowledge the kind permission of Clifford Geertz for use of his comment on epistemology at the beginning of this book. It is reprinted by permission of the *Bulletin* of the American Academy of Arts and Sciences. In addition to my co-authors, a number of individuals have contributed to this effort. Some were available as commentators on the developing manuscript and they offered their ideas and criticisms in numerous and helpful ways. Others, not directly connected to the work of writing, nevertheless provided much valued personal support, especially during times that were bleak. Most particularly, I am grateful to Carol C. Green who has been patient and sympathetic throughout. Morally and materially she has subsidized this work and I thank her. I also wish to thank Michael Austin, Ann Metcalf, Trevor L. Chandler, Linda Wilson, Andrew Callium, Margaret Gibson Marshall, and old friends Lawrence Epstein and Gary T. Henderson. Sandy Brown very capably typed the manuscript. While the responsibility for my words is my own, some part of each of them is here.

James W. Green
Seattle

PART ONE
CULTURAL ASPECTS OF SOCIAL SERVICES

CHAPTER ONE
ETHNICITY AND SOCIAL SERVICES

Cultural variation among human populations is one of the most enduring character-istics of our species. It is a fact of our past and present, and we can be assured of it in the future. Yet this fact stands in opposition to one of the most persistent and stable cultural themes in our national life: the belief that ours is a society without the disruptive divisions of class, caste, or provincial interest that plague people and governments in other parts of the world. The recent expression of almost faddish interest in ethnicity and in finding one's "roots" in faraway places hardly challenges the pervasive melting-pot notion that we are all, under the skin, essentially the same, desiring and seeking similar things. In this view, ethnic differences are orna-mental embellishments of only marginal significance to the aspirations we all share as Americans.

A more sobering view is that cultural differences reflect fundamental varia-tions in what people hold to be worthwhile, and that as long as these variations persist they will invite comparison and questioning of the practices and values of the larger society. Cultural differences and their defense are often perceived as threatening, particularly when claims to ethnographic distinctiveness are asserted and celebrated by persons of distinctive "racial" or ethnic background. It is dis-concerting to acknowledge that members of historically stigmatized racial and ethnic groups often do things their own way, not just because they have been ex-cluded from mainstream institutions by prejudice and discrimination, but because they find the values and institutions of the larger society inferior to their own.

The preference for cultural homogeneity, be it expressed as ethnocentrism, racism, or some other principle of exclusion, runs deep in any society. In a multiethnic society such as our own, it is a source of conflict in relations between groups and between individuals. This issue is a particularly troublesome one in social services, where social workers often deal with individual problems of the most intimate and personal kind. As professionals with the authority and power of their position, they can have enormous influence in guiding people's choices and influencing their values. But that creates a dilemma. Should an assumption of melting-pot uniformity, a belief in the essential similarity of people's needs and desires, underlie the worker's suggestions for problem resolution among ethnically distinctive clients? Or should the worker attempt to encourage problem resolution in terms of ethnically distinctive values and community practices, matters the worker may not fully understand or even support?

The argument made here, and made very explicitly, is that social services can and should be provided to people in ways which are culturally acceptable to them and which enhance their sense of ethnic group participation and power. This means that the worker, the service agency, its policies, and supportive educational and training programs all have the obligation to meet the client not only in terms of the specific problem presented but in terms of the client's cultural and community background as well. That obligation is most difficult to meet where the worker, the agency, its policies, and its educational programs are representative of the interests of only one of the significant groups in our society, namely English-speaking whites of predominantly middle- and professional-class origins.

But difficult or not, there are a number of reasons why social workers should be concerned with cross-cultural relationships in their work. First, ethnic and minority group clients are entitled to competent, professional social services, as are all other persons. Because of the prominence of consumer movements and of political and economic demands for better delivery of social services, minority clients can be expected to become more critical and outspoken about how they are treated in the future. The inadequacy of existing services is suggested by the growing number of programs and agencies oriented to the problems of specific ethnic groups, often managed and staffed by members of ethnic and minority communities. Similarly, minority professionals are becoming increasingly visible in social work. Like their clients, they look forward to an end of tokenism, both in services and in professional employment. They expect and sometimes insist that programs and policies change to accommodate their concerns and those of the people they represent. Nonminority social workers, especially those who cannot perceive that changes are coming and who may not be prepared for them when they arrive, may find themselves more a part of the problem than contributors to solutions. That would be an awkward position for individuals and for a profession explicitly committed to the welfare of others.

There is a second reason why social workers should give careful attention to the nature of cross-cultural contacts in their professional work. That reason, simply, is a history of gross insensitivity to the cultural differences manifest in their clients. Examples are not difficult to find. In 1973 a survey was conducted among a group of social service workers in Alaska, workers who had daily contact with a number of urban Eskimo (Jones 1976). The findings of that survey reflected a variety of worker attitudes toward the Eskimo. For example, one worker observed that "Natives have been improperly socialized. They haven't even been socialized to drink properly" (Jones 1976: 335). Despite the fact that the Eskimo have survived for thousands of years in one of the world's most harsh environments, another worker stated confidently that "Natives have no long-range goals. They don't understand anything about planning for the future." Although the Eskimo have been long known to anthropologists as a people with a finely developed sense of humor and decorum, one that assures emotional survival in tiny living spaces during the Arctic winter, one worker told an interviewer that the "Natives have no psychological awareness; they don't know how to verbalize and express their emotions." He added that in his work with Eskimo clients, "it doesn't matter what they say because our central task is to teach them to verbalize and express emotions: nothing can deter us from that" (ibid.).

It would be too generous to refer to these comments as instances of simple misunderstanding or ignorance. They are, rather, blatant expressions of racism. The fact that they were embellished with psychological jargon or presented authoritatively as official "expertise" does not make them less vicious or hurtful. Nor is the problem ameliorated by the fact that "good intentions" and a "desire to help" motivated the people who offered these remarks. Motives aside, the comments reflect an ethnocentric and condescending quality in worker relations with Eskimo clients. If the survey comments appear to be extreme and unrepresentative of the social service profession generally, they did not seem so to the people who made them.

A third reason for examining cross-cultural encounters in social work has to do with how the profession has conceptualized its involvement with ethnic communities generally. Despite years of work with minority clients, practitioners have rarely considered in any systematic way what their relations to minority communities ought to be. Where there have been descriptions of social work among minority clients, as in the social work journals, the individual characteristics of clients or their problems in communicating with service workers have been emphasized. Little attention has been given to the cultural background of minority clients or to how that background influences the way social services are used. Even so-called "ecological" approaches have been generally limited to immediate family relations or personal networks, with little reference to the cultural setting in which family and social life are embedded. Nor do most texts in the field make much reference to ethnicity as a factor in human services, community organization, or policy and planning. Indeed, most discussions of ethnicity, culture, and minority status in social work can be found only in isolated research reports, in obscure program evaluations, and in angry position papers. They often occur in obscure government documents or published conference papers which are not widely distributed and are difficult to find. The relative invisibility of ethnicity in the social work literature belies its importance to minority group clients and to the social work profession as a whole.

The fact of regular and continuing contact between social workers and persons of minority background, the apparent ignorance of cultural differences attending many of those contacts, and the absence of a conceptual framework within social work for accommodating cultural variation all seem to suggest a need to look at the idea of ethnicity insofar as it is important to the delivery of culturally responsive social services. Our problem, then, is to define a model for cross-cultural social work. It must be one which is applicable to all cross-cultural encounters, regardless of the ethnic or cultural identity of the participants. It must organize ethnographic information on clients in a systematic way. It must be useful for a range of social service activities—be they oriented toward children, the aged, the handicapped, or the abused. The model must suggest hypotheses for direct services and policy research, and its training implications must be made explicit. With such a model, it should become possible to critique and to improve services to ethnic and minority clients in ways that are responsive to their ethnographic heritages and their cultural preferences. We can begin by clarifying some of the concepts that will be important throughout this book.

CRITICAL CONCEPTS

Various terms are used to describe and account for the difference among human beings. Some are useful, some are not. The least useful concept is that of "race," and we will have little use for it here. While perceived differences in "race" may be socially meaningful to the participants in a cross-cultural encounter, "race" as such has no standing as a scientific or analytical category. A race is not a culture, although that belief is common with many people. The word "race" is associated with a set of Euro-American folk concepts which are indiscriminately and widely applied to groups of people who, because they are culturally and sometimes phenotypically or physically different, have been labeled as something less than fully human. "Races" exist only to the degree that phenotypic characteristics of individuals, such as skin color or hair form, are given prominence as criteria for allocating or withholding social and economic benefits. In nature there are no "races," only populations of organisms which can be described in terms of such natural forces as selection, genetic change, and reproductive characteristics. Race is really a social concept, not a biological one, and it serves no purpose other than to make and justify invidious distinctions between groups of people.

Unlike "race," the concept of "culture" is of considerable importance for advancing our understanding of ethnicity. But the term lacks clear, specific, agreed-upon meaning. There are literally hundreds of definitions of "culture" (Kroeber and Kluckhohn 1952). Some are cognitively oriented, stressing what is known and shared by the members of a group as their collective "cognitive map" of reality. In this perspective, culture is viewed as knowledge, and the study of culture is taken to mean the study of meaning (Spradley 1972, 1979). Other definitions emphasize behavior and customs and their transmission from generation to generation. For some, culture is said to be an expression of the possibilities inherent in the way people use their material resources (Harris 1968). But like the terms "life" in biology or "gravity" in physics, the word "culture" has to be given some fairly precise meaning before it is useful as an analytic tool. One could argue, for instance, that in cross-cultural relationships, culture can be thought of as those elements of a people's history, tradition, values, and social organization that become implicitly or explicitly meaningful to the participants during an encounter. For instance, if a white practitioner discussed with an Indian client the removal for adoption of the client's child, the very fact that the interview was conducted in English would be culturally meaningful to the client, if not to the worker, because English is the language of the dominant society. An equally explicit cross-cultural feature of the relationship would be evident if the client proposed that the child be placed with grandparents who understand Indian culture, rather than removed from the community. The culturally sensitive worker would recognize the client's proposal as a reference to an entire set of group-specific values on the role of older persons as having authority and providing advice to younger adults as well as to children. A cultural element—intergenerational family patterns within the group—would have been introduced into the encounter.

This definition of culture, as being made up of those things which are relevant to communication across some kind of social boundary, is an established one in studies of ethnicity (Barth 1969). It has the advantage of being more precise than most. It also suggests where one must look in order to discover cultural differences. It assumes that some of the things that characterize the background and experience of each individual are, at least at the moment of communication, more important than other things. This is particularly critical in the assessment of client problems and, as we will see, in "individualizing the client," one of the critical tasks of social work intervention. It is this sense of culture, then, as something identifiable in people's behavior and thinking and something which can be anticipated in encounters with them, that we have in mind when we use the term "culture."

The word "minority" refers to something altogether different. Minority status persons need not be perceived by others as ethnically distinct, although they often are. (Indeed, there is considerable debate among black scholars as to whether the distinctive characteristics of the black community derive from cultural features of African origin or are a consequence of minority status and exploitation in America.) Nor must persons of minority status be an actual numerical minority, as the women's movement has made quite clear. Minority standing refers to power, not numbers, and the degree to which the individuals who are identified with some group may be denied access to privileges and opportunities available to others. One could speak of minorities as "communities of interest" (Weaver 1977), those who may share a similar set of values, lifestyles, and expectations, but whose most common and definitive trait is that they are exposed to a similar set of limiting political and economic circumstances. In this sense, the term "minority" refers to social and economic disability, not to cultural differences. Categories such as "black" or "Native American" contain a multitude of groups and cultures. But most blacks and most Native Americans compose a "community of interest" when, as minorities, they cannot take for granted equitable access to opportunities or rewards.

Finally, what of social class? If all minority groups were not only culturally distinctive but also self-contained social classes, within a single hierarchy of social stratification, then the tangle of conceptual terminology would be less confusing. But the fact is that cultural distinctiveness and minority status can be found at many social "class" levels. The concept of class is most commonly used to describe a population according to such objective traits as education, income, occupation, and sometimes religious affiliation. But individuals may act in accordance with their perceived class interests in some situations and in accordance with their cultural preferences or minority identity in others. However useful the notion of class may be for categorizing people for some purposes, by itself it may not be adequate for a full appreciation of human differences as they relate to direct, face-to-face, social service encounters. This is because there is so much more about the individual that the social worker must know than the objective criteria of education level, job classification, or similar features. Beliefs, values, behavioral expectations, communication styles, and related characteristics of the individual are important, and these belong to what is usually thought of as cultural background. The individual's social class identification is an addition to these more fundamental features, not a summary of them.

It is clear, however, that none of these terms—culture, minority, or social class—are entirely adequate in describing the problems that occur between workers and clients in cross-cultural encounters. All the terms overlap with one another in important ways, yet they are not interchangeable. "Culture" has been used too often to refer to anything that seems "different" in the looks, behavior, or values of others. In this way, it serves as an after-the-fact "explanation," not as a guide for analysis and understanding. "Minority," referring to power, does not really concern cultural variation. There are many culturally distinct people who are minorities and many who are not. The idea of "class" is difficult to apply in pluralistic societies and is so general that it does not help us to understand group differences occurring within same-class levels. Recognizing, then, that there are terminological and conceptual problems involved in defining and discussing class, minority, and cultural differences and that we will not be able to resolve them all here, we can ask instead a more limited question: Is there a concept of cultural variations that could be particularly useful in understanding cross-cultural social service encounters, regardless of the social characteristics or the relative power of the groups or individuals involved? We will argue that the concept of ethnicity, as it has recently been developed among anthropologists, is useful in that way. Properly understood, it can enable social workers to better understand the relationship of their profession to distinctive cultural and minority communities. It can assist them in a critique of the adequacy of existing social services. And it may suggest ways in which cultural information can be integrated in social work practice. The idea of ethnicity represents a uniquely cross-cultural approach to social work intervention.

CONCEPTS OF ETHNICITY:
CATEGORICAL AND TRANSACTIONAL

⟜ Within the social sciences, a variety of approaches has been devised for analyzing ethnicity, and numerous definitions have been proposed. Common to most definitions are three elements. First, members of an ethnic group have a sense of a shared past and similar origins. The historical accuracy of their origin beliefs is not important. Simply that such beliefs are shared and discussed is enough. Second, members of an ethnic group believe themselves to be distinctive from others in some significant way. Again, the strengths with which those beliefs are held is more important than their accuracy. Third, ethnicity is most important at those times when members of differing groups are in contact. A comparative experience is necessary, so that individuals become aware of their own cultural uniqueness in their relations with others and can then act upon that awareness.

– Based on these generalizations, a number of explanatory models to account for ethnicity have been devised. For convenience, we can think of them as falling into two broad categories: (a) those explanations which treat ethnicity as a categorical phenomenon, and (b) those which approach ethnicity as a transactional one (Bennett 1975). The differences between these two approaches are significant in accounting for cultural variation, and they have differing implications for matters of practice and policy in social services. By categorical explanations of ethnicity, we mean those which explain cultural difference according to the degree to which individuals or groups manifest specific, distinctive traits. Because individuals may dress, talk, eat, or act in specified ways, they are categorized as culturally different, and that difference is named. A categorical account of ethnicity is pigeonholing one. Differences are "explained"—in fact, they are only enumerated—by listing the traits that make group X different from group Y. By contrast, a transactional definition of ethnicity concerns the ways in which people who are communicating maintain their sense of cultural distinctiveness. Behavior in cross-cultural encounters, particularly behavior which emphasizes difference, is the sign and substance of ethnicity. Categorical definitions of ethnicity tend to equate a culture, a population, and a group as though these were identical and overlapping categories. Transactional approaches to ethnicity focus on strategies for defining and preserving cultural differences. Categorical definitions of cultural variation are structural; they name discrete categories and fill them with cultural content or "traits." (Traits, of course, then become the fodder of stereotypes.) Transactional definitions treat ethnicity as an element of behavioral and cognitive participation in the decisions and symbolic constructs which supply meaning to communication (Bennett 1975: 4).

◄ Popular notions of ethnicity, particularly the two that dominate American thought, are examples of the categorical approach to cultural variation. Both the older "melting-pot" ideology and the more recent theory of cultural pluralism assume that ethnicity exists as the survival and embodiment of a series of distinctive or "ethnic" traits historically associated with particular groups. In the melting-pot model, however, that diversity is expected to recede as each group adopts selected traits from the others and gradually submerges its own distinctiveness. Eventually a new, singular, national social identity, one without the divisiveness associated with "race" or class, is expected to appear. That this has not happened, and probably will not, seems evident, as pointed out by Glazer and Moynihan (1963) years ago. While the melting pot model no longer has credence in social science, in much popular thought it still provides a basis for making judgments about others and, in that sense, it often functions as an ideology (Wellman 1977). Thus, groups or individuals are described as more or less "acculturated" or "assimilated," a reference to the extent to which they are presumed to have given up their claims of ethnic uniqueness in favor of the generalized cultural characteristics thought to be typical or desirable for the larger society. There is often associated with this kind of explanation an implicit scale of degrees of acculturation. Individuals who retain their native language, food preferences, or occupations are said to fall at the "traditional" end of the scale. Those who appear to have given up entirely their ethnic lifestyle are "integrated" or "assimilated" into the larger community.

⤙ The melting-pot approach, with its assumptions of acculturation and assimilation, is severely limited, however, as a way of understanding cultural differences, and it will not well serve the culturally sensitive social worker. First, there is no historical evidence that the variety of groups that make up American society are merging into a homogeneous whole. Acculturation for Native Americans, for instance, has really been a euphemism for cultural genocide. (If the word "genocide" seems too strong, the statistics of Indian mortality over the past two or three centuries should be reviewed, or the impact of federal land and education policies on Indian peoples investigated.) Similarly, efforts to preserve ethnic distinctiveness rather than to submerge it can be found in the bilingual education movement among Spanish speakers. It is especially strong in California and the Southwest and among some Native Americans as well. The issue is not simply the right of Hispanic children to be taught in Spanish in classrooms. What is at issue is preserving cultural identity and protecting Hispanic values, because those values are important to people as a way of organizing their lives (Arvizu and Snyder 1977, Gibson and Arvizu 1977). Melting-pot acculturation as a long-term national trend simply has not and does not now exist.

⤙ Second, the acculturation and assimilation approach is offensive to the idea of delivering culturally sensitive social services, because it suggests a uniformity of agreement in the larger society, and subsequently between client and worker, as to which things in life are desired and which are not. Culturally responsive social programs and intervention require exploring alternative values and resources available in the client's own community and helping the client to identify and use those resources, while at the same time monitoring the outcome of any intervention, using criteria appropriate to the client's community and its expectations. To substitute the worker's personal or professional standards for judging outcomes, without reference to the values and institutions indigenous to the client's back-ground, would be to impose solutions that may not meet the client's own interests.

⌐Cultural pluralism, a more recent innovation in popular thinking about eth-nicity, is also based on the categorical approach and, as such, shares the limitations of that model. It stresses the distinctiveness of ethnic groups and the need for them to live in a kind of separate-yet-equal harmony. Unlike the melting-pot view, the pluralist response to ethnicity is based on an appreciation of cultural differences. The argument is made that the ethnic group provides the individual with a primary basis for loyalty and affiliation; that ethnic differences are good in themselves; and that ethnic differences contribute strength, not weakness, to the larger community. While this argument has powerful appeal, particularly for persons of liberal or hu-manistic persuasion, it is not without problems. It can and has been used as a kind of "enlightened" cultural relativism, rationalizing the exclusion of some groups from full social and political participation. An example is the once-popular "culture of poverty" theory, which was used to explain why "they" are not like "us" and to justify programs that attack "their" problems, problems which may be as much a part of the larger society as of a particular group.

─The categorical approach always requires that the outsider view the ethnicity of others as a combination of traits that those others exhibit: their "color," their musical styles, their food, and sometimes their poverty. If the fashion of the times romanticizes these things as "their" way, this provides a justification for doing little or nothing to change debilitating circumstances. It also diverts attention from the fact that many people live as they do because to some extent the larger society permits them few alternatives. Carried to its most extreme, one could argue that slave plantations, Indian reservations, and World War II detention camps for Japanese-Americans were examples of pluralism. Obviously, no one thinks of them that way, because they were imposed through force by one group on another. But rural slums in the South for blacks and in the West for Indians have been viewed by the uninformed in terms of ethnic quaintness and authenticity. Pluralism, by itself, is not an approach which will help us to understand the significance of ethnic and minority group status for the individuals concerned. Rather, it is an intellectual device for categorizing ethnic groups and, like the melting-pot ap-proach, it is limited, because it does not focus on the character of the relations between ethnic groups and the larger society, or on those between ethnic clients and social workers.

⌐ In the transactional approach to ethnicity, the approach to be argued here, the relations between the larger society and persons who identify themselves with an ethnic group are of central interest. The descriptive cultural traits that fascinate the adherents of the pluralist and melting-pot views as quaint and curious are not significant except to the extent that they influence intergroup and interpersonal cross-cultural relationships. As cultural content, such traits as skin color or food preferences may and often do become important as political and cultural symbols to be used in asserting a group's claims to resources or demands for respect. But what is critical to the transactional conception of ethnicity is not the inventory of cultural traits as such. Rather, it is the boundaries that groups define around themselves, using selected cultural traits as criteria or markers of exclusion or inclusion. Social boundaries, then, not categorical bundles of specific cultural traits, define ethnic groups. The inventory of cultural content—ceremonies, technology, language, religion—often has a symbolic function in separating one group from another. But it is the lines of separation and in particular how they are managed, protected, ritualized through stereotyping, and sometimes violated that is of concern in a transactional analysis of cross-cultural diversity.

The transactional approach to ethnicity is primarily associated with the work of anthropologist Frederik Barth (1969). He has argued that one of the serious limitations of the categorical approach is that in its emphasis on cultural content as the marker of distinctiveness, it overlooks the problematic nature of ethnicity in interpersonal behavior. For it is where individuals confront culturally different others that their sense of cultural distinctiveness becomes most important. The ways in which that distinctiveness is defended, asserted, preserved, or abandoned amount to the stuff of ethnic identity. To understand ethnicity, therefore, one must examine the values, signs, and behavioral styles through which individuals signal their identity in cross-cultural encounters. That requires analysis of what Barth calls "boundary maintenance" (1969: 11), rather than the mere listing of cultural traits. Ethnicity is to some degree, then, a situational phenomenon, and it is this situational approach to the issue of cultural difference that would seem to be particularly useful in social services.

From   Barth's concept of the importance of interaction across group boundaries as the defining characteristic of ethnicity, a number of consequences follow. First, relations across group boundaries generally tend to be rigid and stereotypic, that is, they are highly ritualized. This assures that actors in cross-group encounters can more or less predict the behavior of others and can carry on the business at hand without having to learn fully one another's culture. Obviously, the more rigid the boundaries between groups, the more stereotyped the encounters will be. The castelike relations between blacks and whites have contributed enormously to stereotypes and protective maneuvering on both sides of the racial line. Effective cross-cultural communication requires working through and then beyond the etiquette associated with these stereotypes.

— A second idea deriving from the transactional or boundary maintenance model of ethnicity is the recognition that ethnic group formation is an ongoing process, one with political and economic consequences. Despite the ideology of the melting-pot, in which all differences are submerged through contact, the group boundary model suggests that where people can find advantage in making distinctions among themselves, they will do so. This need not be viewed as a cynical or devious characteristic of the human mind; rather, it is evidence for the fact that loyalty to groups and participation in particular styles of living are the most important resources of human beings in their struggles to protect and advance their own welfare. The rationalizations for distinction-making will vary, however. Genetic (so-called "racial") differences have been an historically significant rationalization in our own culture, particularly in relations between blacks and whites. Religious differences, as in Ireland, or beliefs about "impurity," as in India, may also be evoked. The specific nature of the beliefs or rationalizations is less significant than the fact that they continuously evolve and are utilized to justify differential behavior toward individuals presumed to be "different" in some important way. Far from melting away under pressure of acculturation, therefore, ethnic distinctions are defined, redefined, and reinforced as a result of continuous intergroup contact.

Finally, by focusing on how individuals achieve identity through group membership and the manipulation of group boundaries, the transactional model suggests that one's ethnicity is something which, within limits, can be manipulated. (Ethnicity is not a permanent feature of one's identity unless relatively fixed physical features, such as skin color, are given a prominent and stereotypic role in the explanation of group characteristics.) The degree to which a person is "acculturated," therefore, is situational rather than absolute and can be modified to suit the needs of different kinds of cross-cultural encounters. This observation has profound implications for how the manifest ethnicity of individuals in one relationship carries over into their other relationships. One can be more or less "acculturated" as the situation demands, and that is something about which the culturally responsive practitioner would have to be aware in dealing with clients. Individualizing the client would require an accurate perception by the worker of how the individual manages the symbols of ethnicity in a variety of cross-cultural as well as same-cultural relationships.

SOCIAL WORK-ETHNIC
GROUP RELATIONSHIPS

If it is the manipulation of boundaries between distinctive cultural groups that is crucial to the understanding of ethnicity, then the persons who mediate boundaries are critical social actors in the communication of information and the regulation of resources as they affect those groups. In the social science literature there are numerous terms for such persons: mediators, facilitators, ombudsmen, cultural brokers, go-betweens, and the like. In their work with minority clients, social workers are often mediators responsible for gaining on behalf of their clients the things that individuals cannot get without such assistance. But there are a variety of ways in which a mediation function can be expressed, and each of these ways presupposes a concept of ethnicity, an implicit if not explicit value orientation, and a matching intervention style on the part of the practitioner.

At least four modes of intervention within minority groups can be defined. Following Cowger (1977), we will identify these as (1) group advocate, (2) counselor, (3) regulator, and (4) broker. (See Figure 1-1.) Of course, these categories can and do overlap on occasion, but they do suggest ways in which the variety of social work-ethnic group encounters can be understood. We want to use this four-

FIGURE 1-1.   Four styles of social work intervention.

fold division of professional-client relationships to consider some of the implications of ethnicity for social service activities.

— First, the practitioner can adopt an advocacy approach in relations between an ethnic or minority community and the larger society. This is sometimes described as a radical response (Statham 1978). It assumes that conflict is inherent in minority-dominant group relationships and that the dominant institutions of society must be challenged and changed. The client's problems are viewed as the result of unfair and unjust practices and an inequitable distribution of resources. One example of this approach can be found in the work of Cloward and Piven (1975), who charge that schools of social work train students to acquiesce to the organizational demands of social work bureaucracies. These demands, they maintain, place the perpetuation of the agency above the legitimate needs of clients. Established service organizations tend to blame the victim, through explanations of psychological deficiency, instead of providing services to help change the oppressive social and economic circumstances that are part of the victims' problems. Citing the example of health care, they call for turning the discipline against the powers that be: "Social workers are used by hospitals and their medical rulers to appease anxious or dissatisfied patients, to cool out the mark. What we ought to do instead is to challenge the doctors and hospital authorities, and encourage patients to do the same" (Cloward and Piven 1975: xxxiv).

The important issue raised by the advocacy approach is the culpability of dominant institutions—including the institutions that provide social services and social service education—in the problems experienced by minority clients. It is difficult to think of a single problem that is not paired in some significant way with an accepted practice in the larger society: drug misuse and intensive commercial promotion of medications; slums and the investment practice of banks and landlords; job discrimination and the rhetorical insistence on maintenance of standards in hiring and promotion. Social work has been criticized for ignoring the political, social, and economic forces that contribute, in both direct and indirect ways, to the problems that clients bring to workers. In a distinctively cultural approach, a wholistic or ecological perspective would be important. Culturally sophisticated workers would be expected to have familiarity with the mechanisms by which large, impersonal institutions both limit and regulate the lives of their clients.

While many instances of advocacy intervention could be described, one good example is provided by Jacobs (1974a, 1974b, 1979) in her work with a midwestern black community in establishing a neighborhood health center. In that community, infant mortality rates among black children were considerably higher than those for nearby white children. The established health organizations attributed this difference to underutilization of existing health services by the black population and an unwillingness by expectant mothers to comply with the advice of their physicians. Jacobs' research-advocacy team discovered a different set of circumstances, however, which contributed to a high infant mortality and to other health problems as well. These included explicit acts of racial stereotyping by white physicians in reference to their black patients; collusion among white-dominated health organizations to exclude black physicians; and adoption by health providers of a white model of health services, one which was crisis-oriented rather than preventive. At the same time that she documented these problems, Jacobs was able to examine the health care preferences and behavior of community residents. Working with black patients, clients, and a variety of black health professionals, she was able to assist in the development of health care practices that were more closely aligned with community expectations. The work was time-consuming and difficult, but it resulted in a high level of trust between Jacobs and community members and in a demonstrably useful program of health care. It also demonstrated the utility of an explicitly cultural orientation toward analysis of an issue. Long-term problems in the transactions between the white health care establishment and black patients and conflicts between the conceptions of health care prevalent in each group had contributed to a serious health problem. Jacobs' work as an advocate unraveled, in effect, the pieces of that problem, thus enabling the community to better plan its own initiatives.

Schensul and Schensul (1978) have suggested that advocacy as an approach to intervention involves a number of skills and techniques, including research capabilities, knowledge of community institutions, in-depth awareness of community values and of community relations to the larger society, and an ability to promote linkages between community institutions. The key issue in advocacy, however, and the one which Jacobs addressed very early in her work, was that of identifying the person or persons to whom the advocate must be accountable. Once it was established that the needs of patients and clients had priority, and that research, planning, and service delivery must meet those needs, it also became apparent that maximizing the contribution of community residents would be critical to success. The ability to identify and utilize such information would characterize the culturally responsive service provider acting in the role of advocate.

In the second approach, social service practitioners intervene by focusing on the client's specific problems, particularly on client feelings and behavior and on ways in which more positive responses might be made. This is the typically clinical style of intervention, with the practitioner functioning as a counselor. In this mode, professional practice is often viewed as neutral or diffuse in terms of its larger social implications. The target of change is the individual, and the change is achieved through "one-to-one" or small group relationships, in "treatment" sessions taking place in an environment set aside for that purpose. The practitioner's first responsibility is to the client, not to the community as such. This approach, as Cowger points out, is codified in the National Association of Social Workers' statement of ethics, a statement which makes clear that the social worker's first responsibility is to the client and secondarily to society at large: "I regard as my primary obligation the welfare of the individual or group served, which includes action for improving social conditions" (Cowger 1977: 27). To change social conditions is often interpreted as subordinate to the goal of changing clients. While the clinical model has the advantage of recognizing that individuals do have problems that must be addressed through supportive personal services, it often slights the institutionally generated sources of individual difficulty, those that the worker as advocate attacks directly. Since the sources of personal stress are likely to persist long after individual or small group therapy sessions have been terminated, one of the important contributions of the clinically-oriented practitioner is preparing the client to better understand and manage problems which cannot be expected to go away.

But culturally sensitive counseling is not a well-developed area in social services research and training. This fact is surprising, in that counseling has been a growing interest in such fields as education and pyschology and has a number of applied implications, particularly in those government and business programs involving contact with people in other countries. Anthropologists, while they have not specifically focused on the interests of social workers, have also done extensive work in the area of interethnic communication (Ross 1978). The clear need for social work now is to devise research procedures which will identify communication patterns in different ethnic groups as they are manifest in social service encounters and develop protocols for teaching appropriate communication skills. As ambitious as such an effort may appear, it seems quite minimal when one reflects on the number and needs of minority clients nationwide. The alternative is to rely on the clichés and euphemisims of the language of "empathy," "caring," and "engagement," of "openness" and "eclecticism."

Vontress (1976), a black psychologist, has provided examples of some of the problems involved in using well-known counseling techniques in cross-cultural encounters. Self-disclosure, for instance, is particularly difficult in relations between white counselors and black clients, since it presumes a degree of trust that blacks generally have no reason to extend toward whites. Short-term, task-oriented styles of social work may conflict with the emphasis on personalism in social relations, a trait common among blacks and among whites, especially in rural areas of the South, and common to many Mexican-Americans and Puerto Ricans. While brief contacts with a large number of clients may be desirable from the point of view of agency administrators, they may be ineffectual with clients who feel that time spent "just talking" is an important way of entering a relationship.

Obviously, examples of this sort could be compiled almost endlessly. Such a compilation, however, would not lead to a satisfactory way of thinking about cultural differences. It would simply make operational the categorical approach to ethnicity by producing lists of traits and procedures to be memorized and pulled forth whenever a client of the right ethnicity appeared at the worker's desk. Such pigeonholing would be stereotyping to an extreme degree. As an alternative, Mayes (1978) has identified some of the characteristics he feels describe those who, in their personal and professional work, are effective in intercultural relationships. These include critical insight into the characteristics and limitations of one's own cultural background; cognitive and attitudinal openness to evidence of cultural difference in others; a sense of adventurousness in exploring with others what cultural differences mean; flexibility in adapting to and utilizing the learning styles of others; and a very large measure of informed skepticism toward all diagnostic and assessment procedures when these are applied to persons who are culturally different from "mainstream" whites. He concludes that the effective cross-cultural communicator is one who adopts a value stance in which he or she can "understand, believe and convey that there are no 'culturally deprived' or 'culture free' individuals and that all cultures have their own integrity, validity and coherence" (Mayes 1978: 39).

As a statement of principles and goals for cross-cultural counseling, these are worthy ones. They concern a style of rendering service that is not adequately addressed by the NASW Code of Ethics (1980). But there remains the task of defining what these injunctions to culturally responsive service mean in day-to-day encounters with specific clients. Cultures differ in the way decision-making is structured, in the life events that are emphasized, in how the developmental cycle of household and family units are ordered, and in how individuals and households react to crises and to external interference (Sundberg 1976). That kind of information, of critical importance in making an intelligent response to the needs of others, is yet to be compiled and presented in a framework suitable for training social workers. Clearly, it will have to come from a variety of sources, including academic research and publications, intensive participant-observation, and detailed consultation with ethnic and minority social workers who are able to articulate the diverse values and lifestyles of their own communities. Then the counseling mode of cross-cultural social work will have acquired the theoretical and empirical basis it must have in order to contribute to resolving the problems brought to social workers by ethnic and minority group clients.

– A third mode of intervention is that in which the practitioner is seen as an extension of the larger society, in effect a kind of regulator, concerned with helping clients change by modifying their behavior or attitudes. Resocialization of clients, especially involuntary ones, is a standard strategy here. There is an important social control function connected with this intervention approach, one that clearly reflects society's mandate that some kinds of problems be addressed and be either corrected or controlled. In the area of child abuse, for instance, the idea of serving the "best interests of the child" may be viewed as one of changing family discipline practices. The worker may indeed act as a counselor to an abusing parent, but the aim of intervention is to modify family patterns. How these patterns are modified, in what direction, and under what authority are critical issues that often reflect the powerful role of the worker in a regulatory stance.

It is this regulatory function of social work that is often cited by ethnic community leaders as evidence that the profession is more committed to protecting the status quo than assuring just and fair treatment for those who need it most. Whatever the merits of these complaints, the issue that these critics raise is an important one, and it goes beyond mere rhetoric. It concerns how deviance, discontent, maladaption, and nonconformity are to be defined and then judged; who is qualified to make such judgments; and toward what ends change is to be directed.

Deviance occurs in all human societies, from the largest and most complex to those that are relatively small and homogeneous (Edgerton 1976). Furthermore, all societies have means of controlling nonconformity in order to uphold the standards of conduct that are acceptable to the majority. In a culturally diverse society such as our own, two opposing tendencies bear on this issue—the tendency for uniformity and "equality" in the regulation of individuals who commit offenses and the more recent, almost faddish, interest in cultural pluralism and "alternative" ways of controlling behavior. The former represents the imperatives of agency and administrative convenience; the latter often appears as populist, antiestablishment rhetoric. Social workers sometimes find themselves caught between these tendencies, when legal and administrative codes require the imposition of specific procedures and penalties and ethnic communities make demands for different kinds of intervention and regulation. One of the most dramatic instances of this kind of conflict is that involving child welfare work and Indian children. Since the early 1800's, the federal government has been involved in the removal of Indian children from their families. A 1976 Association on American Indian Affairs report showed that one out of every four Indian and Native children has been separated from his or her family and is living in substitute care. Eighty-five percent of these children are in non-Indian placements (Blanchard 1979: 200). The majority of such placements are with foster homes, adoptive homes, and religious institutions. The underlying assumption of these removals has been that in some critical and damaging ways the families of these children are unable to provide proper care. What constitutes "proper care" is both a legal and a cultural issue, and in many instances it has meant an insistence on conformity by Indian people to non-Indian norms.

Few Indian children are taken away from their homes simply on the grounds of neglect or abuse. More often than not, they are removed after allegations of "social deprivation" and assertions that emotional damage will be suffered if they continue to live with their families. But when separation occurs, responsible tribal authorities and agencies are not always consulted or informed of the actions, families are rarely advised of their rights, nor do the natural parents always understand the nature of the documents or proceedings involved (Blanchard and Unger 1977). Once removed from their families, Indian children are kept in substitute care for long periods of time; they lose their ties with their Native American culture, and sometimes their locations are unknown to their own parents. Agencies frequently contend that returning such adoptees to their parents would adversely affect the children, and so they act to terminate the natural parent's rights completely. Often overlooked by courts and social workers are local Indian families who could provide substitute care if the worker knew of them or was willing to enlist their aid in the placement.

Several observers have noted that imaginative and resourceful Native American family and child services have been designed and implemented by tribes and Indian communities, and that many more could be developed. Shore and Nicholls (1975), for example, describe a community-based children's home and child welfare program among members of a Plateau Indian tribe, founded on the idea of enlisting the support of the extended family and community. Services include intensive outreach family counseling and a group home for Indian children that provides short-term sheltered care, long-term placement, counseling, and minor medical treatment. The staff for the program is 90 percent Indian, and emphasis is given to providing child care in close proximity to parents and with outreach programs that assure continuing parental involvement. Decisions to place children are made by the Indian community itself and only with assurance that the affected children will return to their families within a short period of time.

The success of such community-based programs, with their largely Indian staffs, many of whom may lack the degrees and credentials that come with extensive, formal training in classrooms, suggests both the resilience and the generative capability of indigenous individuals and institutions. It also suggests something of the ethical dimension of social services. In regulating others, in supplying corrective services, in acting to manage the expression of deviance, to whom should social workers and their professional organizations be accountable? This is a cultural as well as a political issue, since many Indians as well as other minority persons view social work as an oppressive, policing type of activity. The culturally alert worker will need to be able to defend counseling, placement, and related professional decisions in terms of the larger issues that are entailed in regulating others. What is deviance? Who is to judge? Toward what ends ought changes be made? To whom are those ends acceptable? In whose interest are regulatory services provided?

The fourth mode of social work intervention is that in which the practitioner functions as an intermediary or broker between the individual and society. There is a symbiotic relationship in which the practitioner can assist the individual client with resolution of a problem while at the same time working to make changes in the environment. This approach stresses the dual responsibility of the practitioner to both individuals and society. It also suggests that the client is capable of perceptive evaluation of a problem and that problems can often be handled within the context of the social and cultural resources of the client's community. Intervention is aimed at both the community and the individual. The broker mode of intervention can be particularly appropriate with minority clients, since they may be hostile to the regulatory approach, and traditional counseling methods may be inappropriate in terms of community values or communication styles. In fact, social workers who are themselves minority persons and who work with minority clients provide the best example of what brokerage in social services involves.

Minority professionals occupy a middle ground between their profession and the communities they serve. While nonminority practitioners may experience few conflicts between personal and professional values, minority social workers must confront numerous value dilemmas in their professional practice. Unlike their white counterparts, minority professionals are often bicultural and bilingual. They have grown up in and continue to live in contrasting cultural worlds. Where their primary identification lies with their "home" culture, they speak the language, observe the customs, and often live and participate in the life of those communities. But because they live and work in a bicultural milieu, they often experience a duality of roles and expectations, and they are obliged to honor two systems of norms and values, what Norton et al. (1978) have referred to as the "dual perspective." On the one hand, they are able to explain to clients the intricacies of existing services and can assist them in gaining access to resources. They can serve as advocates for minority group interests. But they are also credentialed in a profession that represents the values of the dominant culture, one that demands in its code of ethics "precedence to my professional responsibility over personal interests," the "practice [of] social work within the recognized knowledge and competence of the profession" and "support [of] the principle that professional practice requires professional education" (NASW 1980). All of these propositions are in potential conflict with the interests of ethnic communities, and at some point minority professionals must reconcile the claims of their professional identities with those of their ethnic affiliations if they are to be effective in both worlds. Accomplishing this goal is an elusive task.

A certain degree of ambivalence is sometimes felt toward minority professionals in social services. The minority professional is in a position to lend badly-needed expertise in legal aid, health care, political advocacy, and the like to his or her community. On the other hand, the requirements of professional advancement in the larger society can place a formidable barrier between such practitioners and their minority community. The attainment of a professional university degree for the minority person is a validation of membership in the professional middle class. Rodriguez (1974) has argued that for a minority person upward social mobility may entail both a sense of cultural alienation and a personal identity crisis. Not surprisingly, some minority professionals ignore the problems of their communities in the interest of professional advancement. In the eyes of the community, however, the valued criteria of effectiveness may be less a matter of professional degrees and certification than of community involvement, visibility, and a proven "track record" of accomplishment in community activism.

The problems confronting the minority practitioner are complex and numerous. The social work profession itself has only recently become aware of and actively concerned about the special needs and potentials of ethnic minority clients. Minority students newly recruited into professional training programs have encountered curricula without significant ethnic minority content or sensitivity to the problems of minority communities. Courses of study often ignore the cultural aspects of social work practice and appear to be oriented primarily to the psychosocial needs of a white, middle-class, client community. The minority professional thus is socialized into a profession whose primary values reflect those of the dominant culture, and he or she must demonstrate competence in skills that have not been adapted to the experience of minority clients.

Efforts to remedy this problem have been sporadic and largely piecemeal, but increasingly, ethnic and minority communities are taking the initiative in the development cf service delivery models (Morales 1976, Souflee 1977, Solomon 1976). For example, in task force reports issued by the Council on Social Work Education from 1973 to 1974, minority social workers criticized existing models of social service delivery as culturally biased and inflexible. They added that while "Social workers are taught 'empathy,' 'to begin where the client is,' and to view the client's situation 'nonjudgmentally' . . . [t]hese principles have been operationalized in the past on the assumption that there was congruence between the client system and the dominant system" (Norton 1978: 4). Operating from a dual perspective, however, minority professionals are in a position to appreciate the limitations of power in the communities they represent and the limitations of understanding in the programs and the treatment techniques offered by established social service organizations.

As distressing as these problems are for minority social workers, they are typical of brokerage roles in many societies. The concept of a cultural broker (Wolf 1966a) contains a number of elements shared by all brokers, whether they be political activists, religious functionaries, or minority social workers. Most importantly, brokers function where there are significant gaps in the institutional arrangements of society. They handle problems where "official" organizations and their representatives are not active. Brokers commonly develop extensive interpersonal networks in both the dominant and dominated sectors of a society, and, as we have noted, the conflicting demands made by these opposing constituencies results in a painful balancing of values, priorities, and personal interests. Cultural brokers often serve as buffers, modifying the impact of adminstrative decisions and procedures on ethnic constituencies. But brokers also provide a mechanism of diffusion for new ideas that may modify the practices of those who hold power. Their role is thus a creative as well as a protective one. Cultural brokers may also develop leadership and authority in their own right and move to consolidate in stable, powerful organizations the mass of informal linkages and allegiances that they have cultivated in the multiple cultural and political worlds they inhabit.

Viewed in this way, the brokerage role in social services is an important and necessary response to the failure of established social service organizations to meet the legitimate needs of minority clients. Minority professionals are a resource to both the professional and the lay community. From their unique vantage point as cultural brokers, minority professionals can use their experiential and cultural backgrounds, as well as existing knowledge of the social sciences, to convey information about the minority community to their white colleagues. They can serve as a liaison between existing self-help and community resources and the larger society, using funds and their expertise to organize a useful response to the problems of their clients. They can work through the intricacies of social service programs on behalf of minority clients and serve as an important link between those resources and minority communities. Finally, they can help devise more effective methods of service delivery for the communities they represent. The creativeness of minority practitioners need not supplant or negate existing organizations and resources. Rather, new methods can enhance the effectiveness of all social service providers.

SOCIAL WORK AS
AN ETHNIC COMMUNITY

We have argued that ethnicity is best understood as a transactional feature of the relationships between individuals. Four separate ways by which social workers often relate to clients have been examined in light of that perspective. We are now in a position to consider the elements of a model for culturally sensitive social services, that is, services in which ethnographic information about the cultural background of individuals is used in efforts to resolve client problems. However, before proceeding to develop the components of that model, we need to consider what our discussion of ethnicity suggests about the community of social workers—itself a special kind of group.

  – All ethnic groups are ethnocentric, in the sense that they place some values above others, emphasize certain ways of doing things above others, and use their preferences as criteria for making judgments about the worth and correctness of other people. This is expressed in what Barth has called "boundary maintenance activity," one of the principal mechanisms by which ethnic group members preserve a sense of distinctiveness and identity. Is social work like an ethnic group in being idiosyncratic in its values and in its practices? Or, rather, do its principles and operational methods transcend narrow ethnocentrism, serving as universal guides for insight into the problems that afflict human beings? One way to approach this question is to contrast some of the values, expectations, and procedures commonly associated with helping relationships in particular ethnic communities with those to be found within the field of social work. One clear example of such contrast, although not the only one that could have been chosen, is that of the relations of social workers with American Indians.

  Noninvolvement is a fundamental value in many Native American communities, and it is a value with which social workers as help providers often collide. One Indian social worker, Jimm Good Tracks, has commented that "all the methods usually associated with the term 'social work intervention' diminish in effectiveness" when applied to Indian clients (Good Tracks 1973: 30). The more traditional in orientation the client is, the less likely it is that intervention by a white social worker will have any positive effect. This is because "no interference or meddling of any kind is allowed or tolerated, even when it is to keep the other person from doing something foolish or dangerous" (ibid.). This perspective contrasts markedly with that of the dominant culture and with that of the professional culture of social workers, in which direct assistance of one kind or another is an act highly valued and praised.

Wax and Thomas (1961) have illustrated this contrast between the ways whites and Indians approach similar problems. When confronted with threatening and anxiety-provoking situations, for instance, whites might be motivated to act quickly and directly. They may engage in physical actions or verbal coercion, but often the principle underlying their response is to "do something" before a situation gets "out of hand" and out of control. Indians are more likely to confront unpleasantness by quiet observation and, if necessary, withdrawal. What looks to whites like avoidance may in fact be careful scrutiny and cautious weighing of possibilities. Escape from a hostile or dangerous encounter comes not by attempting to change the situation, as whites might prefer, but by removing oneself from it. Indians are unlikely to respond violently unless pushed well beyond reasonable endurance. Far from being a "flight from reality," avoidance and withdrawal from threatening circumstances are culturally sanctioned responses which both preserve the individual's sense of integrity and avoid intruding into the affairs of others.

Personal integrity is also protected by refusing to do what is beyond one's knowledge or capability. Among whites, there is something heroic in reaching beyond one's grasp and something honorable in persisting at an "impossible" task until it is done and done well. To many Indians, particularly those of traditional orientation, wisdom is in not attempting that which can be better done by others. There is a strong reluctance to take action that might result in failure, leaving one looking a fool, or action that would impinge on the skills or prerogatives of others. Noninvolvement requires that if something should be done—an object repaired, for instance—it will be done by the persons most able to do so and at the time convenient to them. Others will not make special demands. Similarly, direct requests are avoided. If individuals need something, they will go for it on their own. If they are incapacitated, others will act for them. But need and action will not be anticipated, as it often is among whites who actively seek opportunities to be neighborly or to "help out."

Indian communities, particularly traditional ones, live with low levels of the kind of direct coercive action that whites accept in their social relations. Voluntary cooperation is the way most tasks are completed. This is reflective of the egalitarian nature of Indian lifestyles. The expression of opinions in a direct way, "assertiveness" as a technique in managing others, and "standing out" in a self-appointed manner are regarded by many Indians as extreme forms of rudeness. However well-intended or gentle, intrusive behavior by whites in matters of Indian concern will be quietly noted and may be greatly resented. That resentment will be manifest in withdrawal into silence and perhaps physical removal. Short of violence, ignoring the presence of intrusive individuals is a strong form of Indian disapproval.

The operation of the value of noninterference is probably nowhere more puzzling to outsiders than in Indian concepts of time. It is often said that the white man's time is clock time, while that of the Indian is social time. There is a sense in which this is true, but most whites have misconstrued that generalization to mean that Indians lack a sense of the importance of time altogether. Such a conclusion is not justified. Philips (1974) has described how the Indian sense of time is shaped by a distinctively Indian sense of the progression of events, such as public ceremonies, private conversations, or informal gatherings of friends. To non-Indians, activities such as these are perceived as having beginnings, midsections, and closing points. At each stage, the participants know where in the progression of the event they are located. Verbal signals and mannerisms, but also mechanical things, such as clock time and the scheduling of other events, make that progression clear. But events in Indian terms are demarcated more by the availability of appropriate persons to carry them out, and they depend on the willingness of individuals to come forward to participate. Thus many Indian activities are open-ended and indeterminant and may appear to whites to have confused or ambiguous boundaries. To Indians, there is no confusion at all. As Philips notes, an event cannot happen until the correct persons to engage in it are present. They must participate without coercion, and they must constantly monitor their own actions, so that they are coordinated and not interfering with what others are doing. This concept reinforces the notion of egalitarian interpersonal relations. It respects the nonhierarchical nature of community organization. But it also reveals how, in a seemingly simple thing like marking time, a world view at considerable variance from European perspectives is expressed. The emphasis on people, not the location of the hands on a clockface, as a basis for determining when something is to occur represents an organizational strategy which "maximize[s] the possibility that everyone who wants to participate is given the chance when he or she chooses to and in the way he or she chooses to" (Phillips 1974: 107). "Indian time," therefore, is not simply a remnant from the preindustrial tribal past but an expression of a distinctive cultural reality that is both complex and subtle. Living by Indian time is both a rejection of white America's mechanized sense of the timing of events and an adherence to a person-centered way of organizing and experiencing the world.

It should be apparent that there are major contrasts, if not conflicts, between the white world and Indian communities. Many clients neither share nor do they desire to participate in the values and customs of whites, and in some instances they find traditional social work intervention techniques offensive. This should be particularly evident from our discussion of the value of noninvolvement. How then can social workers who wish to be culturally sensitive to the wishes of their Indian clients offer services in ways that will be helpful and may even be appreciated?

A positive approach to social work in Indian communities might be made up of at least three elements. (1) Non-Indian workers must demonstrate the patience and willingness to do humble helping tasks until such time as they are accepted for more intimate yet restrained involvement in Indian concerns. The burden of proving one's potential value to the Indian community is always on the worker (and by extension, the worker's agency), and this period of testing can be lengthy. (2) Settings such as clinics, schools, employment counseling centers, and other places that assist Indians with their relationships with the dominant society are the places where social workers can be most helpful. Indian-white encounters are the areas in which Indians are most likely to request and appreciate help. Internal family or community matters are beyond what most Indians will recognize as the worker's sphere of authority and capability. The ethnically sensitive worker will respect that Indian sense of propriety and move cautiously. (3) Wherever possible, Indians should be encouraged to become their own advocates and intervention agents. Particularly among nonreservation Indians, the outreach functions of social work agencies can be greatly enhanced by relying on Indian workers, whether or not they are credentialed professionals.

It is apparent, even from this brief example, that there are many potential conflicts between social workers and clients from Indian groups—conflicts in values and in ways of behaving. Yetman and Steele have pointed ou that such conflicts may be inevitable, since "ethnic groups are inherently ethnocentric, regarding their own cultural traits as 'natural,' correct, and superior to those of other ethnic groups who are perceived as odd, amusing, inferior, or immoral" (Yetman and Steele 1971: 12). In viewing social workers themselves as an ethnic group, then, what are this group's values and behavioral preferences—the things that might make it appear as "odd, amusing, inferior, or immoral" to clients from ethnic communities—and how do these proclivities restrict the universal applicability of its concepts and techniques in providing services? Many researchers have noted that the essential ingredients of all professions are a commitment to rationality, universalism, disinterestedness, and functional specificity (Becker and Carper 1956; Cogan 1953; Goode 1957). That is to say, the cultural themes that are characteristic of a professional group include (1) an emphasis on reason rather than tradition as the authority for undertaking action; (2) the uniform application of services to individuals, regardless of their standing in the community; (3) the availability of those services to whomever needs them; and (4) the directing of those services to a specific issue or problem, without the intrusion of the service provider into inappropriate areas of the client's life. The historical evolution of social work from volunteer charity organizations and settlement houses to its present-day professional status illustrates the central importance of these elements.

In the early history of the profession, a concern for professional knowledge and skill was paramount in the minds of social work's proponents. The development of casework as the nuclear skill and differential diagnosis as a scientific base for changing individuals and social conditions underscored this concern (Lubove 1969). So, too, did attempts to develop casework practice along the lines of psychosocial and diagnostic methodology, including the adoption of clinical psychiatric models. Like most professions, social work evolved its associations and schools of professional training to serve not only as recognized and legitimate modes of entry into the field but as forces to socialize practitioners into the evolving norms and values of the profession itself. Prior to the establishment of the first schools of social work, formal training was not a requirement for employment in social agencies. With the advent of professionalization, however, came the demand for uniform standards. Like other professions, social work also laid claims to a discrete body of empirical and theoretical knowledge and operated from a position of community-sanctioned authority. The profession was guided by a regulative code of ethics and a distinctive culture, marked by its own values, norms, and symbols (Greenwood 1957).

Early social work educators looked upon professional training not only as education in technique but also as a socialization process, in which students would be exposed to the full array of social work values and norms. The development of an acceptable terminology of casework method, norms of professional conduct, commonly agreed upon principles and values, and a growing emphasis on technical expertise, affective neutrality, and the service ideal enabled the profession to enhance its image as a scientific helping enterprise. (To a large extent, this emphasis on professional status continues to be a concern today, leading some critics to view social work as a profession still in search of an identity [Richan and Mendelsohn 1973].)

Trained and socialized in this professional "subculture," practitioners are often inclined to view their treatment modes as having universalistic applicability to a wide variety of client problems. Typically, when certain treatment techniques fail with some clients, particularly ethnic or minority clients, it is the practitioners' skill or lack thereof that may be faulted, not the appropriateness of the intervention techniques themselves. But practitioners cannot safely assume that their own criteria for normative family functioning, childrearing, or psychosocial adjustment are necessarily congruent with those of minority clients and communities. In fact, often they are not. When social workers utilize culturally uninformed approaches in group work or casework, without regard to ethnic differences, they impose the values and behavioral preferences of one group and its history—their own—on another. Bluntly put, this is applied ethnocentrism. Each of the two cultures represented in a social service transaction is an ethnic entity, representing a traditional culture and a professional one. What is troublesome in this relationship is not that it is somehow "wrong," and that ethnic clients would be best served by ethnically similar counselors and advocates. It is that all too often the professional value assumptions and behavioral expectations of social workers are taken as the only standards that need govern the ethnic client-worker encounter. The lengthy and formal inculcation of these assumptions and expectations, along with the specialized jargon associated with them, that are involved in established social service training programs almost assures this unfortunate result.

The culturally responsive worker, therefore, must be one who is capable of viewing the worker-client relationship as one like any cross-cultural encounter, wherein the particularistic perspective of each partner toward the transaction is a limited and limiting one. It is limited in that large areas of the life of the other are unknown and will probably remain that way. It is limiting because each side brings to the transaction a set of assumptions, or prejudices, which predetermine what is important to be heard and remembered and what is not. The lack of congruence in these assumptions and prejudices, normal enough among people of similar cultural backgrounds, is exaggerated in cross-cultural encounters. Neither the worker, responding purely from the framework of social work's paradigms and language, nor the client, drawing from the received tradition of an ethnic or minority community, is in a position to fully understand the common sense meaning of the world of the other. Boundary maintenance activity—retreat to the vocabulary, concepts, clichés, and protective ideology of one's own group—assures that the representatives of the two ethnic traditions will remain largely unknown to one another.

CONCLUSION

We can see, then, that there are several very large implications that derive from our definition of ethnicity as a transactional phenomenon and the practitioner as a mediator across group boundaries. First, concerning the four modes of relating to ethnic groups and individuals, the ethnically responsive practitioner can shift from one to another as the needs of the situation change. What is important to note, however, is that each style reflects a different value stance, reflects different intervention assumptions, and has different consequences. Virtually any mode can be useful or useless, destructive or ameliorative, demeaning or liberating.

Second, a distinctively cultural approach recognizes that in some ways the social work profession is like an ethnic or minority group itself. It has a distinctive set of implicit and explicit values, recognizable language, an internal organization with criteria of recruitment and advancement, its own set of institutions, and a history that includes its special struggles, accumulated folklore, and cultural heroes. Most importantly, like ethnic groups, it has had and continues to have its own transactional activities. These activities occur in its relations with other professional groups, such as doctors, nurses, and psychiatrists, as well as during encounters with minority clients. This means that social work, like any other group, has a self-interest to pursue (Handelman 1976). Whether or not that interest is always consistent with the welfare of ethnic clients as they see it is an issue about which the ethnically competent worker would be concerned. It must be examined in every cross-cultural encounter.

Finally, the theories of human behavior and human needs that are taught as global explanations to be applied universally to all clients should be seriously questioned. Such theories are part of the technical knowledge and received traditions of the professional group of social workers. But their applicability to persons from other groups is always an open question. When such theories and treatment procedures are presented to minority clients as superior insights into human behavior, they function as an ethnocentric projection of professional doctrines. The transactional model draws attention to the fact that boundaries between groups have two sides and that for any group, including the professional group of social workers, boundary maintenance is a protective as well as an identity-defining activity. Its relationship to furthering client interests should be thoughtfully considered.

CHAPTER TWO
HELP-SEEKING BEHAVIOR

Despite what appears to be general acceptance of the notion that there are cultural differences among the people seen by social workers and that those differences are important, it is surprising to find a general lack of genuinely cross-cultural conceptualization within social work. That theoretical deficiency is matched by a methodological one as well. There are few training techniques, evaluation schedules, or case studies in which the salient features of cross-cultural intervention are defined and analyzed. Instead, there are highly abstract directives, urging that workers give credence to the ethnic sensitivities of their minority clients, paralleled by a slowly growing mound of case and client data, usually in the form of anecdotes or lists of "cultural traits" that are intended to illustrate what it is that makes culturally distinctive clients different. The prospect for these two trends—admonition to good will and the piecemeal accumulation of raw data—is likely to be a perpetuation of existing social services, without the corrective of ethnographically informed policies, planning, and service delivery. The need, then, is for critical examination of the relationship of ethnicity and social services.

The approach adopted here attempts to meet that need by adapting to human services some of the insights and procedures developed by sociologically and culturally oriented researchers in the health disciplines. It should be made clear, however, that we are not proposing a return to medical models for social service workers. Rather, the issue is that some medical sociologists and medical anthropologists are beginning to undertake culturally grounded studies of patient or client populations. These happen to be medical studies; but the cultural orientation of these researchers has taken them well beyond traditional medical model thinking. For instance, there is a growing research literature on such topics as folk theories of disease causation, ethnic (as contrasted to scientific) disease taxonomies, indigenous curers, illness behavior and patient roles, values and expectations of health and normality, the utilization of indigenous pharmaceuticals, cultural factors associated with pain, divination and diagnosis, and culture-specific behavioral disorders and syndromes. Much of this work has been carried out among remote and exotic groups. Some studies have involved class and ethnic groups in this country. Because not all peoples make the rigid separation of physical health and social and psychological well-being that characterizes Western thinking, it is logical to explore the possibility that cultural models relevant to patient help seeking and service utilization in medical settings may have implications for the things that transpire between client and worker in social service settings as well.

The model, called here Help-Seeking Behavior, is an adaptation from the work of Arthur Kleinman (1973, 1974, 1977, 1978a, 1978b, 1978c) and others on what has been called Health-Seeking Behavior. The model as we will use it rests on several assumptions. First, much of what distinguishes one culture from another and distinguishes subcultures within a large pluralistic society such as our own is shown in the diverse ways in which people perceive and report their experiences, including the experiences of stress and crises. Language is of particular importance, since it is the symbolic device by which the flow of that experience is categorized, labeled, evaluated, and acted upon. Shared cognitive and affective events and the language through which they are communicated are the ultimate bases for a sense of common culture and common understanding. Any approach to understanding the distinctive cultural characteristics of the client must begin with the language the client uses to explain what is being experienced. Language is a key to the components of any presenting problem.

Second, the model recognizes that the experience of a problem or crisis is both a personal and a social event. It is personal in that it disrupts the daily routines of individuals by creating discomfort and pain. It is social and cultural in that the labeling of the experience often requires confirmation from others before corrective action can be taken. A culturally sensitive intervention model requires acknowledgment of the role of socially significant others in the diagnosis and evaluation of personal problems. Indeed, lay consultation may be more critical to the client's response to a problem than information and advice supplied by experts or professionals.

The model, illustrated in Figure 2-1, is constructed around a fundamental division between what individuals know and do in response to a problem and what is known and done about the same problem by professionals and "experts" who do not share their client's cultural background. In effect, there is a client culture and there is a professional culture (more accurately, a professional subculture). These are not the same and the significance and meaning of a problem is different in each.

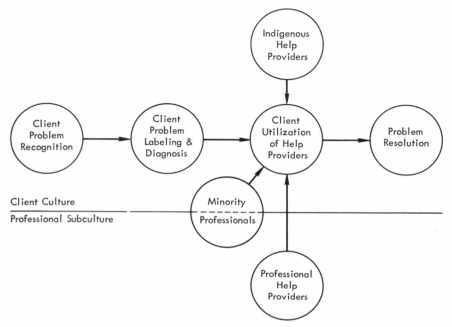

FIGURE 2-1.   The help-seeking behavior model in social services.

We argue that the greater the cultural distance between help seeker and help provider, the greater the discrepancy in perception, labeling, and response to a particular problem.

There are a number of reasons for the dichotomy between the world of the
client and that of the worker, and some have been described by Hayes-Bautista
(1978) in his study of interaction between Chicano patients and medical practitioners. He distinguishes what he calls "stocks of knowledge," lay knowledge and
professional knowledge, which vary not only in their ethnographic content but in
the nature of their organization and application as well. For instance, patient
knowledge about medical matters comes from a variety of sources, including friends,
media, and folklore, and is acquired in slow, random, and unsystematic ways. Over
many years, a patient's stock of knowledge becomes increasingly comprehensive as
new items of information are added. But little of that information is ever discarded
unless it has been tested for its appropriateness during specific illness episodes. Consequently, the stock becomes larger, containing a number of disparate, sometimes
contradictory, bits of information. Lacking depth, it is essentially "cookbook information" that is utilized in ad hoc ways to explain "how things work without making
clear why they do" (Hayes-Bautista 1978: 85). By contrast, the stock of knowledge
of the medical practitioner is marked by a high degree of formality, acquired according to a rigorous learning process and from increasingly specialized rather than

comprehensive sources. Rather than retain information for ad hoc retrieval, the professional seeks to eliminate contradictory bits of information through systematic testing. Clarity, precision, and narrow depth rather than comprehensiveness distinguish the practitioner's stock of knowledge from that of the lay person.

This sociology of knowledge approach is useful in suggesting the difference, even the opposition, between the interpretations and expectations of lay persons and the judgments and procedures of professionals. While the sociological and cultural characteristics of the professional subculture of social workers will be described in more detail later, it should be fairly obvious even now that there is a parallel contrast in the kinds of knowledge held by social service professionals about the nature and treatment of client problems and the perception and meaning of those problems on the part of those who bear them. This is obvious if we think of the ideal of the human service worker as one who, while consciously developing trust with the client, also looks for information that will aid in the clinical assessment and diagnosis of the case. Evaluation of observations and of information offered by the client is made on the basis of long learning and familiarity with methods of treatment and their likely success with certain kinds of cases. There is often an established "procedure" for handling the kinds of things that trouble clients, and part of the worker's job is to set that procedure in motion. But from clients, especially minority clients, may come different beliefs and expectations about what is to happen during the procedures for "treatment," or even of what the problem happens to be. Clients most certainly have a distinctive view of the professional's capability, authority, or interest in them, and this view may contrast sharply with what the worker assumes is going on.

All of these things suggest that the cultural boundary that separates the worker from the client and the professional subculture, its organization, and its operating principles from the ethnic or minority community and its history and styles of life is a feature of every social service encounter. The nature and degree of the cultural distinctiveness of the worker and the client is always an open question; the reality of it is not.

In the remainder of this chapter, we will describe the major components of the Help-Seeking Behavior model as it pertains to the client's culture. Those components include (1) the client's recognition of an experience as a "problem"; (2) the client's use of language to label and categorize a problem; (3) the availability of indigenous helping resources in client communities and the decision-making involved in the utilization of those resources; (4) and client-oriented criteria for determining that a satisfactory resolution has been achieved. In all of these components, the contrast between the client culture and the values, assumptions, organization, and procedures of the service subculture is basic. To make that contrast and its meaning for clients as well as service providers evident, each of the client-oriented cultural components of the model will be illustrated with examples from the ethnographic and human service literature. All of the examples are intended to show that informed ethnographic understanding is critical to planning and delivering culturally responsive social services.

1. The Client's Definition and Understanding of an Experience as a Problem.

The experience of a problem by a client is due in part to exposure to debilitating or disrupting circumstances, such as an illness, loss of a job, or a death in the family. But the culturally distinctive interpretation that is made of those objective circumstances is also a significant part of the experience. This is particularly true where issues of mental health are involved. Any culture provides a repertoire of explanations for problems, explanations related to etiology, symptom recognition, the course of an illness, the assumption of a special role for the sufferer, expectations concerning treatment procedures, and a definition of desirable outcomes. These explanations amount to a "cognitive map" (Wallace 1970) that is more or less shared by members of the culture, by which they organize and act on the information concerning a problem. This map or "explanatory model" (Kleinman 1978a) is part of the conception of the problem that the client brings to the therapist.

But is the "explanatory model" of the client, the lay interpretation of an issue, simply an accounting of a personal difficulty that contrasts in its accuracy or insightfulness with that of the trained service provider? Or is it something of a different nature altogether, indicative of a pattern of perception, thought, and explanation that is quite apart from the assumptions of problem recognition and resolution accepted by the professional? This question goes to the core of the notion of cultural differences. If clients simply "don't know" how to interpret and resolve their problems, or simply cannot articulate their concerns, then cultural considerations can be excluded from the worker's plan of action for them. If, however, clients "know" and articulate on the basis of conceptions distinctive to persons who share their cultural background, then the worker's own perception and appreciation of that fact is critical in formulating a culturally informed response to the clients' difficulties.

We take it for granted that until shown otherwise ethnic or minority clients have a distinctive perception of the world, one which is a mix of idiosyncratic and historically received elements. There is adequate evidence for making this assumption. Indeed, the idea that variations in world view and differences in perceptions of reality are associated with distinctive cultural communities has been a central philosophical and scientific preoccupation of the social sciences, and particularly of anthropology, for a long time. Thus, Ruth Benedict (1934) wrote of "patterns of culture," suggesting that all cultures have their own implicit, governing values, which are evident in a people's myths, rituals, family patterns, and behavior. Other anthropologists have elaborated on this notion of the distinctiveness of the world view in different cultures. Opler (1945) called the unifying ideas of a people their cultural "themes"; Herskovits (1947) spoke of the cultural "focus" as that which governs thought and action in all sectors of society; and Kardiner (1945) described what he called "basic personality structure" as one of the keys to understanding the people of a society. Later anthropologists refined these ideas and developed generalizations on cultural differences that seemed to sum up a great deal and to do so with great economy. Oscar Lewis (1965), for instance, described what he called a "culture of poverty" to depict the poorest people in certain rural areas of Mexico, the slums of San Juan, and in New York. George Foster (1965) has written of the "image of limited good" to explain the behavior and motivations of peasant peoples, and Mary Douglas (1966) has suggested how culturally patterned systems of classification, particularly those that distinguish pure and impure objects and practices, function to create order and control disorder in people's lives. Kearney (1975) has noted that the "world view" of a people, their outlook on life which makes them distinctive from all others, will always include culturally distinctive notions of the self, of others, of classification and relationship, of time and space, and of force or power (Kearney 1975: 248). He further suggests that these elements could be used to develop a "model of world view that would be both cross-culturally open-ended and yet serve as a scheme for cross-cultural comparison"(Kearney 1975: 248). It seems self-evident, then, that to understand others one must first understand something of the distinctiveness of their perceptions of the world, its operation, and their places in it.

The ethnographic description of Native American drinking illustrates the way a people's fundamental perspective on the world can differ from that of outsiders, including friendly outsiders who want to "help." Zola (1972) has noted that the recognition of symptoms and the concept of "trouble" is not value-free. Problem recognition occurs in a cultural, social, and economic context, and there may be instances where what is perceived by clients as normality or as the working out of some inevitable sequence of events is to the professional an instance of pathology, requiring intervention and corrective action. The question that must be asked at this stage of the help-seeking behavior model is: "What is a problem?" It is clear that what has been a "problem" for the white community may be something else for Indians.

Native American Drinking.   No people have been more stereotyped in reference to drinking behavior than American Indians. The orthodox view on alcohol and Indians is that of a whole continent of uncivilized tribes incapable of resisting the white man's "fire water" and reduced by it, along with warfare and the reservation system, to near-total loss of their lands, livelihood, and dignity. This perception has remained, despite the shift in emphasis on alcoholism as a disease rather than a moral failing of the individual. Some Native American leaders have agreed with these views, calling drinking a "most grave problem" (Locklear 1977: 203) for all Indian peoples. The question posed here, however, is not that of the seriousness of the problem but of its nature. If drinking is a problem for American Indians, what kind of a problem is it? How is it experienced, perceived, and acted upon in Indian communities, and in particular, what is its meaning within the context of those communities? Those issues must be understood before effective ameliorative actions can be undertaken.

In its most naive form, speculation on Native American drinking has assumed that Indians are possessed of an inordinate desire for the white man's liquor, coupled with an unfortunate genetic incapacity for dealing with it. Neither of these beliefs is true. More sophisticated propositions have associated problem drinking and alcoholism with the social disorganization created through white contact, particularly where access to economic rewards is blocked (Graves 1967) or where individuals feel that they have no sense of belonging to either traditional or white communities (Ferguson 1976). Such studies suggest that the incidence of Indian drinking can be better taken as a measure of the pressures of culture contact, not as an indicator of biological deficiency. This does not explain, however, what drinking means to Native American individuals, nor does it offer insight into the social context of drinking behavior. Yet these are the things that must be investigated in order to know how the problem is identified and its seriousness gauged.

An alternative approach to the "social breakdown" thesis is one which views drinking behavior, first, as an extension of cultural traditions deriving from precontact as well as postcontact times and, secondly, as a category of learned behavior specific to differing tribal and cultural groups. This approach has been developed by MacAndrew and Edgerton (1969) in what they call the analysis of "drunken comportment." They argue that in the conventional wisdom of studies of drinking behavior, it is assumed that the affects of alcohol on human beings are everywhere similar. That is, as more alcohol in consumed, there is a progressive deterioration of sensori-motor functions and superego controls. Alcohol is presumed to have a "disinhibiting" effect, with results that are predictable: jocularity, lewdness, aggression, and overt expression of things normally concealed or at least suitably managed. Alcohol as a "superego solvent" reduces normally decent individuals to something less than honorable.

But if one looks at the historical and ethnographic record of drinking practices among American Indians, a more complex picture emerges. There is instead an infinite series of gradations in drinking practices among the great variety of tribal groups, ranging from those who became boisterous and violent when "under the influence" to those who remained sedate or only titillated while inebriated. Among some groups, such as the Menomini, religious ceremonies focused on the attainment of visions and dreams, and alcohol was used, often generously, within carefully controlled ritual settings to advance that aim (MacAndrew and Edgerton 1969: 118). Lemert (1954) noted that there was little aggression associated with heavy drinking among the Northwest Coast groups he observed, and Levy and Kunitz (1974), in a careful and thorough study of drinking in the Southwest, found that the Hopi who abjured public drunkenness were very heavy drinkers in the privacy of their homes. They also found that Hopi drinking contrasted markedly with that of the neighboring Navajo and Apache, both of whom practiced public drinking and the public intoxication that went with it. In Canada, Kupferer (1979) found that drinking among the Cree of Ontario contributed to a sense of community solidarity. Because they valued individual autonomy and normally shunned emotional intensity in their relationships, weekly drinking was an occasion for relaxed animation and the venting of strong feelings. Clearly, one cannot conclude that there is a uniform effect of alcohol on all Indian individuals nor a homogenous response to alcohol by all Indian groups.

To account for differences, MacAndrew and Edgerton (1969) argue that drinking behavior occurs "within limits," limits which are culturally defined and which individuals know and observe even while inebriated. Most importantly, they suggest that, not only in Indian societies but in all societies, alcohol use occurs during special "time out" periods, in which rules of normal comportment are expected to be relaxed. Religious ceremonies may be special "time out" periods, and the "within limits" rules that govern them are precisely defined. Occasions of public drunkenness are also "time out" periods, wherein the standards of decorum of the household, the workplace, or the religious ceremonial are not expected to intrude. The "drunken comportment" that is displayed at these times has its own set of understandings which, however benumbed by excess, are not normally exceeded by the drinker (Hill 1978).

How does this work in practice? Price (1975) has argued that there are both positive and negative consequences of drinking among Native Americans, and that there are also external and internal sources of control. The negative consequences—alcoholism, injury through accidents, and the like—and the external controls—police, detoxification cells, government treatment programs—are well known. Less well known are the positive consequences—the activities of "time out" periods—and the internal controls—community expectations and sanctions—that establish the "within limits" rules for drinking activity. We have already mentioned the spiritual significance of intoxication where vision states are valued. But there is also the fact that drinking provides an opportunity for camaraderie, especially for young men new to urban areas and who are unfamiliar with the hazards of such places. For some of these men, a period of freedom, of "time out," before taking up the responsibilities of jobs or permanent settlement in reservation communities is important. Price notes that a 1969 study of alcoholism by the Indian Health Service found that heavy drinking was primarily a young man's pastime, that it occurred infrequently among women, and that it declined rapidly after age forty. Perhaps most important, the study found there are many Indians of all ages who do not drink at all (Price 1975: 20).

Indian drinking, to the degree that it becomes a problem for the dominant society, is handled in two ways. One is by the police and courts. Arrest and incarceration rates for Indians are generally higher than they are for whites, even when whites consume greater quantities of liquor (ibid. 22). The second approach is that of Alcoholics Anonymous. But AA is a white model, not only in its perception and definition of the problem (as a "disease") but of the treatment required (abstinence and public confessions). It cannot be assumed that all Indian communities, be they reservation or urban ones, will find AA perceptions of drinking behavior compatible.

It seems clear, then, that drinking is culturally conditioned behavior like any other; that when it becomes "excessive" it remains regulated by normative expectations of drunken comportment specific to the group; and that when and where drinking is determined to be a "problem" are highly dependent upon the values of the beholder of drinking behavior. One cannot know a priori that a "drinking problem" exists unless one knows the values of "time out" and "within limits" associated with it.

2. The Semantic Evaluation
of a Problem by a Client.

In one sense, a culture can be described by what it is the members of a community have in their heads—the knowledge, information, and beliefs they share with one another. This shared cognitive material marks them as one group, culturally distinctive from others. This view of culture was expressed by Goodenough (1957: 167) as follows: "A society's culture consists of whatever it is one has to know or believe in order to operate in a manner acceptable to its members, and to do so in any role that they accept for any one of themselves. . . . It is the forms of things that people have in mind, their models for perceiving, relating and otherwise interpreting them. . . ." Even if one is not willing to accept the argument that culture is equivalent to what people know—and some anthropologists take that position—it remains true that a signficant part of what is known in any society is linguistically labeled and communicated in speech. Identification of linguistic labels, therefore, and exploration of their meaning to members of the culture are critical to understanding some significant portion of the world as members of a specific culture view it.

We have suggested the importance of understanding the social context within which the client experiences a problem. But the meaning of a problem for the client is not simply in the fact that a disruptive personal event has intruded upon his or her daily affairs. Its meaning is in what the client makes of that disruption and in what it suggests to him or her about how reality is constructed and what can be done about it. It is the meaning of a problem, not simply its occurrence, that must be of interest to the culturally responsive worker.

The arrangement of cultural knowledge in any society is a matter of categorization and the appropriate use of folk categories and folk knowledge in communication. Categories and the linguistic labels that identify them may be of several types. Categories called "domains" are basic ethnographic units, the major classification of items in a culture. Thus, the semantic label "family" refers to a cultural domain. But there are differing kinds of families, and the variations among them are important. These variations are the "attributes" of the members of the domain. Thus, in American popular culture we have the domain of "families," and we recognize such attributes as "nuclear," "broken," "extended," "mixed," "single parent," and the like. The attributes themselves can be more minutely divided, in order to give finer shades of meaning. Thus, "single parent" families may have an adult male parent, adult female parent, biological parent, or adoptive parent. Similarly, an attribute such as "mixed" can be further subdivided. In its most general usuage, the folk attribute "mixed" refers to adults of differing "racial" groups ("race" being another folk domain, one rigorously applied in American culture), but it may also refer to married adults of mixed religious preferences. The complexity of the domain "family" is made more evident when we appreciate that in our culture native speakers also use the term in a metaphorical sense to apply to nonfamily entities. Thus, a speaker may suggest that the members of a large corporation ought to treat one another as "one big happy family."

This latter usage of the folk label "family" suggests one of the critical features of folk thinking and the semantic labels for folk categories. That is, semantic labels have what have been called both a "referential meaning" and a "social meaning" (Spradley and McCurdy 1975: 541). The referential meaning of "family" is its dictionary definition or, when more precision is required, the kinds of definitions that might be found in a sociology text on family life. The social meaning, however, refers to the community of speakers who use a particular semantic label, the occasions on which they use it, and their sense of appropriateness in its utilization. Appropriateness has to do with subtle shades of meaning and the fact that only persons thoroughly familiar with the culture will understand and appreciate those meanings when they are heard. This level of understanding is called "communicative competence" (Gumperz and Hymes 1972), and its use suggests that the speaker (and possibly the hearer) are intimately and intuitively familiar with both the referential and the social meaning of a semantic label.

The cultural knowledge of the individual has been referred to as the individual's "cognitive map" by Wallace (1970) and, in Kleinman's health-seeking behavior approach, the patient's "explanatory model" (1978a). Kleinman's usage is more limited and more precise, since it does not attempt to be a global concept but has to do only with the domains of illness and health. Thus, it is more useful for thinking about social service clients. We could argue that in coming to the worker with a specific problem having to do with the health of a child, for instance, the client has an implicit "explanatory model" of how the child became sick, what the symptoms are and what they mean, what has been observed to be effective with such symptoms before, why certain therapeutic procedures are deemed useful or not, and why some kinds of health advisors are preferable to others. All this conceptualization of the health problem is something that the client knows, whether or not he or she can articulate it well.

The section that follows explores exactly this point—the complex features of an explanatory model of illness and health that is at some variance from biomedical knowledge. Yet it is cultural knowledge that is widely shared among Spanish speakers in the United States who are of differing social classes and of diverse geographical locations.

Hispanic Disease Categories. Among Spanish-speaking persons in this country, beliefs and knowledge about disease derive from at least four sources (Saunders 1954: 141). Medieval Spanish traditions were brought to the New World by colonizers, and these influenced and were influenced by indigenous Indian groups. Elements of Anglo popular traditions, particularly as these are evident in mass media and advertising, and "scientific" or biomedical knowledge are also part of the body of medical concepts shared by Hispanic persons. But Hispanic disease concepts are not equivalent to those of Anglo biomedicine. They have their distinctive etiology, nosology, symptomotology, and treatment methods. An examination of several major categories of disease, as they are defined by many Spanish-speaking persons, will reveal something of their cultural significance for Hispanic patients.

Hispanic disease categories do not rest on a dichotomy between physical and mental sources of *enfermedad,* or illness. Rather, they come from a notion of disturbed balance in one's physical and social well-being. As in the ancient Hippocratic system, the individual in a healthy state is believed to be a harmonic mixture of contrasting elements: hot and cold, wet and dry, and the various "humors" of the body. The ethnosemantic labels for three significant disruptions of this balance are *empacho, mal ojo,* and *susto.* These medical categories have been described in a number of studies carried out in Latin America and in communities in this country (Martinez and Martin 1966, Madsen 1964, Clark 1959, Saunders 1954, O'Neill 1976). The descriptions provided by Rubel (1960, 1964, 1966) are particularly useful, because of his emphasis on the social functions of these disease concepts.

Empacho is a physiological condition, affecting both children and adults, in which the manifest symptoms of stomach pains are believed to be caused by food that cannot be dislodged from the side of the stomach. The food is said to be in the form of a ball, which can be broken up and elminated through back rubbing and the use of purgatives. A diagnosis of *empacho* is made only after other problems, such as indigestion, have been eliminated.

Mal ojo is the result of dangerous imbalances in social relationships, and, in its advanced form, can be fatal. Its symptoms include bad headaches, sleeplessness, drowsiness, restlessness, fever, and, in severe cases, vomitting. The individual's sense of equilibrium is in danger of being disturbed in any encounter with others. If one is the subject of covetous glances, admiring attention, or intense interest by another, *mal ojo* is likely to result. The eyes of another are the virulent agent for initiating the condition, although evil intent need not be present. Children are particularly susceptible to the looks of adults, and women may be exposed to danger from the glances of men. This unnatural bond of power that one individual may hold over another may be broken by prayers, gently rubbing the body with a whole egg, or by having the perpetrator touch the head of the victim, thereby draining off the threatening power of the relationship.

The *susto* syndrome has a number of characteristics widely dispersed among both Spanish and Indian cultures in Latin America. *Susto* means fright, and a victim of *susto* is one who has lost some of his or her spiritual essence as a result of an upsetting experience. The source of the fright may have been trivial or truly life-threatening, but the symptoms are the same: depression, lack of interest in living, introversion, and disruption of usual eating and hygienic habits. The cure requires coaxing the lost spirit back into the individual's body. This is done through prayers, body massage, spitting cold water over the patient, and particularly by "sweeping" the body with small branches while "talking" the spirit back to where it belongs. Curing is usually undertaken by someone familiar with the condition and known to be successful in treating it. The family and patient are consulted as part of the diagnostic process to determine that *susto* is in fact present. Not all frightening experiences lead to *susto,* but many can, and a link between an earlier experience and manifest symptoms must be established before treatment can begin.

One view of these "folk" illnesses, particularly the methods of diagnosis and treatment, is that they are simply historical survivals from older, now discredited, systems of medicine. They persist only in impoverished, backwater areas, due to lack of better alternatives. Another view, however, is that they are consistent with the culture in which they occur. They express an underlying logic through which Hispanic persons find meaning and sense in the world. Rubel (1960) has argued that the experience of stress is common to all these disease states. In small communities, where one's position in life is a matter not only of economic holdings but of reputation and the respect and esteem of others, challenges in the form of unwanted endearments or jealousy and envy are highly stressful. *Mal ojo* is resolved, balance is restored, when the unwitting perpetrator of the disease touches the victim, assuring that there is no intent of inappropriate desire to control the other. Stress is also experienced when individuals are unable to meet their role expectations. Children who feel they have disappointed their parents, particularly in a culture which emphasizes the notion of family honor and the shame that disrespectful behavior entails, may well develop the symptoms diagnosed as *empacho*.

The role stress theory of *susto* has been refined by O'Neill (1976), who suggests that it takes two forms: rationalized and precipitating fright. In the rationalized form, there is a lengthy time period between the onset of symptoms and the experience of fright. In addition, fright is usually initiated by nonhuman agents such as an attacking animal or the accidental breaking of household utensils. The patient explains the appearance of symptoms by locating a frightening experience in the past that is deemed to have been causal. This is not, however, an irrational, post-hoc procedure. Rather, the patient uses this explanatory principle to define himself or herself as sick, thereby utilizing the sick role in order to withdraw from the relationships that generated the stress. In this way, the sense of failure in role expectations is institutionalized and a means of treatment is made available.

Precipitating fright, by contrast, involves human causes, and in this form the appearance of symptoms is rapid. Confrontations with others, exchanges of insults, or threats of violence are all events that challenge the individual's sense of self-control and decorum. Loss of control and of balance in personal relationships precipitates the fright symptoms. This is most likely to happen within the family or among kin, where the frustrations of daily life serve as tests of the individual's ability to preserve a sense of calm and composure. The appearance of symptoms is a signal to all that a withdrawal and the easing off of tensions and hostilities are necessary in order to restore the normal order of relationships and the sense of balance and self-control of the patient.

Far from being irrational manifestations of folk superstitions, then, the *susto* syndrome is a culturally-based apparatus, couched in the language of health and illness, by which Hispanic individuals adapt to the stresses of everyday life. For *susto* sufferers, both rationalized and precipitating frights "serve to validate the problems in culturally meaningful terms, which facilitates the rehabilitation of the individual in social context" (O'Neill 1976: 61).

How widespread are these beliefs among Hispanic Americans in the United States? Martinez and Martin (1966) found that in a sample of urban Hispanic housewives, virtually all their respondents had heard of the diseases we have decribed, and 85 percent of them knew therapeutic measures for treating the symptoms. In addition, 95 percent either had experienced a folk illness or knew someone who had. It is significant that Martinez and Martin reported their findings in the *Journal of the American Medical Association.* Physicians are not usually called upon to treat *susto* or *mal ojo,* because, as the housewives in the survey pointed out, doctors neither understand these diseases nor are they trained to treat them. As long as that situation persists, patients will seek help from alternative health providers who better understand the reasons for their problems.

3. Indigenous Strategies
of Problem Intervention.

There is an enormous range of help-seeking activities in all cultures. Those activities are guided for the most part by lay interpretations of a problem and by informal consultations with persons who are already within the troubled individual's network. Some types of lay intervention and help seeking will be more familiar than others: reliance on family members and friends; solicitation of advice from a minister, pharmacist, or faith healer; use of special diets or drugs; exercise or meditation to effect some kind of change; resort to religious or secular rituals to manipulate unseen forces. There are also help-seeking activities distinctive to specific groups in our society, such as the utilization of *curanderos* among many Spanish-speaking persons and the active use of religion in the treatment of illness in some black communities. The degree to which many whites rely on television commercials and the popular media as sources of guidance for problem identification and resolution has also been a topic of research interest (Bauwens 1977).

The point to be emphasized is that in virtually all communities, including highly urbanized ones that are well supplied with professional healers and therapists, there are many alternative sources of help. Indeed, professionals may be the least and the last consulted. Especially where minority communities view the social service system as a threat or as a source of social control, social workers may well be the last resort in the chain of help-seeking contacts.

In pluralistic societies such as our own, one of the critical problems in providing social services is the relationship of the dominant provider system to indigenous alternatives. Where professionals are recruited, trained in specialized techniques, indoctrinated in the ideology and folklore of the profession, certified, and licensed, the social distance between them and their clients and between them and the community-based sources to which clients may turn is enormous. Questions of legitimacy, popularity, prestige, and cost are all considered by potential clients in the choice of a help provider. The lack of legitimacy of many social workers in minority communities can be expected to have severe consequences for the intervention process. That issue can be met in part, however, if the worker undertakes to utilize rather than to replace existing resources. If there are individuals or local organizations with histories and reputations for providing assistance, the worker should seek them out, determine what needs they meet and how, and work to deliver services in a complementary manner. The social worker may never enjoy the prestige of such persons or groups, but he or she can work to complement indigenous helping resources.

The black community is one in which these issues of legitimacy are of major importance. The social service establishment has not always served that community well and, as noted in Chapter 6 on the black family and social work, black critics have been harsh. Social services agencies evolved out of the needs of poor European immigrants in large eastern cities while black churches sought to address the problems of poor rural blacks. Blacks had always been a part of the American social landscape. They always had been poor, and their problems did not seem amenable to the psychodynamic approach that became popular in much of social work. But blacks had many of their own sources for help and for specialized advice on personal concerns. Many of these sources persist in both rural and urban areas today.

Black Community Resources.   For a significant portion of the black community in the United States, and in many rural, largely white areas, there exists a common set of beliefs about health, illness, and general well-being derived from old European and African sources. The African origins of these beliefs are bodies of knowledge common to the west coast of Africa during the time of slave trading in the seventeenth and eighteenth centuries. European origins are just as old and were brought to North America by the earliest immigrants. There is no generalized name for this system of knowledge, although terms like "witchcraft" or "spiritualism" have been used. In its contemporary form in the black community, it is a consistent, self-contained set of principles for accounting for the problems that beset individuals. In addition, it is associated with a set of practitioners who, under certain circumstances, provide effective assistance to those who seek it.

This system of belief has been studied by a number of anthropologically-oriented researchers, not only in this country but also in the West Indies and in Africa (Snow 1973, 1974, 1977, 1978; Whitten 1962; Wintrob 1973). It is thus very widespread and, in its geographical dispersion, surprisingly homogeneous as well. It is based on a fundamental division of illness, mental as well as physical, into two kinds: that which is natural and that which is unnatural. It is important to understand this distinction, in order to appreciate the power of those individuals who are recognized within their own communities as proficient healers.

Natural illness results from failure of the individual to properly care for the body. It may also come about as divine punishment for one's misdeeds. In either event, a lack of wellness is due to an improper relationship with natural forces. Cold air, strong drafts, misuse of alcohol, or poor diet can all be responsible for illness and can signify the individual's inattention to basic health and hygiene requirements. Similarly, illness that is a consequence of the displeasure of God results from failure to respect principles of decency and morality as they have been established by Biblical and church authorities.

Unnatural illness, however, is the result of evil influence. Such illness may range from obvious physical ailments to psychosomatic symptoms to problems commonly classified as mental health concerns. But they are all similar, in that their origin is in the evil intentions and the evil actions of others. Unlike natural illness, unnatural illnesses are initiated by a human agent against a victim and fall outside the orderly domain of the universe established by God and nature. Various terms for this activity are "hexing," "rootwork," "fix," "*mojo*," and "witchcraft." It is believed that evil intentions and evil actions are efficacious because all events in the universe are interconnected, and if one knows the interconnections and how to use them, one can have a measure of influence and control over others. It is this wrongful use of power, not the knowledge of occult things per se, that is evil. Thus, the individual who suffers an inexplicable physical or mental problem has reason to believe that someone else is the cause of it. It is important, therefore, to find a specialist who can identify the source of the problem and who knows how to deal with it.

Clearly, neither mental health specialists nor biomedically oriented professionals are in a position to respond to individual complaints based on this kind of conceptualization of illness and misfortune. But there are individuals in the black community who are effective as far as they and many of their clients are concerned. These healers are variously known as psychics, "rootworkers," counselors, "root doctors," conjurors, and sometimes witches. Snow (1973, 1978) has described in detail the skills and procedures of a woman she calls a "voodoo practitioner," and what is remarkable are the similarities of her techniques to those of mental health professionals. The woman's practice was located in her home in the downtown section of a large southwestern American city. Her clients included blacks, whites, Indians, and Mexican Americans. Snow had difficulty locating the woman, because she is known only by word of mouth. Yet her place of business is similar to that of many doctors, counselors, and other professionals. She had an office, in which she kept 9-to-5 hours, and patients met her in a waiting room. The woman had received her training from her grandmother, an individual who also possessed special powers of healing and who was widely known in the local black community for her skills. The training consisted of learning ways to utilize her "gift" in helping others, a gift with which she was born and which could not be obtained in any other way. Portions of her therapy involved touching and massage, but much of it involved talking through a problem with the patient. Using an idiom with which most black patients were intimately familiar—the personalities and events of the Bible—she was able to illuminate the source of personal difficulties and ways of coping with them.

Snow's practitioner made the critical distinction between natural and unnatural forms of illness, claiming no special medical skills for those problems which were clearly within the domain of medical providers: "Now an unnatural sickness—well, that's a person that's sick in the mind. Mentally sick. Doctors can't *find* that. They X-ray and they can't find it. . . . And yet they are *sick,* mentally sick in mind. And then, I'm a *counselor,* I counsel them. . . . I give 'em medicine you know, through their mind. I call that spiritual medicine" (Snow 1973: 278). Judged by the enthusiasm of her patients and the size of her clientele, this practitioner was very successful in her community. She did not compete with established medical professionals, since both she and her patients recognized that she dealt with problems which such practitioners were not trained to handle. Furthermore, she had an intimate knowledge of the pressures of life in the black community and of how poor people are vulnerable to forces they cannot control. Many of her patients came to her after having seen professional counselors, having been disappointed in the kind of treatment they received, and having concluded that professionally trained experts cannot treat the kinds of problems that afflicted them.

It is important to note, as Snow does, that these beliefs in unnatural illness are not simply the legacy of prescientific superstitions. It would be a serious error to interpret them that way. Rather, unnatural illnesses "are those which have to do with the individual's position as a member of society. . . . Some arise from the tensions and anxieties of everyday living. . . . Hostility in interpersonal relationships, on the other hand, may cause the individual to become the target of witchcraft" (Snow 1973: 272-73). Where social relationships are strained because of the problems of poverty, discrimination, and exclusion from full participation in the larger society, beliefs in the efficacy of evil influences are a reasonable response to the daily problems of living (Rainwater 1970).

Foster and Anderson (1978) have identified a number of the characteristics of healers and curers, traits which they believe are the marks of such individuals in all cultures. They include specialization, selection and training, certification, projection of a professional image, expectations of payment, and an ambivalent public image. Snow's practitioner fits all these criteria. She has a specialized store of knowledge—the treatment of unnatural mental and physical illness—and she was specially selected and trained for her task. That selection came about through the influence of her grandmother, but it was also a divine choice. "I was born just exactly with the gift," she said, and with that phrase Snow appropriately titled her article. Certification of competence was oral, in the testimony of patients, and did not require framed certificates issued by hallowed institutions. Further, this healer conducted her practice as a business and, as she herself admitted, her public image was a mixed one. Some in the community accused her of manipulating dark and forbidden forces. Yet she responded that she was simply implementing the power, the "gift," that God had given her.

To the extent that Snow's respondent had success with her patients, it must be attributed not only to her personal skill in counseling others but also to the sense of legitimacy as a helping person that she enjoys in her own community. It is this legitimacy which outsiders, stationed within agencies which are themselves outposts of larger, alien bureaucracies, cannot hope to obtain simply through formal training and completion of specialized, degree-granting programs. Outsiders can acknowledge, however, the importance of indigenous help providers and, to the extent feasible, attempt to learn something of their methods and the reasons for their success. Cultural awareness does not require imitation of the skills of knowledgeable insiders, however desirable that may sometimes be, so much as it presupposes an honest sensibility as to who and what is really helpful for persons seeking advice on matters that trouble them deeply.

4. Culturally-Based Criteria of Problem Resolution.

One of the core tasks of a care system, according to Kleinman (1978a: 87) is the "management of a range of therapeutic outcomes." This is a particularly difficult issue in social services, where intervention and treatment efficacy are difficult to define. That difficulty is compounded where cultural differences contribute to failures in communication and misunderstanding of intent. In transactions with clients, particularly minority clients, social workers have traditionally responded to this problem in two ways, neither of which is useful in enlarging the worker's sense of cultural awareness.

One response has been to focus on the idiosyncratic characteristics of each client, taken one at a time. Differences in ethnicity, race, or power between the client and the worker are underplayed or ignored altogether. The rationalization for this strategy is the often-expressed desire by workers to "individualize the client" and get straight to the diagnosis and treatment as expeditiously as possible. There is a great deal of support for this position in the social work literature, and, indeed, it is one of the implicit if not explicit value and ideological components of the social work professional subculture (Levy 1976). But from an anthropological perspective, this orientation all too often has the effect of stripping the individual of just those things that may be the strongest supports to a healthy sense of individual identity and capability: culturally based communication styles; cultural values associated with the preservation of health; the use of resources; subtleties in family roles; standards of reputation and respectability with family or peers; and patterns of demeanor and conduct that vary, given the occasion or the status of others present. To perceive the client's individuality as something beyond, behind, or irrelevant to these things leaves only as insubstantial ephemera of what the individual must really be like. It also leaves open the possibility for easy stereotyping within whatever theory of human behavior the worker brings to the client encounter, be it Freudian, behaviorist, or eclectic. Pursued vigorously, the decision by the worker that he or she need only "individualize the client" in order to come to a full understanding of the client's needs and possibilities is really a decision to ignore the greater part of that individual's biography.

The other response is the urge to find cultural "reasons" for client behavior, problems, and styles of self-presentation that cannot be accounted for in any other way. In this approach, whatever it is that clients do or say is viewed as causally related to "their culture." Sometimes social workers, relying on common, everyday explanations for cultural differences, may make superficial, stereotypic judgments about their clients. Typically, the more difficult it is to explain the behavior or problem in question, the more intense the search for cultural explanations. This is particularly likely if the explanation uncovered is one which will satisfy curiosity about the beliefs and strange customs of others (Neutra et al. 1977). This kind of reliance on cultural variations—variations that are known anecdotally rather than as part of a systematic effort to comprehend the meaning of ethnicity for clients— suggests the truth of the cliché that "a little knowledge is a dangerous thing." Lacking an organized, comparative framework for accommodating ethnographic data, isolated and anecdotal information about ethnic differences are the worker's primary source of knowledge about culturally distinctive clients.

The resolution of this difficulty is largely a matter of matching familiarity with the cultural background of a client with a cultural intervention style that can lead to treatment goals within the client's framework of understanding. If the worker is knowledgeable about the recent history and the day-to-day experiences of the client's home community, there is little likelihood that inappropriate intervention approaches and goals will be pursued. Similarly, the worker who is alert to cultural variations within the client community will have some sense of how individuals might respond to specific communication styles or therapeutic techniques. Of course, the greater the cultural difference between the worker's background and that of the client, the more the worker must learn in order to be effective in cross-cultural encounters. The recent immigration of Southeast Asians to this country, particularly the Vietnamese, provides one example of how social workers can respond to clients in a way that builds on principles of cultural awareness.

Asian Immigration.   The evacuation of Vietnamese from South Vietnam in 1975 represented a major challenge to social service organizations in many parts of the United States. Unfamiliar with American culture and the English language, many Vietnamese discovered too late that what they thought was to be a temporary retreat before returning to their homes was to become instead permanent exile and relocation in a strange country. Many apparently came to accept the fact that their future would be an American one (Kelly 1977). But this acceptance was not easy, given the suddenness of their emigration and the difficulties of life in the refugee camps (Rahe et al. 1976). The need for social services, both advocacy and long-term counseling, was and still remains great—a need that is complicated by the fact that the refugees came from a culture with little tradition of publicly sponsored social service programs and considerable stigma associated with the kinds of problems that practitioners in this country are trained to help resolve.

The stark cultural differences separating Vietnamese and Americans suggest the importance of service providers acquiring both an overall background knowledge of Southeast Asian peoples and some guidelines for using that knowledge in professional practice. Both of these objectives can be met through a careful study of the cultural history of the immigrant population and the translation of predominant cultural themes into service techniques and objectives. The results can and should be the resolution of individual and family problems in a way that is acceptable and useful to clients. We will briefly suggest here the types of skills and knowledge that would be important.

As is true of most areas of the world, the population of Southeast Asia is culturally diverse. Excluding tribal peoples, of which there are numerous distinctive ethnic groups, there are two major civilizations in the region (Keyes 1977). Buddhist-oriented traditions evolved as the result of extensive borrowing from India. This borrowing was followed by the cultural infiltration of people from southern China. Consequently, refugees from Burma, Thailand, Cambodia, or Laos would most likely be affiliated with a Buddhist world view. The Vietnamese, by contrast, represent a distinctly Chinese tradition, one influenced more by Confucian ideals and Chinese patterns of social organization. The historic Vietnamese "push to the south" along the eastern edge of the mainland led to a lengthy period of instability and conflict, a condition which still persists. Part of that conflict involved colonizing activities by the French, whose influence is seen in the importance of Catholicism in the country.

Having noted these major variations, it is important to mention several general themes that are common to the region. One is the exceptionally high value placed on family life. The Vietnamese pattern is based on a Chinese model of the patrilineal extended family, one in which the senior male has high status as head of the family unit. In predominantly Buddhist areas, less emphasis is given to lineality in family and kinship structure, although the predominant importance of senior males is often preserved. A second similarity is the role attached to fate in everyday affairs. The Buddhist notion of karma suggests that all life involves suffering, but that the individual can reduce his or her share, at least in any future existence, by the performance of meritorious acts. To some degree, one can influence one's own fate through morally upright behavior and thoughts. Salvation is the ultimate reward. The Vietnamese view excludes the possibility of salvation or of modifying one's fate. The world simply is, and harmony in this life, not salvation in some future one, must be the individual's goal. Since there is no escape from fate, preserving a sense of harmony and balance is a goal, particularly in the "five fundamental relationships of society," those between ruler and ruled, father and son, husband and wife, older brother and younger brother, and friend and friend (Keyes 1977: 195).

The refugees from Vietnam were a special, perhaps atypical, segment of Vietnamese culture. While many came as family groups, rather than as lone individuals, most refugees were young, half of them under the age of eighteen. Almost 50 percent were Catholic, over a quarter were Buddhist, and two thirds were from highly educated, well-to-do, urban and professional households (Montero 1979). Confronted with American cultural traditions and jobs that were for the most part menial and low paying, they were certain to face adjustment difficulties. A number of problems have occurred repeatedly.

Many Vietnamese have experienced disturbing readjustments in family roles, a matter of particular interest to social workers. Under more crowded, less affluent, living conditions, inherent strains in family life have become more apparent. These include potential conflict between the wife and her mother-in-law and the resultant strain for the husband, who must balance important filial obligations and responsibilities toward his wife. Similarly, the strict obedience expected of children in their relations with parents, relatives, all adults, and older siblings is challenged by American practices, which foster a sense of independence, assertiveness, and inquisitiveness. The American sense of autonomy in action conflicts with Vietnamese notions of subordination of personal interests to those of the family group. Finally, physical violence, drinking, divorce, open criticism of others, and direct, face-to-face confrontation are all highly offensive. Yet they are increasingly part of the experience of refugees, who must cope with economic marginality and with uncertainty about the meaning and consequences of their actions, and who sometimes live in isolation from other Vietnamese (Vuong 1976).

A culturally sensitive approach, by which social workers can work with their Vietnamese clients, has been developed by Ishisaka and his associates (1977). It contains a number of steps, the most important of which involves a lengthy period of trust-building, without direct reference to family problems; separate discussions with individual family members; scaling of expectations to the realities of American life; negotiation of revised expectations between family members, still meeting separately with the worker; and the generation of multiple ways by which these revised expectations may be met. Many of the steps utilize cultural principles concerning fate, family roles, and other cultural precedents for handling guilt, depression, and paranoia, as well as problems with police, courts, schools, and employers. The goal of this program is to promote "bicultural adjustment," that is, "Individuals who speak with no evidence of shame regarding their unique cultural backgrounds; who indicate an unapologetic understanding that Americans behave in ways that are sometimes confusing, and who do not show excessive anxiety in novel American situations. . . ." (Ishisaka et al. 1977: 18). Such an individual would be capable of expressing positive sentiments toward his or her own ethnic heritage and would at the same time feel no need for either condemnation or uncritical acceptance of the culture of the dominant society.

IMPLICATIONS OF THE MODEL
FOR SOCIAL SERVICES

The Help-Seeking Behavior model for provision of services to culturally distinctive clients contains the following components: (1) group-specific criteria of problem identification; (2) group-specific linguistic categories of problem labeling; (3) lay helping strategies for problem resolution; and (4) group-specific standards for knowing that a problem has been successfully resolved. It should be apparent that these are all cross-cultural categories. They are applicable to any group or community. They also require the worker to think in cross-cultural terms, and this requirement has major implications for how workers approach their tasks. At minimum, it may mean some adjustments in intervention techniques and perhaps even in professional values. The culturally responsive worker, functioning in a service system designed to accommodate culturally based, help-seeking patterns, might be characterized in the following way:

1. Capable of thinking about clients in terms of group characteristics—both group strengths and potential sources of conflict—as well as in terms of individual pathology and individual problem resolution. Since the concept of culture applies to groups, not to single individuals, the capacity for linking cultural components to individual behavior is a critical task. Stereotyping or reliance on culturally devoid psychological explanations is antithetical to cultural awareness.

2. Willing to undertake an examination of group strengths as they are understood by group members. This may require modification or abandonment of some established theories and interpretations of how or why clients experience the problems they do and what the worker can do about it. It also

means that clients ought to be viewed as potential teachers of the workers as well as recipients of services. Such an attitude toward clients could result in a substantial modification of the client role in the service system.

3. Open to utilization of indigenous sources of help. This is not only a cultural issue; it is an explosive political one. It suggests granting credence for intervention effectiveness to lay practitioners, who may lack formal training and recognized credentials or degrees. These are often people whose skill in their craft most social workers could never match. How these "unofficial" help providers are to be acknowledged and their skills utilized remains a difficult and unresolved problem for the social work profession.

4. Willing to acknowledge the role of both lay and professional helping activity in client intervention, combined with rigorous efforts to compare the quality of each. This is especially difficult, since the evaluation of services in institutional settings is often complex. It is much more problematic when investigating the quality of care provided outside controlled settings. Yet even where methodological issues can be resolved, the political ones of comparing the work of trained professionals with indigenous helpers may be insurmountable. This is one area where minority practitioners can make important contributions to identifying the components of culturally sensitive intervention skills.

5. Accepting of definitions of successful intervention that are meaningful to clients and their community but which may on occasions be only incidentally meaningful in terms of agency accountability, agency managers, program evaluators, or professional service standards. There may always be a conflict between the interests of the client and the client's community, on the one hand, and the agency, its needs and the demands of professionalism on the other. But the worker still needs to recognize that where these conflicts occur, the real problems experienced by clients and client communities are too important to be lost in agency and office politics.

In summary, the Help-Seeking Behavior model is a way of thinking about social services from the perspective of the client and the client's culture. It is applicable cross-culturally, and the sensitive and alert worker can use it, regardless of the work site. What is required is a willingness to suspend temporarily all professional or agency priorities, in order to look at the worth of the services provided from the perspective of those who are the recipients. The model raises questions as to what alterative sources of help may exist and how those sources can be encouraged and complemented by professionals.

Finally, the model suggests that the road to cultural awareness requires much effort and learning on the part of the worker. The kind of person the worker happens to be—open, caring, empathic—is not sufficient without the acquisition of cross-cultural sensitivities as well. A sustained effort, aimed at recognizing cultural modes of behavior and responding appropriately, is required. The skillful worker will learn to recognize predictable patterns in client interaction; the same worker will also know how to individualize the client in relation to those patterns. That is the prime attribute of the worker who, in the next chapter, is defined as ethnically competent.

CHAPTER THREE
CROSS-CULTURAL
SOCIAL WORK

Cross-cultural social work is the utilization of ethnographic information in the planning, delivery, and evaluation of social services for minority and ethnic group clients. Defined in this way, it means much more than simply contact with clients who are culturally or racially different from the worker. It means adequate preparation for and alertness to those cultural features of the client's background which influence the outcome of a social service encounter. It is the quality of the service encounter, and particularly how a social worker begins to acquire the knowledge and skills appropriate for working with clients from ethnically distinctive communities, that concerns us here. Our contention is that traditional social service training methods must be supplemented by field-oriented learning techniques similar to those that have been developed by anthropologists and others for whom cross-cultural understanding and communication are critical. Entering unfamiliar communities, working with key respondents, utilizing the general approach of participant observation to identify culturally distinctive helping patterns and—in the following chapter—interviewing skills that generate culturally sensitive information will all be considered.

There are several reasons for the need to acquire cross-cultural knowledge and capabilities in social work. First, many workers know little of the cultural characteristics of their clients. This is not surprising, since it is only recently that minority concerns have appeared in the curriculum of social work programs. Yet unfortunately much that passes for "cultural sensitivity" training, be it in formal education or on-the-job workshops, is trivial at best and tokenism at worst. It is necessary, therefore, to propose ways of acquiring cultural information and of utilizing it in a systematic way. The anecdotal approach to acquiring knowledge about the values, preferences, and expectations of culturally distinctive clients is simply inadequate.

Second, among most Americans the expression of prejudicial attitudes in public and professional settings is much less acceptable than it used to be. In educated circles, at least, bigotry is boorish. But institutional forms of insensitivity and discrimination persist. As we noted in the chapter on ethnicity, institutional forms of mistreatment are harder to see and more difficult to correct. That is partly due to the fact that sometimes individuals benefit in direct or indirect ways from the status quo. Privilege is at stake. But institutional practices which are long established also carry the authority of tradition. Tradition can be used as a dogma— "we have always done things this way"—and thus serve as a rationale for the continuing of program and agency practices. A cultural approach to social services, however, makes explicit the dichotomy between the values and procedures of those who provide services and the values and responses of those who receive them. Two kinds of traditions—those of the profession and those of the client community—are clearly juxtaposed. This makes it possible to identify and then change institutional as well as individual deficiencies in social services in ways that take into account the characteristics of those served.

CROSS-CULTURAL LEARNING

It is commonplace in much of social work, especially in those areas involving direct encounters with clients, that the successful worker must establish rapport and develop empathic relationships in order to further treatment objectives. Truax and Mitchell (1971), for instance, found empathy, warmth, and genuineness to be frequently reported characteristics of individuals considered effective in assisting others. A number of training approaches have been devised to facilitate the acquisition of these "helping" capabilities (Ivey 1971; Danish and Hauer 1973). The literature on skills development in social work is very large, covering many kinds of intervention activities, and we will not review it here. However, such approaches generally stress the student's enhanced perception of verbal and nonverbal cues, attentiveness to emotional states during interaction, and styles of questioning and responding. Typically these training approaches suggest to the learner rather general categories of desired behavior ("self-involving," "encouraging," "assertive," and the like) and pose problems with which the learner can practice intervention and relationship-building techniques. One assumption of many of these training efforts, although it is rarely stated, is that the designated "helping skills" are uniformly applicable to most if not all clients and to most client problems and that the worker need only refine these skills in order to develop the warm, trusting relationship that is the mark of the professional in working with others.

We will argue here, however, that such techniques as displaying and building rapport are not in and of themselves a sufficient basis for working with minority clients. While personal qualities of warmth and caring may well be important as work styles, they are not in themselves an adequate basis for comprehending what it is that troubles another individual or for knowing how that individual may be helped. Rather, what is needed is a set of training experiences that can be adapted to a variety of cross-cultural situations and by means of which the learner can acquire the relevant knowledge for working successfully with minority group clients.

But how does one learn about another culture? A child learns the patterns and pieces of a culture as they are presented, somewhat randomly and over a long period of time. A monocultural adult entering an unfamiliar social world is forced to learn the same way. Events and objects appear which are strange at first, then recede into the background as their places in a culture context become familiar and are taken for granted. The adult's advantage over the child is the capacity for critical assessment of the pieces as they are presented. The disadvantage is that learned prejudices act as blinders to much that is going on. Critical assessment can proceed at several levels, all of which are necessary in acquiring ethnic competence.

The framework developed by Taft (1977) includes useful steps for acquiring knowledge of other cultural systems. The first level of learning is that of cognition. One must simply learn what members of the culture know—their beliefs about their history, values, and ideology, and in particular how they judge their relationships to the world. The accuracy of their beliefs and knowledge is not at issue; consequently, it is futile to rely solely on library research to find out about these kinds of things. What matters is what people believe to be true, since that is what is most real to them and is the basis on which they act. What is held to be real is, in any culture, orderly and for the most part reasonable to the group members. At the cognitive level, then, the task of the ethnically competent practitioner is to try to determine the orderliness of beliefs and behavior as the members of the culture perceive it. That order is expressed as "common sense," the taken-for-granted things that people rarely question. For example, there are ways of treating children, of serving food, and of offering greetings that are "right," as well as ways that are "wrong" according to perceived notions of propriety. The worker will simply have to learn—by reading, listening, watching—what those things are. An alertness to the regularities of conduct and the presence of mind to find out what they mean to the participants is essential.

Second, there is an affective tone associated with beliefs and knowledge. Sometimes that tone is identifiable in the overtly expressive features of a culture —singing, dancing, eating, arguing, playing, and working. Affective tone can also be discovered in the subtleties of offhand comments, facial expressions, joking relationships, exchange of favors, and styles of demeanor. In all cultures, people play largely predetermined roles: those of spouse, child, friend, or co-worker. How they play their roles, however, how they make those expressive gestures that Goffman (1959) called the "presentation of self," is a clue to the affective characteristics of a given culture. Those characteristics are likely to be complex and difficult to perceive, but they represent gut-level realities of experience that no practitioner can choose to ignore. To appreciate them fully for oneself as a cultural outsider is perhaps impossible, but to be able to recognize them and respond appropriately in a cross-cultural encounter is essential. Rapport comes with a willingness to learn something of the cognitive orientation and affective expressions of a people, to recognize these and to respond in kind. Rapport derives from an intense effort to learn the cultural setting of others; it does not come from patronizing urges to project oneself into the shoes of another.

What this suggests is that the competent practitioner may on occasions attempt—with a great deal of caution and humbleness—to simulate culturally appropriate role performances when invited to do so. This is, as Taft notes, the "ultimate test of enculturation" (1977: 136). One can know about things and respond to feelings of the members of an ethnic group. But until one can act appropriately and have the act recognized by others as culturally genuine, the broadened understanding that comes from having moved in two cultures is never really achieved. Perhaps this performance level of capability is beyond what most practitioners really require for their jobs. Yet it would be difficult to argue that a profession committed to "helping" individuals with their intimate problems of interpersonal and family relationships could ignore the cultural realities that are the context of those problems. A performance-level response of cultural awareness represents a depth of comprehension of others that surpasses the usual injunctions about patience, genuineness, and honesty in client-worker relationships.

There is a need to define this capability, for it represents the essential, critical characteristic of the worker who knows, appreciates, and can utilize the culture of another in assisting with the resolution of a human problem. We will refer to that capability as "ethnic competence." To be "ethnically competent" means to be able to conduct one's professional work in a way that is congruent with the behavior and expectations that members of a distinctive culture recognize as appropriate among themselves.

It is imperative that our definition of ethnic competence be understood for both what it says and what it does not say. It does not say—and we must be emphatic on this point—that the trained individual will be able to conduct himself or herself as though a member of a culturally distinctive group. That is clearly absurd, and to offer such a capability as a personal or professional training goal would be highly misleading. It would also be manipulative and patronizing, as some individuals might correctly point out. Rather, the definition implies an awareness of prescribed and proscribed behavior within a specific culture, and it suggests that the ethnically competent worker has the ability to carry out professional activities consistent with that awareness. It does not propose that trained individuals are those who can mimic the behavioral routines and linguistic particularities of their minority clients. Nor does it rule that out. Its emphasis is on the trained worker's ability to adapt professional tasks and work styles to the cultural values and preferences of clients.

ETHNIC COMPETENCE

Given our definition of ethnic competence, we need to specify what the concept includes. There is a small but growing body of literature on cross-cultural communication and cultural awareness. It covers a variety of fields, including counseling with foreign students, preparing corporate executives to conduct business in foreign countries, and researching the verbal and nonverbal behavior of culturally distinctive individuals in psychology laboratories. Little has been written on cross-cultural counseling and communication for social services specifically, and much of what has been written is either anecdotal or of a narrow, clinical orientation. There is a need, therefore, to identify some of the characteristics of effective cross-cultural communication, particularly as they might apply to social work, and to suggest ways that workers can acquire the knowledge and skills that contribute to cross-cultural capability in their professional work.

In some ways, it is easier to define what cross-cultural sensitivity is not than to pinpoint what it is. Pedersen (1976) has described what he calls the "culturally encapsulated counselor," the individual who is unable or unwilling to engage the client on any but the counselor's own terms. Such a counselor capitalizes on the status differences that separate him or her from the client and uses these differences to establish a coercive or authoritarian relationship. The client's living circumstances or personal problems are evaluated according to criteria more suitable to the personal or professional milieu of the counselor than to the day-to-day experiences of the client. Encapsulation is often evident when the counselor has been socialized into a set of professional values and theoretical orientations that stress the characteristics of the client in isolation, with only minimum reference to larger social groups, especially groups other than the family. Pedersen notes that a "technique-oriented job definition further contributes toward, and perpetuates, the process of encapsulation" (1976: 24) by dogmatizing theoretical orientations and closing off any consideration of alternative ways of working with clients. The encapsulated counselor is more committed to a set of beliefs, to "process" and technique, and to professional and institutional loyalties than to the concerns and background of individual clients.

Effective cross-cultural communication, the kind we have in mind when we speak of ethnic competence, must in some way be different from the portrait of communicative arrogance contained in the notion of encapsulation. The list below, adapted from Mayes (1978), suggests what some of the differences might be and it defines some of the features of ethnic competence. These features refer not only to the personal attitudes and attributes of the individual's supplying counseling services but also to the organizations that back them up, the way they are trained, and the ways they learn about and communicate with those whom they seek to assist.

1. Ethnic Competence as Awareness of One's Own Cultural Limitations

One of the implications of the model of help-seeking behavior is that the more similar the cognitive and affective characteristics of the client and the worker, the greater the chance for effective communication. In addressing this issue in the medical context of relations between patient and physician, Kleinman (1978a: 88) has noted that: "Viewed from the perspective of the cultural system . . . professional practitioners talk about sickness in a sector-specific language of biological functions and behavior, whereas patients and families, even when they incorporate terms from the former, talk about sickness in a culture-wide language of experience." Where highly sensitive and private issues are the topics of discussion, as they often are in social services, the cultural differences between client and worker can be just as easily magnified.

Stewart et al. (1969) list five value assumptions which are characteristic of "mainstream" American culture and which they believe are dominant in much of the planning and delivery of mental health services. These values are (a) active self-expression (b) equality and informality in social relationships (c) achievement and accomplishment (d) control of self and one's destiny while in pursuit of a better future, and (e) individualism and autonomy experienced in democratic, nonauthoritarian relationships with others. Admirable as these values appear to be, especially to persons whose socialization has included years of public education and advanced training in university programs marked by liberal, humanistic learning, they may not be the values of those whose immersion is in a subculture more oriented toward day-to-day problems of survival or those who participate in a community that has preserved old, even ancient, traditions transplanted to an American setting. For instance, a client's sense of propriety in discussing intimate matters outside the family might conflict with the notion of "active self-expression," particularly when that expression is with someone not of the client's ethnic group. Nor can it be assumed that the ability to articulate to others one's most private feelings is a sign of a positive mental state. It may not be appropriate for the individual in some cultures to independently "assert" himself or herself with others. Similarly, we could not take it for granted that all cultures have a notion of "personal growth" tied to expectations of individual accomplishment.

What all of this suggests is the applicability of the old anthropological cliché of cultural relativism. Cultures are in fact different. Students occasionally get a sense of this when they participate in "values clarification" exercises. And as useful as these may be, they are not a substitute for live confrontation with people who are in a world different from one's own. While some may not agree that these five postulates do indeed define the core values of mainstream American culture, they nevertheless provide a perspective with which to compare the contrasting values and assumptions of the social work profession and the traditions and concerns of people in ethnic and minority communities.

2. Ethnic Competence as Openness to Cultural Differences

The belief that "underneath we are all the same" and that we all share a basic understanding of what is good and valuable in life might well have been added to our list of common American values. These beliefs derive from the melting pot ideology, with its assumption (and hope!) that the cultural differences that separate people are less important than the things that unite them, and that manifestations of differences are best underemphasized in order to assure tranquility in social relations. Even at a time when the word "pluralism" has become a fashionable one, as a description of a personal sense of tolerance and appreciation of the idiosyncrasies of others, it remains true that cultural dissimilarity is less highly valued than is cultural homogeneity. In fact, the promotion of cultural differences, and the privileges that may or may not go with those differences, is viewed by many as threatening. This is dramatically clear when themes of ethnicity are explicitly linked with proposed changes in the distribution of status and power (as in the Black Power movement) and in the realignment of economic privileges (as in Indian land and fishing claims). Cultural differences are threatening even on the symbolic level, as when seemingly "assimilated" individuals insist that their children receive instruction in languages other than English when these are used in the home. The deliberate acceptance and appreciation of cultural differences have rarely been promoted in the educational, religious, or political institutions of the larger society. It is not surprising, therefore, that this lack of acceptance should be reflected in an awkwardness and a hesitancy in providing social services to ethnic and minority communities.

The acceptance of ethnic differences in an open, genuine manner, without condescension and without patronizing gestures, is critical for the development of an ethnically competent professional style. In face-to-face counseling, that means, among other things, that the worker must have a sense of how the social artifact called the "counseling relationship" fits into the normative expectations of the person being counseled. Does the client perceive as normal or acceptable a deeply personal conversation with a near stranger, one having a great deal of authority and one who is a representative of another, possibly dominant, ethnic group? Is the worker expected to give something of value—advice, goods, an eligibility rating— in return for a proper show of deference or need? What does the client expect to happen during and after an encounter? Clarification of expectations in the counseling relationship is the first step toward generating a discussion of the meaning of cultural differences as far as it relates to the provision of a service. That clarification need not turn on such obvious and abstract questions as "What does your Indianness mean to you?" But it ought to start with some acknowledgment that both the client's and the worker's ethnic and cultural identities may be important to what each of them expects to result from the counseling encounter. The skill with which this is done, of course, depends on the maturity and capability of the worker. But it is an essential skill, in that it makes clear to both worker and client that the latter has something more to contribute to the discussion than an explication of a problem; the client also possesses a heritage that contains clues as to what can be done, and it is the client, not the worker, who may be in the best position to appreciate how that heritage can be utilized in the problem-solving process.

3. Ethnic Competence as a Client-Oriented, Systematic, Learning Style

All cross-cultural encounters are potential learning experiences. They may result in the discovery of new information or in an enhanced understanding of something not fully appreciated before. Systematic learning depends on whether the worker-as-help-provider is willing to adopt the role of worker-as-learner.

The concept of ethnic competence makes the assumption that the client, however plagued by personal problems and uncertainties, knows a great deal which can be elicited and used in whatever therapy seems appropriate. The difficulty for the professional may be in accepting a learner relationship toward the client in addition to the investigative and advising tasks of counseling.

The kind of flexibility required for learning from clients is not often taught in professional education programs such as social work, education, or health. The distinctive nature of ethnographic sensitivity lies in the fact that the remarkable is sought in the most commonplace and that one's professional obligation is to discover the cognitive and affective weight of even the most mundane objects and events. To achieve that level of insight means that the professional must be willing to be "trained" by the people who are his or her respondents (Pelto and Pelto 1973). There is little in American higher education or in the subculture of professionalism to support that kind of perspective toward clients, patients, or others who seek advice. The worker who adopts ethnic competence as a training goal, therefore, not only must deal with the natural hesitancy of minority groups to reveal community secrets to outsiders but may also have to confront the prejudices of professional colleagues.

4. Ethnic Competence as Utilizing Cultural Resources

Individual responses to authority and dependency, the sense of autonomy in action and decision-making, and openness to communication are expressions not only of personal idiosyncrasy but of cultural conventions. Even where the worker is familiar with such conventions in a general way, there remains the problem of assessing the individual client's relation to them and planning how these conventions—cultural resources, really—can be utilized on behalf of the client. The ability to help a client recognize and make use of resources, be they people or ideas, is one of the critical tasks of the ethnically competent worker. It is what Solomon (1976) has called "empowerment." It encourages the client to draw upon the natural strengths inherent in all cultures and communities and thereby reduce dependency on social services (Handelman 1976).

Cultural resources are probably those least used by professional social workers in their encounters with clients. There is a tendency to think of resources as the network of community social service agencies and resource utilization as the referral process by which clients are linked to the social service system. This is only the visible and obvious part of the human service network, and for many clients it may be the part to which they go only as a last resort. Clients may have relied first on family, friends, voluntary organizations, ministers, pharmacists, or bartenders for advice and assistance. They may have struggled with a problem in more private ways, through reading, contemplation, prayer, talking to themselves, or watching soap operas on television. They will have made choices and decisions about the nature of a particular problem and how they will or will not deal with it. In all of these things, troubled individuals will have relied upon the beliefs and values that are part of their particular heritage and, when they have turned to others, they will usually have gone to those who share in their traditions.

It is not reasonable to conclude, therefore, that clients can be expected to improve upon their abilities to manage their lives without recourse to the things that they know and have done in the past. If, for instance, the client's background includes an acceptance of a powerful but informal role for older adults in directing the affairs of an extended family, spread over multiple households, as is the case among some black families (Martin and Martin 1978), then the worker needs to know that ethnographic fact, so that the utilization of that resource for a client can be planned.

The capacity for individualizing the client within a specific cultural matrix is the genius and the challenge of effective cross-cultural social work. To do so, the worker must know the resources available to the client and how they may be best used. The term *resources* here means not only the network of community agencies and referral services. It also means the institutions, individuals, and customs for resolving problems that are indigenous to the client's own community. Indeed, these indigenous resources may be the most important for resolving on a long-term basis whatever problem brought the client to the worker's attention in the first place. Because such resources are part of the community as an ongoing entity, they are less likely to fade away as public policies and governmental funding levels change. Community resources will be available to the client after professional consultations have been terminated. It is critical, then, that the worker know what these resources are and how they can be most productively utilized. That kind of learning requires moving out into the community, not just as a worker representing an agency and its interests, but as a learner of the subtleties of communication, expectation, and participation in the cultural world of the client.

5. Ethnic Competence
as Acknowledging Cultural Integrity

There is a tendency for those raised in the Anglo-Saxon tradition to think of faraway cultures, such as those studied by Margaret Mead, as examples of whole and intact entities, while dispossessed and displaced Indian or West African cultures are but shattered remnants, ripe for assimilation to a melted-down American norm. In catch phrases such as "culture of poverty," "multiproblem families," "cultural deprivation," or "the black problem," the prejudicial view of failed cultures is expressed. Yet all cultural traditions and all extant communities are by definition rich, complex, and varied. It is only the superficiality of the contacts that generally occur among persons of differing ethnic backgrounds that conceals subtlety and nuance and makes difficult the appreciation of difference.

The idea of the holistic, integral nature of all cultures is a philosophical one, but it is also a practical, empirical matter. For instance, McFee (1968) has described how, in his research among the members of one group of American Indians, some of his respondents shifted their frame of reference when interacting with whites and shifted back again when dealing with highly traditional members of the reservation community. In his striking metaphor of the "150 percent man," he found individuals who behaved 75 percent Indian among other Indians, and 75 percent white in certain relations with whites. Clearly, simplistic descriptions of acculturation as a one-way continuum from Indian to white culture masked a great deal of the complexity of Indian-white (and many Indian-Indian) encounters. Similarly, the terms so often applied to individual deviance—marginality, partial assimilation, culture loss—seemed inappropriate for describing the lives of 150 percent men. McFee's point, and it is an important one in thinking about the nature of the exchanges between worker and culturally distinctive clients, is that any culture, including seemingly very traditional ones, contains a complex repertoire of responses, and that this repertoire may be expanded by contact, even destructive contact, with other cultures. Thus, a once isolated culture may become, in some ways, an increasingly differentiated one. Differentiation, not replacement of one set of traits by another set, is the critical social process. It can include the acquisition of new technology or the modification of old values, and it most certainly fosters an elaborate etiquette of cross-cultural encounters. To recognize new forms of social complexity as they emerge in the behavior of individuals and to value the capacity for creative response to social change is to acknowledge the integrity and capability inherent in all cultural traditions. This view of cultures, as sources of creative complexity rather than substitutive replacement, is the essence of ethnic competence as a personal and professional orientation.

Yet to state the matter as simply and obviously as we have here is to propose an outlook radically different from the policies and attitudes which have governed contacts between whites and nonwhites in the past and which, for the most part, continue at the present. There remains a gross unwillingness, in American society at large and in social service programs specifically, to take seriously the notion that a multitude of life ways is as acceptable as the homogeneous norm represented in the national media. Perhaps it is our heritage of racism, of genocidal policies toward Indians, and of easily ignited fears of "yellow peril," together with the continuing expression of ethnic and racial antagonism by cults and hate groups, that prevent the resolution of these old antagonisms in just ways. For us in social services, however, the need remains great to examine the philosophy and procedures of our programs to assure that they do not perpetuate the inequities of the past.

FIRST STEPS TOWARD ETHNIC COMPETENCE

The five characteristics of "ethnic competence" described above should help to orient our professional work toward the needs of minority clients. By themselves, however, they are only propositions about a general way of thinking and acting. The route to awareness of the role of culture in human behavior requires direct observation and participation in naturalistic settings, away from the confines of offices and their imposing routines. For instance, the practitioner who has failed to attend a black church service or talk with a black minister might not understand black clients. The worker serving Indian clients should witness how extended families take care of their children and their elderly and how ritual practices are used for preserving traditional ways. He or she should try to understand through participant observation the problems that individuals face in leaving reservations to find jobs in the Anglo world. These activities cannot be observed from behind the desk of an agency office nor can they be understood through classroom exercises or short-term workshops alone. Nor can very much understanding be acquired through hasty consultation with minority social workers or minority group leaders. Ethnic competence means moving beyond the description of one's job functions and learning about clients through direct observation and even participation in their everyday routines.

In becoming a learner of another culture, however, one cannot operate alone or without guidance. There is often a temptation for the excessively eager person to want to attempt to slip unobserved into another community for purposes of "study." This usually creates a false sense of knowledge and insight, as it is really a kind of academic voyeurism, not a serious effort at cross-cultural learning. Rather, the learner must enter as the guest of a member of the group or culture involved, a member who understands the learner's goals and who agrees to act as a guide. In addition, the task of preparing to meet with a cultural guide is a lengthy and sometimes tedious one. It requires extensive study of documents and popular reading material related to the group in question. Only after extensive preparation and establishment of rapport with one or more guides is the learner in a position to begin anything that approximates participant observation.

We will describe these three steps in cross-cultural learning—background preparation, use of cultural guides, and participant observation—but it is important first to comment on the role of minority professionals in the learning process.

People who are in regular contact with persons ethnically distinct from themselves and who work well with them depend heavily on informed and informative insiders. Their use of cultural guides is not occasional, occurring only at times of social or political crisis. Rather, their consultation and advice-seeking are ongoing activities and are important parts of their professional styles. While it seems obvious that white practitioners ought to have this kind of relationship with minority professionals, the idea of the key respondent or cultural guide is hardly limited to white-nonwhite situations. Black workers may and do encounter Asian or American Indian clients, for instance. But all workers must be alert to the potential for exploitation in the key respondent relationship. Many minority workers will rightly view infrequent requests from white workers for cultural guidance as another form of tokenism. However well-intended, some white workers may be surprised when minority professionals express irritation at requests for information on why "their people" think and act as they do. The resolution of the problem can be found, in part, in a genuine and committed long-term, rather than episodic, effort to learn about the culture of ethnically distinct clients. The procedures that are described below are some steps in that direction. We discuss ways of making the initial approach to persons in an unfamiliar culture, the role of the cultural guide in providing information and additional contacts, and the technique of participant observation as it can be utilized by social service workers.

1. Entering an Unfamiliar Community

In a discussion of doing social research in naturalistic settings, Johnson (1975: 76) notes that successful entree into the field is not the beginning of a project so much as the consequences of careful preparation and planning during a pre-entree phase. The same can be said for the social worker's efforts to become familiar with the community in which he or she will be working. Without knowledge of the community served, social services cannot be responsive in a positive way to the needs of clients. And without careful preparation, entrance into the community for the purpose of acquiring that knowledge cannot be the exciting and interesting experience for the worker that it can and should be.

The task of learning about an unfamiliar community often appears to be one of the most difficult and also the most threatening aspects of acquiring ethnic competence. It seems difficult, and in some ways it is, because most of the time most people are not required to deal with persons unlike themselves except on a short-term, instrumental basis. Contact with ethnically distinctive individuals, at least for most whites, is limited to commercial transactions, on-the-job activities, and random encounters in public places. For these kinds of encounters, the rules of decorum usually require studied indifference or cautious politeness; personal opinions about race or ethnicity, however benign or prejudiced, are not allowed to disrupt the superficial agreeableness of such encounters. It requires a real effort, therefore, to show more than a casual interest in others, especially an interest that requires one to seek out culturally distinctive persons in their own homes and neighborhoods.

There are two procedures to be followed in planning to enter an unfamiliar community. The first is preparation through study of available research and documents; the second is a series of visitations for the purpose of what we will call "social mapping." These two procedures should be carried out at the same time, prior to developing contacts with community members and prior to the extended interviews that will be carried out with key respondents.

At least three sources of data for study are available on culturally distinctive communities, and all three should be utilized extensively. First, ethnographic accounts in the form of scholarly monographs are available on almost every ethnic group in American society. Indeed, it is difficult to think of any group that has been overlooked by sociologists or anthropologists in their pursuit of a "new" people to study and write about. Many ethnic groups have produced their own researchers, so that it is not even necessary in most instances to look up the publications of white scholars. There is a small but growing number of minority persons who have written eloquently and imaginatively on the culture of their home communities. The perspectives of these writers should be part of any background reading program.

A second source is the literature on ethnicity and on race relations that has developed within social work itself. This literature appears in the recognized, established journals and sometimes in off-beat, less easily located publications. It focuses on the issues confronting minority persons in social services and on the problems that exist in developing sensitive and useful services for minority clients.

The third source is the documentation that pertains to a specific community or region. Because of the number of studies conducted by the government at all levels, and for all kinds of reasons, it is unlikely that any city or county totally lacks descriptive information on the minority groups resident there. The problem with this resource is difficulty of access. It is often buried in the files of government agencies, some of them social service agencies, and one would first have to learn of their existence even to ask where they were located. Such sources, however, are crucial for what they reveal about the conditions of life in many communities, and they are usually worth the trouble to find, read, and analyze.

The task of the worker is to find and assimilate as much of this background information as possible. There are two reasons for doing so. The worker cannot begin to appreciate what is going on in a community, or why, without digging into the sources at each of these levels. Each has something important to say that cannot be learned any other way. In addition, background research and reading provide an initial familiarity, however limited, that can help reduce the sense of anxiety and uncertainty about what will be discovered during community visits. To avoid the necessary homework that must precede community encounters is, quite bluntly, to slight the seriousness of the job to be done.

The second procedure is that of visiting the community for the purpose of social mapping. Social mapping, according to Cochrane (1979), is identifying and recording the cultural resources of a community. It is making a kind of inventory at the macrosocial level. The elements of a social map include (1) identification and location of all ethnic groups in an area; (2) description of the social organization of the community; (3) description of the beliefs and ideological characteristics of the residents of the community; (4) recording of the patterns of wealth, its accumulation, and its distribution; (5) description of the patterns of mobility, both geographical and social; and (6) information on access and utilization of available human service providers (Cochrane 1979: 20-45). From a social service perspective, the development of a social map represents an effort to relate the findings of ethnographies, social service research, and community documents to the specific characteristics of the area that the worker seeks to understand.

The product of this procedure should be a document containing one or more real maps and information on each of the six items listed above, all provided in such detail that a stranger to the community could read it and gain some general sense of who lives in the area, how they live, what they believe and do, and how they make use of social services. The document should also make clear the outstanding needs of the community as they are perceived by the residents themselves.

There is a good reason for taking the time to do all this background investigation. Most social service workers become aware of the characteristics and the problems of the communities they serve only after a lengthy period of involvement. The pressures of the work place, which require the worker to begin with clients almost immediately, mean that the process of learning the more general attributes of the community is delayed. Furthermore, information is usually acquired only on a piecemeal basis and as a consequence of doing other things. Obviously, this is neither an efficient nor a reliable way of learning. Social mapping, however, is an activity that is highly focused and one that results in a tangible product. The development of the social map becomes, for some, its own reward. In addition to the benefits that accrue to the serious student of the community, the map is something that can be expanded, revised, and utilized with other workers in the agency as a part of their job orientation or performance evaluation. It becomes, then, a device for quickly introducing outsiders to the complexity of a given community and for planning improvements in the design and delivery of culturally sensitive services. It replicates in a small way the "community study" method that has been so productive in the development of cross-cultural understanding in the social sciences generally.

2. Key Respondents

Key respondents are those individuals who are knowledgeable about their community and who are able and willing to articulate that knowledge to an outsider. They can be thought of as cultural guides, as persons who are able to adopt teaching roles in order to assist the worker in understanding the subtleties and complexities of a particular community. In his book on participant observation, Bogdan (1972) referred to such individuals as "gatekeepers," as they often have the power to grant access to key persons or institutions in the community. Not all key respondents, however, are of equal value as guides or teachers about their community and its distinctive features. What any individual knows, his or her stock of social knowledge, is obviously a function of many things, not the least of which are the size and composition of that individual's personal network, participation in community organizations and activities, access to community leaders and decision-makers, as well as ascribed characteristics such as gender and age. All of these things facilitate access to some kinds of information and inhibit access to others. In judging the value of a key respondent's knowledge, therefore, the issue is not simply what is correct and what incorrect. The issue is one of determining the meaning of a particular respondent's knowledge, given his or her position in the community. Knowledge is in large measure a matter of social placement, and what one respondent knows may have to be supplemented or modified by what another has supplied.

Simply getting information, however, is not enough. The culturally sensitive observer is often interested in things that a key respondent may take for granted or in details of daily life that the respondent may prefer to conceal. In his well-known dramaturgical model of social behavior, Goffman (1959) distinguished what he called "front region" and "backstage" social performances. Front-region behavior is that which is relatively open and public, where individuals conduct themselves in ways that support recognized standards of decorum. In backstage regions, however, the more hidden and sometimes contradictory features of everyday life are evident, and individuals may behave in ways which, while predictable or rational by certain standards of their culture, nevertheless do not coincide with publicly espoused definitions of reality. Family life, for instance, is relatively well concealed in our own as well as other cultures, and it could be considered a backstage region. It may be, as Leach (1968) once pointed out in an infamous remark, that the "tawdry secrets" of the family constitute one of the most remote and difficult of access backstage areas of a culture. Obviously, a key informant, acting as a culture guide, is not going to be willing to enter into a discussion of such sensitive, often concealed matters with someone who represents an ethnic group or profession that lacks high esteem in the respondent's community. The result is that the worker seeking information is most likely to hear what the respondent believes ought to be told and no more. The solution to this problem is the development of a carefully cultivated relationship of trust, built over a long period of time, so that the learner and the respondent can come to understand and respect one another's position and purposes.

There is a tempting shortcut to working out this kind of relationship with a key respondent. That is to rely on the opinions of persons who are "old hands" in the community but who are members of one's own racial or ethnic group. Such well-established persons are often easy and comfortable to talk with, but there are two distinct disadvantages in relying upon them. First, just because they have long familiarity with a community does not mean that they know and understand it well. Individuals can and do spend years working among persons they little understand, and their longevity is sometimes used as justification for flawed judgments. Second, reliance upon a senior worker or others in an agency for information about the community being served deprives the worker of the direct encounters outside the relatively safe world of the agency that are essential for learning about and appreciating cultural distinctiveness. Knowledge consequently comes to the worker second hand, screened through persons whose ignorance or biases may not be obvious. The information that the learner acquires in this way has the status of gossip and folklore, in this case office folklore, and it serves as a poor substitute for real learning about real people in their own settings.

One other point about key respondents is worth noting. People do not usually give of their free time and energy without some expectation of return. Any relationship between the learner and a key respondent is one in which a "bargain" has been struck, implicitly or explicitly. The respondent may want to aggrandize his or her own position in the community through functioning as the "expert." He or she may have a complaint concerning social services, or social workers generally, so that the appearance of the learner is an opportunity to make those opinions known. Or the respondent may expect special favors at some future time. These things have to be kept in mind by the learner in asking anyone to spend time as a cultural guide or gatekeeper. It would be naive to act otherwise. Consequently, the learner should have clearly in mind what it is that he or she has to offer in exchange for a key respondent's confidence.

3. Participant Observation

Participant observation is an approach to data collection that is commonly associated with anthropology. Unfortunately, the phrase "participant observation" has suggested to many investigators, particularly novice ones, a loose, unstructured way of acquiring information, as though one could somehow "soak it up" just by being in proximity to others. It would be better to think of participant observation as an orientation toward research, rather than a "method" as such. It is an orientation distinguished by the student's long-term commitment to learning detailed characteristics of a community in a way that minimizes intrusion on the day-to-day life of the residents. Obviously, such a definition does not fit most types of psychological and sociological research. The latter in particular, with its reliance on interview schedules, is often of short duration, involving brief and highly controlled encounters, and is one which yields specific but limited data, largely divorced from social context. The great strength of participant observation is that it makes possible an understanding of the subtle meanings attached to behavior by the members of a culture. Its weakness is that it produces information that is not easily quantified or manipulated.

In participant observation, as in any learning activity, the investigator must have some idea of what kinds of information are important and what kinds are not. One cannot use participant observation successfully by approaching the subject with a blank or "open" mind, although inexperienced researchers often attempt to do so. The help-seeking behavior model of social services suggests some of the kinds of things the learner ought to be looking for while participating in and observing the round of community life. The heart of the indigenous therapeutic system is the encounter between a person recognized in the community as a helper and the individual with a problem or complaint, and it is one place that an investigator should be looking in order to find what is useful and effective with clients and what is not.

How might participant observation be used as an investigative style in this instance? First, the observer must solve several logistical and access problems. Once it is determined, with the assistance of a cultural guide, that there are persons in the community who specialize in providing some kind of helping service to others, one such specialist must be located. That is never easy, since for a variety of reasons local specialists may not want contact with investigators from outside the community. This is particularly true where generations of student and academic researchers have entered and sometimes overrun minority communities in their quest for information for term papers and scholarly articles. Since most of these outsiders have been white, there is now a manifest resentment to further intrusion. Where the social worker is concerned, there may be ambivalence toward the role of social work and social service organizations. The learner may have to depend on the cultural guide to act as a third party in finding contacts and making introductions.

Second, the observer will have to prove that he or she is worthy of being given the information that is desired. This is simply a matter of trust, and it may not come easily. Ignorance by the larger world of the secrets of one's community is a form of protective camouflage, particularly in a society with a history of racism such as our own. If the student can make an effective argument that, as a social service worker, he or she can do a better job for the people who live there, it may be possible that a working relationship with a local specialist can be built. (That argument can also backfire, if the activities of the social worker's agency are not acceptable to the host community.) Ideally, the learner would then be able to observe and record information on helper-client encounters and discuss that information with the specialist.

But what should be observed? The third element in successful participant observation is a conceptual framework within which to work. Such a framework is critical to assuring that the learner's objectives in doing the observation are achieved. The theoretical framework identifies what is important, what has to be found, and what issues need to be kept clearly in mind as observation proceeds. Without some governing framework of ideas, hypotheses, propositions, or testable statements, participant observation is little more than sophisticated voyeurism. This means that the observer needs to study community documents and scholarly resources in order to formulate some ideas about what ought to be observed and why it is important to be focusing on the topic chosen. Individuals who fail to develop an informed conceptual orientation to their participant observation inevitably make two errors: They attempt to note and remember all that they see, thus experiencing information overload; or they assume a stylized way of looking and listening around others, one that tells all those in the vicinity that they are being "watched" and "studied." In the former error, the indiscriminate observer invariably complains that the situation was too complex, or that things happened too fast to note all that went on. The latter error is simply one of rudeness, one which has been frequently commented upon by minority persons hosting white students or researchers in their community.

A conceptual framework can be developed through familiarity with previous studies in the area of the learner's interest. Consider, for instance, participant observation among community specialists who have unique helping skills. Foster and Anderson (1978) have developed a typology of healers as they exist in a variety of cultures. They have tried to characterize what may be said to be true of all helping specialists, be they shamans, herbalists, or physicians. In this formulation, all healers are specialists, set apart in some significant way and recognized for their talents. They are also ranked, with those claiming supernatural powers generally ranked highest. They are selected and trained in some distinctive way, and that process legitimizes their claims as to who they are and what they do. It assures those who seek their help that they are dealing with someone of known competence. Part of this selection and training involves some form of certification, whether it is a sheet of embossed paper hung on a wall or scars and regalia that were won from endurance in a difficult initiation ritual. Such specialists have professional images and distinctive ways or styles in dealing with their clients and patients. Such styles may even include distinctive psychological characteristics or mannerisms which patients expect to see during therapeutic encounters. Most specialists expect some kind of payment for the services they have given, Finally, there is high prestige attached to the work of the healer or counselor. That prestige is part of the belief that the specialist has powers far beyond that of others in the community and, further, that those powers are being used to enhance the health and happiness of others.

Taking Foster and Anderson's formulation, a social service investigator might decide that in order to work in a culturally responsive manner with clients in a given community, it will be necessary to locate and understand something of the methods of a community specialist who enjoys local respect. Assuming that problems of access and rapport have been resolved, then it would be necessary to formulate open-ended propositions based on these criteria for describing a specialist. What are the distinctive signs of this person's helping activity? How is he or she regarded in the community, or in varying segments of it? Is there a hierarchy of such specialists, and if so, where does the individual of interest to the student rank in that hierarchy? How was selection and training accomplished, and what is its legitimacy in the eyes of clients or patients? What are the features of the specialist's communication style? Are there elements of it that are common and repeated from client to client and, perhaps, expected by clients as part of the curing or counseling procedure? Can these elements be described and their significance for helping the client be estimated? These are examples of the kinds of questions the participant observer would have in mind while observing client-therapist encounters, while discussing particular helping skills with the respondent, and while interviewing former clients about their experiences with the specialists they chose for help.

Participant observation conducted in this way is a powerful tool for learning the cultural characteristics of an unfamiliar cultural scene. It is not the only research approach that can be successfully used, but it is the one most likely to elicit the kind of information that is useful to the worker who will be confronted with culturally unfamiliar clients. It alerts the worker to subtleties of interaction, communication style, and client expectation that cannot be discovered in any other way. And, as should be evident, it is a technique that requires at least as much discipline as the more structured, highly quantified methods of community study.

CHAPTER FOUR
LANGUAGE
AND CROSS-CULTURAL
SOCIAL WORK

The black actor Ossie Davis once complained that the English language was his enemy (1969). Bigots and discriminatory hiring practices offended him, but so did the language itself. English, he argued, perpetuated in its vocabulary all the habits of mind and verbal responses that are associated with racially founded inequities. Davis's point is obvious enough if one thinks of the slang terms used for labeling members of ethnic groups. But words do more than label. They impose an order on perception; they create categories of things and suggest something of what the categories are worth. Perhaps it was a victory of sorts when "colored" became "negro," then "negro" was capitalized, and finally "black" replaced "Negro." Labels identify, but they may also prescribe and limit the possibilities of the persons to whom they are applied.

Words are weapons, and in Davis's view they have to be handled as such. Misuse of words can be a kind of aggression. Individuals are labeled and boxed into categories that do not apply to them. Or words are used to "mystify" others, to suggest expertness and superior insight on the part of the speaker (Jones 1976). Reliance on clichés, particularly the clichés and jargon of institutions, professions, and higher education, is a common way by which language becomes weaponry. From the point of view of many in minority and ethnic groups, such use of language is threatening and offensive because it is, among other things, the language of power and coercion.

Social workers have not always been sensitive to their use of language with ethnic and minority clients, a criticism now made even within the profession (Sotomayor 1977). Resort to esoteric and jargonistic language in the helping professions has been described as a "zero sum game" by Gelman (1980). He notes that the use of such language by social service workers serves a number of functions, including the demarcation and protection of professional turf; assertion of authority over clients; and pretensions to specialized knowledge when in fact such knowledge may not exist or be fully understood. Esoteric language is one of the "rituals unique to professional culture" (Gelman 1980: 50), and its misuse can have serious and unfortunate consequences for the worker-client relationship. Lee has documented the hostile use of language in social work for describing the poor, noting that "how we talk and think about a client or, perhaps more importantly, a 'class' of clients, determines how we act toward the client" (Lee 1980: 580).

But this same view of language as a cultural product and of esoteric language as one of the significant symbols of a culture or a subculture can be used to the worker's advantage. Like social workers, clients also have specialized or esoteric language, which is reflective of their particular cultural orientations. And, as among social workers, the esoteric language functions to define boundaries, to conceal "inside" information from those who would attempt to penetrate group boundaries, and to preserve a sense of specialness and dignity among those who are familiar with the jargon. In this sense, "language is more than a means of communicating about reality: it is a tool for constructing reality. Different languages create and express different realities" (Spradley 1979: 17).

This chapter describes the significance of language in revealing how people categorize and organize their perceptions of the world and how the worker can use language to learn about a distinctive culture. We view speech as a kind of behavior, and, just as verbal behavior is ordered by the governing principles of grammar, so too every culture has its distinctive "grammar" of correctness in social relations. These are the things that to members of the culture are the "common sense" of everyday life. The task of the culturally responsive worker is to acquire an awareness of the "common sense" of another culture and to utilize that knowledge in the sensitive delivery of services. Language is the means of access to that knowledge.

LANGUAGE AND WORLD VIEW

Linguistic variation is one of the most significant markers of ethnic diversity. People of different cultures may speak entirely separate languages, or they may speak languages that are separate but that have a common ancestor, or they may have a common language, marked by dialectical variations. Even within a single ethnic group, language variations are often used by individuals to express something of the origins, personal values, or social status of the speaker in relation to others within the group. Language is thus a marker of status as well as an indicator of who is and who is not a member of a specific group.

In addition to these social functions, language usage has an important relationship to thought processes. While the connection between speech and thinking is not entirely clear, one important hypothesis in this field suggests that language influences the way people perceive the world, that it has an important role in molding the individual's perception of reality. The linguist, Edward Sapir, argued that language "defines experience for us by reason of its formal completeness and because of our unconscious projection of its implicit expectations into experience" (Sapir, as quoted in Mandelbaum 1949: 578). He suggested that the natural world bombards our senses with stimuli and that these stimuli are sorted according to learned linguistic categories. These categories are in some sense "real" for us and are the tools of thought. Assuming that we require language to think and that languages vary, Sapir felt that it must be the case that speakers of different languages will perceive and therefore construct reality differently.

Indeed, by learning a new language one enters into a different world, wherein the thought and behavioral responses are significantly different from one's own culture. "The fact of the matter is that the 'real' world is to a large extent unconsciously built upon the language habits of the group. No two languages are sufficiently similar to be considered as representing the same social reality. The worlds in which different societies live are distinct worlds, not merely the same world with different labels attached" (Sapir, as quoted in Barnow 1963: 96). Benjamin Whorf, also a linguist, took a similar point of view and argued that the ways in which individuals organize their perceptions of the world do not constitute a uniform process, one that can be assumed to be the same in all groups or cultures. For the individual, the world is not objectively known, but is filtered through a cultural lens, the most important feature of which is language. He agreed with Sapir's statement that the "real world" is constructed according to the received linguistic tradition of a culture. "We see and hear and otherwise experience very largely as we do because the language habits of our community predispose certain choices of interpretation" (Whorf, as quoted in Carroll 1956: 134).

It is interesting to note how and why Whorf came to this point of view. Before he was a linguist, Whorf worked as a safety inspector for an insurance company, and he was impressed that the name for something could influence people's behavior, even when that behavior was "objectively" inappropriate or even dangerous. He noted, for instance, that around gasoline storage drums and pumps, a certain kind of cautious, careful behavior was appropriate in order to prevent fires. But where people worked with "empty gasoline drums," they were careless with handling equipment and with their cigarettes and matches. The phrase "empty gasoline drums" suggested an absence of danger, when in fact the empty drums were at least as hazardous if not more hazardous than the full ones, since they contained highly explosive vapors. Dangerous behavior, such as smoking, was a response to a linguistic cue, not an objective condition. In this way, language habits masked the reality of the situation and substituted a conventional and, in this example, inappropriate interpretation.

Semantic labels are part of the reality-defining process. They are also indicative of sharp variations in the classification and interpretation of behavior. This is well illustrated by an example of an old stereotype and of research involving ghetto residents and how their linguistic labels reflect a world view that is not only different but in some ways in opposition to those views that are applied by the dominant white culture.

Liebow (1967), an anthropologist, was concerned with the problems of poor people in general and of urban blacks in particular. He recognized that much of the academic research carried out among poor blacks had either implied or concluded that they were largely responsible for their own problems. While paying lip service to such factors as racism in the larger society and the problems of unemployment for the poor and often poorly educated, such studies normally concluded that there was something pathological about urban black life itself. The "female-centered family" was usually identified as the scapegoat in these studies, but other things were often cited as well: "faulty child-rearing practices," "illegitimacy," "absentee fathers," "inability to use money wisely," "low value placed on formal education," and a "psychological inability to make future plans and to work consistently toward the realization of those plans." This last factor in accounting for the problems of the poor has often been described as an "inability to defer gratification" and a poor sense of the management of time. Thus, it has been assumed, poor people are poor in part because they have never learned the importance of planning and saving for the future. When they get something in the way of a financial surplus, their impulse is to spend wildly and to come up short before the next payday, or before the next welfare check. Indeed, this is one of the most common stereotypes about the poor and is often used as a justification for keeping assistance programs small.

The terms we have put in quotation marks here are semantic labels, which both classify and "explain" the behavior of the people in question. But the terms are not "objective" in the sense that they represent critically examined, unbiased, and cross-culturally applicable analytical constructs. They are, rather, the linguistic habits of a particularly small segment of the larger society: largely white, highly educated researchers and policy-makers, whose own value orientations derive in part from their participation in highly structured, bureaucratically organized research, teaching, and government institutions. Their language reflects some of the concerns of those institutions: pathology, legalism, analytical understanding, "intervention," and abstract generalization. The issue we raise about them is not whether these concerns are legitimate, since for some purposes they probably are. The issue is whether they are appropriate for understanding the people they purport to describe. How might that appropriateness be tested?

Living in close contact with those he called street-corner men and their families, Liebow looked at these "problems," but from the inside, from the perspective of those involved with getting along on very little. He discovered that to phrase the issue as one of middle-class financial prudence ("deferred gratification") versus lower-class psychological hedonism simply obscured the reality of the situation. From the perspective of economically poor black men and women in urban ghettos, the idea of planning and saving for the future made very little sense.

They could look around at those older than themselves and see what the future would be like, and it was nothing much worth investing in. Most of those who did have jobs were in dead-end positions. No matter how hard one worked at sweeping floors or washing dishes, these things never made anyone anything other than a hard-working sweeper or washer. Liebow's respondents perceived the future only as a continuation of the present, and the life experiences of friends and relatives were evidence for that concept. While the middle-class virtue of thrift may be appropriate for those who have a future to work toward, for those who do not, planning to use money as an investment in the future made little sense.

Viewed from the inside, from the point of view of participants at the bottom of the social and economic system, Liebow found it impossible to conclude that the poor have a hedonistic present-time orientation. The "inability to defer gratification" was not an obsession with present pleasures, but a despair for the future. The poor whom Liebow studied could see very clearly what their future was likely to be, and they made a highly rational calculation that it was not the place to risk what little they had. Thus what appears to the uncritical outsider as a narrowly present orientation toward time is, in fact, an accurate assessment by the chronically poor of their life prospects. In this sense, the poor are as future-oriented as anyone else, perhaps even more so, and they have decided that the demands of the present must be met, because they are not likely to be different tomorrow. Phrases like "inability to defer gratification," "present-time orientation," and the like do not represent objective descriptions of what Liebow observed. Rather, they are, as Whorf suggested, linguistic constructions that stand for the reality outsiders have created to suit their particular interests and needs. Whether or not these language habits accurately depict the real living conditions of the poor must always be taken as a hypothesis, not a fact. It is this use of language constructions, as labels which may or may not accurately depict some segment of reality, that concerns us now.

LEVELS OF UNDERSTANDING

The problem of improving the accuracy of linguistic labels for behavior, particularly labels applied by one group to the behavior of another, is an old one in the social sciences. Late in the nineteenth century, anthropologists who were attempting to develop a scientific approach to the study of culture became aware of the need to overcome the ethnocentrism that was endemic to the descriptions of so-called "primitive" peoples offered by missionaries, government agents, and various travelers and adventurers. Many of the perjorative terms still used to stereotype racial and ethnic groups came from these misinformed descriptions. In challenging these stereotypes, anthropologists insisted on examining behavior and interpreting it within the context in which it naturally occurred and from the point of view of the actors in the situation, rather than from the perspective of uninformed outsiders. Thus the collection of verbatim texts and lengthy, detailed descrip-

mundane as well as exotic customs became a goal for scientific activity. This approach placed a premium on getting information from the "native's point of view" and interpreting it according to the insights of the members of the culture under study. Franz Boas, who taught the first generation of academic anthropologists (including Margaret Mead), and who did extensive field research among the Indian inhabitants of Vancouver Island in Canada, set the tone for this approach by arguing that: "If it is our serious purpose to understand the thoughts of a people, the whole analysis of experience must be based on their concepts, not ours" (Boas 1943: 314, quoted in Pelto and Pelto 1978: 55).

The distinction between "their concepts, not ours" is central to what has become known as "ethnoscience," an approach to understanding behavior through analysis of the language and conceptual categories of a people. The study of language has provided a model for the analysis of cultural features, because just as every language has a distinctive structure, so too each culture is distinctive, one from another. Based on this analogy, an important distinction has been made in social research between *emic* and *etic* levels of analysis. We will use these terms frequently in the remainder of this chapter, so it is important to have their meaning clearly in mind. The word *etic* comes from phonetics, the study of speech sounds. Phonetics is concerned with the description of all possible sounds used in language behavior, regardless of time or place. (An international phonetic alphabet of standardized symbols is used to record those sounds, and it contains, of course, more symbols than are needed for describing any specific language.) Phonemics is the study of those sounds which are differentiated by speakers of a particular language as "real" or "correct" to them. It concerns only the sound categories that convey meaning within a restricted community of same-language speakers. Based on this distinction, then, anthropologists have distinguished two kinds of analysis. An *etic* analysis is one which uses highly abstract, global categories, which are imposed on data by a researcher in order to make a cross-cultural comparison. An *emic* analysis is one which is based on localized, group-specific categories and which is intended to generate an "insider's" perspective of how the world is organized. Etic analyses are useful in making broad-scaled, cross-cultural generalizations or global statements. Emic analyses delineate the structure of a single culture in terms of the cognitive and behavioral categories which are specific only to that culture. Etic approaches normally obscure fine-textured detail in order to achieve generalizing power. Emic approaches achieve their insight concerning individual cultures at the cost of the larger cross-cultural perspective.

An example can help make this important distinction clear. Suppose we are interested in doing a study of child abuse, and we want to answer two kinds of questions. First, we want to know how common the problem is, what kind of people are generally implicated in it, and what is done in other societies to prevent or control it. Second, we want to know something about child abusers themselves and why they do the things of which they are accused. The questions in the first category are posed at an etic level of analysis. To answer them, we would have to agree upon a cross-culturally or cross-nationally valid definition of child abuse, something that so far has been very difficult to do (Parke and Collmer 1975; Korbin 1976). We would need to see a list of the social and personal characteristics that the research literature suggests are typical of child abusers, so that we could compare these to each case identified and studied. Finally, we would need good statistics from all areas of the world, so we could be sure of the validity of our conclusions. The research might lead us to a definitive statement about the frequency of child abuse worldwide, a description of a statistically "typical" abuser, and policy and treatment suggestions for control and rehabilitation of perpetrators and victims in different countries. Our understanding of abuse would be greatly enhanced by this information, information that is at an etic level of understanding, because we have operated at a high level of generality and with definitions and counting procedures of interest to us only as external, perhaps remote analysts of the problem we seek to understand.

The other questions are of a different order. They concern the meaning of child maltreatment to the abusers themselves, how they think that children ought to behave, what they view as permissible discipline, and whatever it is that seems to them to justify the harsh treatment that the law, society, or their neighbors will not permit. At an emic level, the problem for analysis is one of getting the "insider's" point of view, the reasons for which maltreatment of children seems acceptable in specific instances. Here we are no longer working at the level of cross-cultural generalization. Rather, we want the abuser to speak for himself or herself, so that we can explore in depth the symbolic and affective content of what our respondent spontaneously offers. In an emic approach, it is the respondent, not the investigator, who establishes which topics are relevant for analysis. At the end of a period of detailed questioning with a small number of individuals, we may have identified many of the things which account for abusive behavior, at least among those who have participated in the study. Having viewed the world through their eyes, we may be more sympathetic to their plight. But more important, we may have gained real insight into why people mistreat children and what can be done to get them to change their behavior.

Emic and etic styles of analysis are very different, and that difference has been summarized as follows:

> In contrast to the etic approach, an emic one is in essence valid for only one language (or one culture) at a time. . . . It is an attempt to discover and to describe the pattern of that particular language or culture in reference to the way in which the various elements of that culture are related to each other in the functioning of the particular pattern, rather than to attempt to describe them in reference to a generalized classification derived in advance of the study of that culture. (Pike 1954: 8)
>
> An etic analytical standpoint . . . might be called "external" or "alien," since for etic purposes the analyst stands "far enough away" from or "outside" of a particular culture to see its separate events, primarily in relation to their similarities and their differences, as compared to events in other cultures, rather than in reference to the sequences of classes of events within that one particular culture. (ibid. 10)

In social work, the etic-emic distinction can be thought of as the difference between an "experience far" and "experience near" perception of others (Kohut 1971). For purposes of cross-cultural learning, it is the emic or "experience-near" approach that we want to emphasize. There is a very real sense in which social work does not always work at this level of understanding. Global explanations of client behavior, when they are accurate, typify a large number of people at an abstract level of appreciation, and such descriptions may be useful for planning and policy purposes. But because they do not approximate client knowledge and awareness of specific problems, they omit much that is part of client responses to particular problems. Similarly, the technical vocabulary as well as the popular jargon occasionally found in social work substitutes the emic categories and perspectives of social work as a professional culture for the indigenous labels and constructs that structure reality for the client. Yet it is the latter, the ethnographically based observations and judgments of clients, that must be identified and utilized in the provision of culturally sensitive social services. Finding that information involves a special method of interviewing, one that has significant consequences for the relationship of social workers to their clients.

INTERVIEWING FOR
EMIC AWARENESS

In social services work, the goal of the culturally responsive worker must approximate what has been described as "communicative competence," that is, "what a speaker needs to know to communicate effectively in culturally significant settings" (Gumperz and Hymes 1972: vii). To accomplish this, the worker must have a strong grasp of the meanings that are suggested to the client by behavior, events, and other persons in naturalistic or "culturally significant settings." This is an obvious but often abused point. The practitioner for whom the subjective state of the client is a central concern, for whom "getting in touch with feelings" is an important, even a primary, task, may be very limited in his or her efforts to acquire and utilize cultural knowledge. The error of a reliance on "empathy" and "openness" is that it presumes an ability to enter into the sensibilities of another without first learning the context and meaning of those sensibilities. The real trick in cross-cultural social work, as in any kind of cross-cultural learning, is to comprehend what it is that the client knows and how that knowledge is used in the mundane traffic of daily activities. In our emphasis on the emic approach, we are first concerned with meaning, client meaning, and not contrived, a priori "caring responses." What clients say—literally—is a crucial source of data, which must be carefully gathered, using such simple ethnographic interviewing techniques as will elicit in the client's own terms (emics) the meanings attached to personal, family, or other problems typically brought to social workers.

Interviewing in social work has been described as an "action system" (Pincus and Minahan 1973: 118), which is simply a way of saying that it is a distinctive kind of social event, with its own conventions and procedures. These procedures vary, depending on whether the situation calls for a nondirective approach, with free-flowing conversation based on the interviewee's concerns, or for a highly structured setting, where the collection of specific, predetermined data is of first importance. Both approaches have their uses in social work (Jenkins 1975). With each, the worker must be skilled and effective, because interviewing is the "most consistently and frequently employed social work technique" (Kadushin 1972: 1-2).

But what is distinctive about social work interviewing and, in particular, about interviewing with minority clients? Benjamin (1969) has described what he calls the "helping interview," one in which the "primary goal is to help the interviewee. He is at the center, he is the focus; he is all important. Everything else is incidental" (Benjamin 1969: xi). General features of the helping interview include a desire to offer assistance, careful listening, openness and honesty, and an effort to gain rapport and develop empathy. Similarly, Kadushin has attempted to isolate the distinctive features of social work interviewing. He has suggested that they include contact with troubled people, who, in wide-ranging discussions, convey to the worker information that will have both diagnostic and therapeutic value (Kadushin 1972: 13-15). This kind of interviewing, Kadushin suggests, is in contrast to that which is merely data collection for the sake of agency records or research projects.

These approaches have, however, two major limitations that are particularly evident if we begin thinking about interviewing ethnic or minority group clients. (They are limitations, incidentally, that are common to many kinds of interviews, not just those carried out by social workers.) First, the statements that have been made about honesty, genuineness, and rapport refer to interview characteristics that are highly abstract. Consequently, they are difficult to translate into directives for behavior that can be passed on to a learner. Such abstractions also function to perpetuate a belief common to many social service workers—the belief that one need only approach others as an open, patient, and caring person in order to achieve a communication breakthrough and perhaps even therapeutic efficacy. We suggest here that the desire to be a "helping" person, while laudable in itself, is not sufficient to develop ethnically responsive interviewing skills. More is needed than generalizations which stress empathy and caring or sentimentalization of the interview as a profound social event.

The second limitation has to do with the skills that are needed in social work interviewing. Since one really cannot teach people to "care" about others in their professional relations, discussions of interviewing often turn from broad generalizations about rapport to specific techniques. These are frequently described in terms of anecdotes or with reference to the results of controlled studies of interviewing, such as the effects of black and white interviewers on black interviewees. Generalizations about appropriate behavior are then drawn from the anecdotes and the research conclusions, as guides for the students to follow. Techniques, strategies, and tactics constitute one response to the need for going beyond global statements about helping and caring for others (Gordon 1969). They are specific, and therefore they are learnable with a little practice. But the cultural appropriateness of such techniques and their acceptability to ethnic group clients are likely to be highly variable. Interviewing skills that may work well with Puerto Ricans (Ghali 1977) may be quite unacceptable to Japanese-Americans (Kaneshige 1973) or American Indians (Youngman and Sadongei 1974). It becomes evident that it is difficult to speak of any specific interview techniques that can be assumed to be successful with any or all minority clients.

Ethnographic interviewing from an emic perspective, however, is a way to move beyond the limits of culturally bound tactics in information gathering with ethnic and minority clients. It is really an interview technique that is also a process of discovery. "Its object is to carry on a guided conversation and to elicit rich, detailed materials that can be used in qualitative analysis" and it has been described as "intensive interviewing with an interview guide" (Lofland 1971: 76). The notion of the interviewee as a guide has an important implication for the helping relationship. It means that in some respects the interviewer is the student, and the interviewee is the instructor, guiding the student through the labyrinth of the interviewee's mind and culture. Attentive listening means more than just hearing the client out as part of the therapeutic process. It means that the client is in some sense an expert in defining the depth and breadth of a problem, and that the opinions of this expert must be clearly understood before analysis of the problem can begin. (See Jenkins [1975] for a similar example.) Simply allowing the client to ramble at length will not produce information in an efficient way, nor will it increase the understanding of the client's problems by the social worker. The central idea in this type of ethnographic interview is that the social worker channels the flow of the interview by using linguistic features of the conversation provided by the client.

There is no standardized process of ethnographic interviewing. What we offer here is simply a description of a few methods commonly used in cross-cultural encounters. The process is easily described, but it must be practiced extensively to be carried out well. Essentially three steps are involved: planning the interview, conducting it, and summarizing and analyzing the results.

PLANNING THE
ETHNOGRAPHIC INTERVIEW

The technique of intensive guided interviewing assumes that there is something problematic that is of concern to both the interviewer and the interviewee. Unlike interviews with highly structured, closed-ended questions, the intensive guided interview calls for the worker to identify in advance those aspects of the client's life which may be personally and professionally puzzling. These topics are then listed as questions and are arranged in an order that seems to make sense to the interviewer. In some respects, the choice of topic to be used in opening the interview is almost arbitrary, and the specific topic itself may be less significant than the fact that the worker is organizing his or her thoughts around a point of departure for the interview. Lofland (1971) calls this process "global sorting and ordering" of problem areas, and in this process it is best to define and order problems in a way that is straightforward and obvious. "Deep" sociological or psychological presumptions about the "true" nature of the situation are not appropriate here. For example, Lofland (1971: 79) cites the outline of an intensive interviewing schedule that was developed by Davis and Biernacki for a study among former users of marijuana. Note both the simplicity of the outline and the fact that it attempts to organize the interview around questions that may be interesting to the interviewee.

1. First trying marijuana
2. Circumstances surrounding first contact
3. State of being surrounding first contact
4. Conditions for continual use
5. Conditions for curtailment or stoppage
6. Present situation
7. Current attitudes toward usage

Each of these areas can be extensively subdivided, and as more interviews are conducted with similar clients, the list can be expanded. All that is required at this step, however, is for the interviewer to give enough thought to potential interview topics so that they can be listed in a simple and well-organized manner.

In addition to selecting the topics for the guided interview, the worker will have to plan his or her own account of why the interviewee's cooperation is important. Spradley (1979: 58-68) has suggested that the interview be thought of as a "friendly conversation," in which the interviewer makes explicit at the beginning the purposes of the discussion and then offers procedural explanations during the process of the interview as to the ethnographic importance of the information sought. This latter suggestion is particularly important, because it educates the interviewee as to his or her role in the interview, particularly the "guiding" role through a cultural setting about which the worker is unfamiliar. For instance, let us suppose that the respondent is a man who is an immigrant with limited job skills, who has agreed to discuss with you his experience as a resident alien (Green 1973). You have explained that the purpose of the interview is to collect data for a government report on the needs of resident aliens and that you want to tell the story from his point of view. Having your list of general questions in front of you, the interview begins. The explanations of your ethnographic purpose would be offered in comments interspersed throughout the conversation such as: "I want to know as much as I can about your first week in this country, how you survived, and what other immigrants say when they talk about the shock of getting adjusted." That kind of remark establishes your immediate purpose and tells the interviewee specifically what kind of information you want. You will also need to explain your recording procedures: "I want to write all this down, word for word. All right?" The interviewee's role as "tour guide" to the newly arrived immigrant scene becomes clearer. It is reinforced by comments such as: "Would you say that again? I want to get your exact words here, because I'm trying to understand your obvious feelings about that event," or "When you discuss this with other immigrants, do they describe it in the same words, just like that, or do they say it differently?" The latter question moves the interviewee even more closely into the setting of similarly affected immigrants, and he relies increasingly on "insider" information in order to continue the discussion. It lessens his need to "translate" his experience to you as the social worker, a government representative, or someone well educated and holding a white collar job and therefore different from himself.

There is nothing magical or difficult about these kinds of comments. What they do is keep your ethnographic purpose at the center of the interviewee's attention. They reinforce over and over again the message that the interviewee is the expert, the cultural guide; that everything said is important and must be recorded accurately; and that you as the interviewer have a clear purpose in mind, that of getting the client's perspective, the "native's point of view," as explicitly and as fully as it can be articulated for you. The emphasis on guiding the interview, using respondent-supplied cues, can be particularly helpful with respondents who ramble, who are initially distrustful, or who feel they have nothing worthy to say. The procedure, simple as it is, makes the interviewer's communication with the client much more active and productive than the usual bland injunctions to use paraphrasing, interpretation, and "minimal encouragers" (Ivey 1971) as devices to keep the interview flowing.

THE INTERVIEW SESSION

Having established the role of the interviewee as cultural guide, there are a few simple devices by which to keep the interview moving, which will also assure that information of ethnographic significance is collected. These devices are called "cover terms," "attributes," and "sequences."

Neither the worker nor the client can specify in advance everything that will emerge in an interview, particularly one at the early, descriptive stage. It would be presumptuous to assume that one could know in advance which topics are important and which are not. As the interview develops, however, certain phrases and words begin to stand out, either because they are unfamiliar to the interviewer or because they appear to have special meaning to the interviewee. Often these are words in the vernacular of the respondent, but they need not be. These special terms, words that the respondent uses casually and with familiarity, are "cover terms." Cover terms literally "cover" a number of ideas, objects, concepts, or relationships that are part of the client's world. For example, if we were using our global list of questions with the marijuana user and he or she said: "I just got tired of being a pothead all the time," the word "pothead" should be recognized as a cover term. It refers to a special category of persons that is familiar to those in the drug subculture, and it has cultural significance and psychological reality to the speaker. Similarly, in our example of the labor migrant, he might have said: "You can't get into this country legally without a green card, man, it's your ticket to security." The expression "green card" is part of the specialized knowledge both of labor immigrants and the law enforcement officials who have the power to deport people. It is, therefore, a cover term. Cover terms can appear in nearly every sentence uttered by a respondent, and it is critical that they be recorded just as the interviewee used them. They are the basic ethnographic materials around which much of the rest of the interview will be built.

What we have called "attributes" are simply characteristics that are attached to cover terms. As the interview proceeds, the number of cover terms will accumulate at a rapid rate. Introductory, open-ended interviews are likely to generate many of them, more than can be handled in a single session. What the interviewer must do is pick some small number of cover terms and probe to discover the attributes of each of them. For instance, we might say to the marijuana smoker: "May I interrupt you for a moment; I need to know how you would describe a pothead. How is a pothead any different from other marijuana smokers?" This type of question illustrates several features of the ethnographic interviewing style. First, the interviewee is always in the teaching role, and the interviewer is the one who is taught. Second, the interview is controlled by the interviewer, but through use of ethnographic material supplied by the respondent. Third, the meaning of the information to the client is always the central purpose of the interviewing. During the interview, the worker ought to be noting cover terms on a pad, perhaps underlining them, and then leaving space on the page for filling in the attributes. Fifteen minutes of general, introductory conversation often can produce so many cover terms that an hour or two will be required for eliciting the attributes of them all.

A third device is identifying sequences. We need to know where the cover terms fit in the flow of the respondent's daily life, what relationships exist between the terms, and how they are utilized when the client is speaking with members of his or her own culture. Eliciting the attributes of the cover terms gives some sense of their meaning, but one also must know how they are used and how they contribute to the common sense of the client's world view. We might ask the labor immigrant several questions to elicit sequences associated with the cover term "green card": "Tell me all the things you had to do to get a green card." "Tell me all the things you have heard other people do to get their green cards?" "If I needed a card, what would I have to do to get one?"

All these questions put the cover term into the context of its use and meaning in the client's life. Sequences put order into the jumble of cover terms, as the respondent casually moves from one topic to another. The collection of sequences from an interviewee, over a number of interview sessions, can illuminate numerous areas of the cultural life of a client, many of them normally hidden from outsiders. The worker who is familiar with sequences in the lives of drug users, labor migrants, alcoholics, run-aways, and prisoners will not only be familiar with the rationale and rationality of behavior from the client's point of view but will also recognize these sequences as they unfold in the interactions of others. Perhaps one of the most startling and exciting things that can occur when one's sensibilities to the nuances of behavior in another culture are growing is to suddenly see previously unrecognized sequences of behavior in the most mundane and casual of activities. It is at that point that "communicative competence" becomes a possibility and that the social worker can begin to think of ways of working with clients that will incorporate their frameworks of understanding with the resolution of their problems.

SUMMARY AND ANALYSIS

Raw data that have been collected from respondents over a series of interviews is just that—raw data—until some effort is made to summarize them and make an analysis of their significance for a particular social service activity. The first step is to go through the list of cover terms and write them out as fully as possible. All the attributes associated with each term should be brought together in one place, so that the ethnographic content of each term can be fully identified. It is at this point that most investigators will discover gaps in the information so far collected. Thus it is wise to begin the process of summary after the first interview and to continue with it following each subsequent interview. Because data can accumulate rapidly over even a short period of time, the accumulation can soon get out of control. Blocking out the content of cover terms promptly is the only way to prevent information overload.

Second, cover terms and their content must be linked to sequences of behavior. There are multiple levels at which sequences can be described, from the most minute to the most elaborate. The choice of level ought to be determined in part by the ethnographic interests of the investigator. In our earlier discussion of the labor migrant, the questions about the process of acquiring a green card, a process with its legal as well as its illegal components, was an example of a sequence. But other sequences might have been concerned with how the respondent finds a place to live, how he approaches potential employers, what he must do to avoid detection by the immigration authorities, or what he is doing with the money he earns. A simple way to develop sequences is to graph them out, using blocks and arrows to indicate the various stages of an activity and the alternative ways of accomplishing specific ends. The advantage to developing such "road maps" of cultural processes is that the diagrams can be used to check and verify information. When sequences are matched to cover terms, and the terms are supported by detailed descriptions based on attributes, one element of a culture, an element that approximates the psychic reality of the client, begins to emerge in rough outline.

But sequences and their supporting cover terms have to be handled carefully, for they can all too easily lend themselves to stereotyping. Whatever one or more interviewees may have said, each one of them has a particularistic and therefore a partial view of his or her own culture. The investigator must distinguish between that which is offered as an expectation or ideal form of behavior and that which concerns how the business of living is actually carried on. All people have a reper-toire of idealized perceptions about how the world is supposed to work and what their place in it ought to be. But most people also recognize the discrepancies between the real and the ideal, even though they may not make this explicit during a conversation. It is therefore crucial to identify variations in sequences, variations that are acceptable or nonacceptable according to one's respondents. These varia-tions should be explored in subsequent interviews, but they can also be objects of interest in participant observation.

Finally, the lists of cover terms and sequence graphs should be analyzed in terms of their implications for social services. This means returning to the cate-gories suggested by the help-seeking behavior model and determining where, within those categories, the cover terms and the sequences are significant. For instance, many of the cover terms ought to concern the labeling of problem states, and the attributes ought to make clear what these conditions mean to the client. The use of helpers, be they indigenous figures or social service professionals, ought to be outlined in the sequence graphs, with alternative pathways shown and the rationale for each made clear. These are simple steps, and no special knowledge is required to carry them out. What is required, however, is a willingness to spend the time to collect the information and to analyze it carefully for its relevance to the work style of the investigator.

The result of all this effort ought to be some kind of personal guidebook or notebook, wherein the worker continually adds to the data collected about clients. When done systematically, this process can lead to a surprisingly sophisticated ethnographic document, one to which the worker can refer and one which can be used in training. The collection of such data should have at least as high a priority as the all-too-numerous forms that social workers are already expected to com-plete. Carefully prepared information on client values, behavior, and preferences—information that is continuously checked and rechecked in client encounters—is basic to effective delivery of services. Anything less means that workers function in ignorance of what is really happening in the lives of their clients. That condition should be professionally unacceptable. The accumulation and cultivation of ethno-graphic data and the shaping of such data to define the needs of clients and the responses of workers constitute one of the basic tasks of cross-cultural social work.

CONSTRAINTS ON
CROSS-CULTURAL COMMUNICATION

In our model of ethnic group relations, we suggested that each group has its dis-tinctive cultural features, its "ethnicity," which it protects by regulating the charac-ter and quality of intergroup contacts. We also suggested that the subculture of social work professionals is in some ways like an ethnic group itself, with its par-ticular values, knowledge, and patterns of organization. In the area of communica-tion with ethnic or minority clients, that distinctiveness is forcefully, sometimes painfully, evident.

Consider briefly the social setting in which many social work interviews take place. They are usually held in an office, away from the more naturalistic settings of behavior in which most clients are comfortable. They are highly structured events, both in terms of time (with specific beginnings and ends) and in the relative status (usually unequal) of the participants. Emphasis is placed on the immediate problem that has brought the participants together, and there is little time for informalities other than handshakes or cursory comments about the weather. The interview is expected to result in some "outcome"—a verbal agreement, a signed document, a prod to some kind of action—and this "outcome" is expected by the worker to be additive to the ongoing interviewer-interviewee relationship. Finally, the relationship is expected to terminate at some future point, so that the social worker can go on to other, similarly structured encounters with other clients. In short, the brevity and formality of the traditional social service interviewing process suggest that it is a communication style expressive of a certain type of culture, namely, bureaucratic culture. The social service agency is one important manifestation of this culture, and the formal interview is one of its culturally peculiar modes of "communicative competence."

There would be nothing wrong with this as the prevailing style of worker-client communication if social workers, as members of bureaucratic organizations, only interviewed other office workers. But just because minority groups have been largely excluded from participation in the institutions of power, their styles of communicative competence are adapted to cultural settings other than bureaucratic ones. Those settings are the home or the street corner, the store-front church or the neighborhood bar. The people in such places have multiple interests in one another, not a single "problem" to discuss, and they are often of the same or a similar status. A high value may be placed on the freedom to come and go, on entering and leaving conversations, without reference to clock time. In addition, interpersonal contacts in such settings are interesting and valuable to the participants in their own right and do not require an "outcome" or the additive quality of progressing through stages toward an expected termination. The imposition of an agency-oriented, "professional" communication style on a minority client might therefore be regarded, from the "native's point of view," as a highly aggressive and ethnocentric cross-cultural event.

Is there a solution to the dilemma of having to employ a bureaucratically styled form of communication in a setting where its appropriateness and utility are uncertain? For the social worker interested in ethnic competence as a skill for promoting effictive social service delivery, two answers to the dilemma can be considered. The first is to recognize the limitations of all interviewing as a way of learning about others. The guided, intensive interview technique we have proposed, with its emphasis on the ethnographic perspective of the client, goes a long way toward overcoming rigidness and superficiality. But it is still a highly structured linguistic event that is intended in many ways to serve the information gathering and service interests of the bureaucratic culture. The challenge to the ethnically sensitive practitioner is to use the event to expand personal and professional capabilities beyond the superficiality of most cross-cultural social service encounters. That use takes considerable effort, because as a communication activity the usual social service interview is as much reflective of the cultural remoteness of the client from the worker as it is of the worker's desire to develop and maintain a helping relationship.

Second, the ethnically responsive social worker will not be content to develop his or her knowledge of a client community simply through interviews. For example, consider the backgrounds and activities of minority group professionals. Whatever specific helping skills they may have learned in their formal education, these have usually been added to their lengthy personal experiences in naturalistic (that is, nonbureaucratic) settings with minority persons and in cross-cultural encounters focused on topics other than those defined by the job. As we have already noted, minority professionals often make commitments of time and energy to a client community in ways that white professionals do not. They do this because they are a resource to those communities. But they also do it because they know that they must be kept constantly informed of the needs of those communities. As professionals, they do not lose their home-grown communicative competence. White professionals, or minority professionals working in unfamiliar communities, can follow this example and inform themselves by seeking contacts and relationships in their service communities outside their bureaucratically defined responsibilities. In this way, the limitations of all interviewing as a learning technique can be partially overcome.

PART TWO

THE ETHNOGRAPHIC BASIS FOR SOCIAL SERVICES IN ETHNIC AND MINORITY COMMUNITIES

CHAPTER FIVE
CULTURAL CONTEXT AND INDIVIDUAL VARIATION IN SOCIAL SERVICES

Each of the papers that follow develops a perspective on the meaning of cultural differences as they are expressed and as they are experienced by members of various ethnic and minority groups. Each paper also deals, implicitly if not explicitly, with an issue of considerable importance in social services: individualizing the client. Within specific ethnic groups, there is considerable variation in people's behavior and in their commitment to the prevailing values and practices of their fellows. Intracultural diversity is a fact of social life, and it is one which the culturally competent worker must be able to handle. Unfortunately, training in cross-cultural sensitivity has often been built upon what might be called "uniformist assumptions" in the interpretation and use of cultural data. That is, particular cultural traits are identified and treated as though they were typical or uniformly characteristic of a culture. Such approaches, common in both training programs and literature, have been criticized by a number of anthropologists as well as other social scientists (Pelto and Pelto 1975), because they make it easy to apply unthinkingly such labels as "culture of poverty" and "female-centered family" to whole groups of people, including individuals who may or may not exhibit the social and cultural traits that such labels suggest. In a critique of common cultural descriptors for Spanish-speaking people—terms such as "machismo," "traditionalism," "fatalism," and "present-time orientation"—Romano (1968) concluded that such labels have limited explanatory value, because they assume that millions of people are basically alike. Similar critiques of assumptions of cultural uniformity have been made in reference to blacks (Hannerz 1969, Liebow 1967), Native Americans (Graves 1970, Red Horse et al. 1978), Puerto Ricans (Sanday 1976: 63, Fitzpatrick 1971, Steward et al. 1956), and West Indians (Wilson 1974). While broad-scaled, underlying cultural themes are most certainly important in the interpretation of behavior, individual instances of behavior are also the result of situational variables, such as the individual's status within the community (Wolf 1966a), the character of social networks (Mitchell 1969, Collins and Pancoast n.d.), and the organization of households (Bott 1957, Martin and Martin 1978). The problem for the worker is that of untangling cultural and situational factors in order to make sense of the client and the client's problem.

There are two ways to approach the issue and both are important, since neither alone will give the worker a satisfactory grasp of all that is involved in individualizing clients. There is a macroperspective and a microperspective, that of the group and that of the individual, and they complement one another. Sanday (1976) has argued that within a culturally plural society such as our own, individuals can be viewed as belonging to one of four major categories: mainstream, bicultural, culturally different, and culturally marginal. Mainstreamers have assimilated the standardized, most widely accepted values of the dominant society, and they attempt in their behavior to emulate those values. If the individual is white and of adequate economic resources and is given frequent opportunity, the assimilation and behavioral manifestation of those values are largely unthinking and automatic. Members of racial and minority groups may think and act like mainstreamers, they often become mainstreamers, but they do so in spite of the fact that their participation in the lives and institutions of other mainstreamers involves constant testing and challenge of their right to be there, however subtle or unsubtle. Bicultural individuals, on the other hand, may participate in mainstream culture, but they are also involved in important ways with the values and interests of identifiably distinctive cultural groups. Many minority persons in American society, and certainly many minority professionals in social work, would be considered bicultural in this sense. They have a dual commitment, a loyalty to their communities of origin and a stake in the political and economic institutions of the dominant society. They move as the situation dictates between two (or more) cultural worlds.

Sanday's third category is those who are culturally different. They have been exposed to the dominant or mainstream culture, but their primary affiliation and locus of activity are with a distinctive cultural entity. They may avoid contact with mainstreamers but still make minimal use of mainstream institutions, such as employment agencies and social security, and they are exposed to the mass media and mass merchandising. Culturally different individuals are often isolated in geographical enclaves, such as "China towns" or "little Italys," from which they seldom emerge. Indeed, English may not be the language of the home, although they may know it and use it in public settings. The fourth category, culturally marginal persons, are those who have little or no attachment to any identifiable cultural entity. They may come from any ethnic or racial group, but for a variety of reasons—physical or developmental handicaps, geographical isolation, disabling life circumstances, or sheer choice—they are truly alienated and follow a way that is uniquely their own.

The value of this typology, and it must be regarded as a tentative one at best, is that it prepares the worker for making an initial judgment about the cultural placement of the individual client. It is not enough to know that we are confronted with a person who is black or Indian; we must also know where in the typology of intracultural variation that client fits. By utilizing Sanday's four-way cut into the concept of culture to, in effect, "size up" the client, we are refining our capacity to make distinctions. It is important to note here that it cannot be argued, as some may be tempted to do, that locating the individual in terms of this four-way division of intracultural possibilities is simply another effort to pigeonhole people. The client may be as alert to subtle clues that identify and affirm status as is the worker. Indeed, if the client is of a minority group and the worker is not, he or she is probably more sensitive to verbal and nonverbal signals that assign place and establish degrees of social distance. Rather than pigeonholing, the typology can be viewed as a classificatory device that suggests the kinds of options (and limitations) available in a multicultural society, a point about which Sanday is explicit. The issue we are really discussing, then, is one of the kinds of opportunities, in an overall sense, that the client has been able to pursue. If we can clarify that with each client, then we will have been able to make one step beyond bland cultural stereotypes. We will have sharpened our sense of who and what the client is and the meaning of the client's life experience in relation to the problem to be resolved. The alternative is to proceed without any ethnographic information or cultural sensitivity at all and thus in ignorance of the kind of person the worker is dealing with. The worker's assessment, therefore, of the client's attachment to one of the four kinds of cultural expression allowed by Sanday's typology is a first step in individualizing the client's cultural background.

But the individual is more than just a participant in a given culture at a specified stage of its history and more than the manifestation of one of the variations of a particular cultural experience. He or she is a creative agent who is capable of managing cultural resources and manipulating troublesome situations in order to arrive at some personal advantage (Boissevain 1968, Schmidt et al. 1977). The next step in individualization of the client, then, must be some assessment of the degree of the individual's commitment to the cultural principles and practices he or she nominally espouses and of how that commitment is expressed in behavior. At this point, the elements of personality and features of idiosyncrasy, mannerism, and distinctiveness become important.

Examining the issue cross-culturally, LeVine (1973: 27-28) has posed what he considers critical questions in estimating the degree of an individual's conformity to a cultural standard. First, is the individual's behavior general across situations? How consistent is it with the expectations of others and the expectations of self? Second, does the individual adhere to normative standards in private situations as well as in public ones? (Presumably, when one is not exposed to immediate feedback and evaluation by others, there is more room for variation, even violation of cultural norms.) Third, does the individual's behavior adhere to cultural expectations during experiences of pain and stress? If behavior is culturally patterned, and if individuals conform to those patterns even in extreme or threatening circumstances, we can say something of their commitment to the themes of their cultural backgrounds. Fourth, do individuals articulate their understanding of cultural norms and discuss these in terms of a variety of life experiences? If so, that would suggest a preoccupation and self-consciousness with the verbal and symbolic material of cultural tradition. Fifth, do the individual's manifestations of cultural conformity persist even during short- or long-term separations from the community of origin and during sojourns into the nonsupportive atmosphere of the dominant society? Issues of adaptiveness and biculturality are at issue here.

Even if all of these questions can be answered with some kind of assurance that the individual does indeed represent in his or her behavior the themes and symbols of a particular cultural tradition, LeVine notes that there remains one final and most difficult problem:

> It is not only possible but probable that in the same population will be found individuals who perform a practice merely because it is a social imperative and those for whom the practice is more deeply imbedded in their psychological processes. . . . Thus an ethnographic description that tells us most persons in a population behave in accordance with a norm raises more psychological questions than it answers. (1973: 28).

Clearly the task of individualizing the client is a difficult one, requiring the culturally sensitive worker to acquire as much ethnographic knowledge as possible. To assume of an individual who is Hispanic that he or she must believe in the health and illness system associated with *mal ojo* is to use cultural data to stereotype anew. But to know that *mal ojo* is a *variable,* the significance of which must be determined on a case-by-case basis, is to use cultural information in a way that helps clarify the context of behavior and its meaning for the client. It is to use ethnographic information in a transactional rather than categorical sense, a distinction made in the chapter on ethnicity. Cultural knowledge is needed to formulate tentative guesses and to make reasonable hypotheses about a client's relationship to the culture of origin and to the culture of the dominant society. The use of such information as a means of guiding one's own insight rather than imposing new labels is at the heart of cultural awareness and cross-cultural, communicative competence.

Admittedly, making an ethnographic approach to individualizing the client is difficult and time consuming. But what else could it be? The alternative is to deal with human beings as culturally naked bundles of mismanaged psychic energy and behavioral errors. Unfortunately, much of what has passed as cultural awareness training for social workers in the past has been little more than poorly understood and misapplied anthropological anecdotes and gossip, rather than an effort to deal with human beings in their full complexity. Much remains to be done before well-defined training principles and procedures can be established.

THE ETHNOGRAPHY OF
PROBLEM RESOLUTION

Each of the following chapters is concerned with some aspect of help-seeking and help-providing activity in ethnic and minority communities. In addition, each chapter makes available to the reader information of an ethnographic character that is important to the sensitive design and delivery of social services. The chapters should be viewed, therefore, as illustrations of key cultural themes in various communities. These themes are expressed in multiple ways in the lives of the clients and in their perceptions and evaluations of problems. Familiarity with a specific cultural context is a first step in assessing the behavioral and psychological involvement of clients in their own communities and is critical for establishing what in the way of services might be culturally meaningful and personally acceptable. Problem resolution must be founded on reliable ethnographic information, since without it the worker's suggestions for change may be irrelevant to the client's real concerns.

The paper by Leigh and Green attempts to provide a corrective to the long tradition in the social sciences and the social welfare literature of stereotyping black families and life in the black community. Terms such as "female-centered" and "matrifocal" family, "incomplete" and "multiproblem" families, have long been freely used to characterize black Americans. The now infamous "Moynihan Report" (1965) is perhaps the best-known example. The authors summarize some of the recent research in this area and discuss the important work of Martin and Martin (1978), of Stack (1970, 1975), of Hannerz (1969), and of others who have shown that there is much more complexity and subtlety in black families and communities than previous researchers had recognized. The fact that some members of the new generation of researchers are themselves black and present a distinctively black viewpoint contributes to this new level of awareness. So, too, does the adoption by these researchers of holistic, emic research strategies. The paper suggests the importance for the worker of a systematic, ethnographic approach to understanding the internal organization of client communities. Without such knowledge, it does not seem reasonable that solutions to personal or community problems can be discussed intelligently.

Ishisaka and Takagi address a particularly difficult issue, that of developing services for people of widely varying cultural backgrounds. They consider the Chinese, Japanese, and Pilipinos (the latter the preferred spelling) among whom differences in language and customs are obvious and evident. But the times and circumstances surrounding the arrival in this country of each of these groups are significant as well. The experiences of the Chinese, for instance, are not identical to those of other Asian people here. Varying patterns of community organization and family styles within each group reflect this difference. Yet there are commonalities as well, in that those of more recent residence are usually in greater need of social and advocacy services than of long-term counseling on problems of mental health. How those needs can be met, utilizing the cultural expectations of clients, is presented in a particularly insightful discussion of community and personal values.

Ishisaka and Takagi make clear that help seeking and problem resolution are complex and subtle processes, requiring both knowledge and skill on the part of the worker if satisfactory results are to be achieved.

Miller's paper on Native Americans is distinctive in that it is an effort to generate ethnographic insight through careful analysis of a specific issue in a particular population. She studied the problems of urban Indian families in Los Angeles, families in which one or more of the children suffered some kind of disability. Her careful and detailed analysis of how parents identify and respond to disability, of how families become "lost" to the service system, and of how encounters with service personnel sometimes result in misunderstanding is suggestive of the importance of the kinds of insight that the help-seeking approach makes possible. The paper concludes with an outline of intervention guidelines. These should be viewed as useful for practice, but they can also be considered hypotheses. There is enormous variation among Native American cultures, as Miller notes, and intervention approaches applicable to one group or setting may not be applicable to others. The paper opens up this important possibility in a way that should be immediately useful to worker and researcher alike.

Miller's paper is useful for another reason as well. Her work suggests the value to informed social service intervention of ethnographic research. All the authors here note that the ethnically competent worker must have a good understanding of the history, family patterns, values, and lifestyles of the client's community. But the ability to utilize current research findings is equally important, for such findings modify and inform gross generalizations about cultural differences. Background knowledge of client communities, the kind usually supplied in classes and training workshops, must be supplemented by the skills of interpreting ethnographic data and of adapting one's professional style to new information. That concern is evident in Miller's approach to Native American clients.

The historical background of Spanish-speaking people in the United States is central to the paper of Gallegos and de Valdez. They note that many Spanish speakers were never "immigrants" in the usual sense, but rather were absorbed by this country as the result of territorial conquest. The struggle that ensued was for them one of preserving and protecting a place for themselves in a society that denied them even the basic rights of citizenship. That denial extended to social services, Hispanics having been more frequently ignored than included in the design and implementation of programs. It is not surprising, therefore, that Spanish-speaking people have not always utilized even those few services that are available to them. To some degree, of course, they have relied on cultural resources, such as the extended family and the values unique to it. Yet, as the authors note, families do not always function as their members would want them to, and the need for social services can be as great among those with extended family traditions as among those with no family resources at all. Gallegos and de Valdez make clear that little is known about Hispanic clients, of how and why they use or fail to use professional services. It is therefore critical that more research be undertaken and that Hispanic scholars and researchers as well as the consumers of services be part of any effort to improve service delivery.

Despite the diversity of their approaches, each of the authors recognizes the importance of a thorough familiarity with the cultural background of clients. This is a point sometimes lost in the emphasis on "skills" and techniques in social work education. But, as we have already noted, without such information the planning and delivery of services must occur removed from the world as experienced by clients and in ignorance of their sense of need.

CHAPTER SIX
THE STRUCTURE OF
THE BLACK COMMUNITY:
THE KNOWLEDGE BASE
FOR SOCIAL SERVICES
James W. Leigh
and James W. Green

It is difficult to visualize an image of joined hands and common struggle that would symbolize the historical relationship of social work and the black community. Rather, that relationship has run sometimes warm, more often cold, depending on the vagaries of changing theoretical trends and the imminence of political and social crisis. Following the Civil War, the federal government established the Freedman's Bureau to promote the employment, educational, and legal rights of the emancipated slaves. Yet despite the efforts of that agency, for most of the nineteenth century, black Americans were almost totally excluded from social service institutions. Nor did the private charities of that same period have any great impact on or even interest in the problems of blacks. Based in the Northeast and the

JAMES W. GREEN is a cultural anthropologist, having done research on children and migration in the West Indies. He is also interested in medical anthropology in the Caribbean. Other work has included studies in child abuse and the development of training programs for protective service workers. He has done consulting on cultural awareness training with both public and private social service agencies. He received his Ph.D. from the Department of Anthropology at the University of Washington where he currently teaches.

JAMES W. LEIGH received his MSW from Wayne State University in 1954 and in 1961 a Diploma in the Program of Advanced Study at the School for Social Work, Smith College. He has worked in the field of juvenile probation, mental health, child welfare, and social work education. His interests include teaching, consultation, and research in social services for ethnic and racially identified individuals and families. He is an Associate Professor in the School of Social Work at the University of Washington.

Midwest, the Charity Organization Society movement was more concerned with the terrible crowding of northern and eastern cities by European immigrants. Staffed largely by white volunteers of middle- and upper-class origins, the services provided were intended to acculturate European immigrants to American patterns of living as quickly as possible. In addition, those organizations were committed to a view of poverty as a personal and moral condition, one embodied in their distinction between the "worthy" and the "unworthy" poor. Blacks, however, were viewed as a group apart—a caste—physically present in American society but culturally distinctive because of appearance, origins, and the experience with slavery. Such a caste could not be expected to acculturate to mainstream lifeways. It was unlikely, therefore, that during the period of Jim Crow racism the plight of several million blacks would appeal to the sense of mission of charity-minded organizations.

It remained for the settlement house movement of the 1880s to resume what the Freedman's Bureau had tried to do before its demise in 1872. Settlement house workers advocated changing the conditions of poverty rather than the morals and manners of the poor. Their emphasis was on providing a setting within which the poor would be encouraged to create their own distinctive style of community. In this respect, no determination concerning "worthiness" was made. Consequently, those blacks who began moving into northern cities at that time were welcomed in settlement houses. The workers there, almost alone among whites in their opposition to discrimination, aligned themselves politically with black leaders and participaged in the founding of the NAACP and the National Urban League. Both of these groups stressed improvement of social conditions, the former through legal changes, and the latter through work with community groups and social workers.

When Freudian psychology and psychiatry first became prominent among social workers, immediately after World War I, social work's interest in black people began to diminish. As the country's most depressed and oppressed minority, their problems of simply surviving were overwhelming and massive. Not only were there too few resources to meet such a need but the problems that were presented did not appear to be amenable to change through the newly popular counseling and psychotherapeutic techniques. The worker who had provided direct services at the settlement house was transformed into the clinician, directing psychic discovery. Thus, "when the profession embraced psychological conflict as paramount in problem-solving activity, blacks were deemed poor candidates for therapy because of the concrete nature of their problem . . . " (Solomon 1976: 78). Nor, in the view of many, was there any reason to expect change in the conditions of such people. Popular stereotypes and the doctrine of Social Darwinism linked social potential to genetic and "racial" characteristics. To the degree that the black community endured the worst that northern slums and southern sharecropping made available, individual blacks were viewed as capable of living with poverty and as incapable of rising above it. Psychological intervention by social workers would not help.

It is important to note that the neglect of problems faced by the black community was also justified on what were felt by many to be valid scientific grounds. After the Civil War and into the twentieth century, theories of race difference stressed "innate" attributes presumed to be characteristic of peoples of varying origins. Among blacks, these so-called racial attributes were presumed to include limited mental capabilities, obsession with immediate gratification, inability to learn the characteristics of other "higher" cultures, and lack of interest in self-improvement. This concentration on the presumed negative characteristics of a given group were explained by a notion of social change peculiar to and flattering of white Victorian-era thinkers: all races, it was argued, evolved at different rates toward higher levels of physical and mental perfection. By examining the cultural characteristics of different races, and by making physical measurements of brain sizes among other anatomical features, one could "scientifically" determine how far along the scale of evolutionary development a particular race had progressed. According to the comparisons that were made, the white "races" of Europe (really different nationalities) were the most highly developed, those of African background the least advanced.

This kind of theorizing was spurious to an extreme degree and was rejected by some anthropologists and biologists as simplistic stereotyping, without scientific standing of any kind. Yet, as stereotypes, these notions of restricted development persisted in popular ideas of racial differences. The belief that black people were conditioned by their genetic inheritance to develop only an inferior culture suggested that there was really very little justification for attempts to change, through social services, what seemed to have been established in nature.

With the emergence of the civil rights movement of the 1960s, however, the profession was reminded of the needs of the black community and of the history of deficiencies in service provided to black clients. Indeed, not only was the adequacy of services a point of contention but racism within social work itself also became an issue. An important editorial in a 1964 issue of *Social Casework* announced that problems in the relationship of the profession to blacks could no longer be ignored:

> The relative dearth of literature on the racial factor in casework treatment, . . . and the conspicuous absence of research on the subject suggest that repressive psychological mechanisms may be at work. Perhaps it is difficult for a profession committed to humanistic tenets to engage in honest appraisal of possible disparities between its ideals and its accomplishments. (1964: 155).

This statement was a welcome one in its honesty in recognizing the potential for racism within an avowedly "helping" profession. But the statement was also a manifestation of the limited understanding of racial issues typical of many professionals, evident in the curious if not quaint way the etiology of the problem was described: "repressive psychological mechanisms may be at work." As a psychological view of the origins of the problem, racism within social work was attributed to wrong attitudes, to ignorance, and to fear and guilt. The question of institutional sources of racism was not addressed.

The *Social Casework* editorial did inspire, however, a proliferation of research activities and articles on how racism was a possible factor in social services. Typically, the center of this new research interest was the client-practitioner relationship.

The literature analyzed, often in psychological terms, the complexities of cross-racial encounters between white workers and black clients (Fibush 1965, Bloch 1968, Simmons 1963); black workers and white clients (Curry 1964); and the problems of racially mixed service settings (Lide 1971, Fibush and Turnquest 1970). The significance of race in interviewing (Kadushin 1972) and in clinical work was also discussed. While not without their value, most of these studies concluded that racism in some form did indeed exist in social services, that it created problems of communication and worker effectiveness in interracial relationships, and that some of the problems could be overcome when people learned to cope with their feelings about race and when the worker proved to be both trustworthy and helpful in assisting the client.

But has this kind of response, with its emphasis on interpersonal encounters, been an adequate one for the profession? Is race simply a "factor" to be recognized and added into existing intervention formulas for working with clients? Is it sufficient, as one social worker has proposed, "to examine and loosen these 'repressive psychological mechanisms' by means of an honest appraisal" (Lide 1971: 432)? The reply of some black social workers and of many black critics of social work has been a qualified if not a negative one, and they have called for something more ambitious. Their concerns focus on three issues.

First, black critics have argued that traditional, individualistic approaches to problem solving with black persons can do little toward improving the lot of the black person in our society. Intervention based on psychodynamic theories is at best a palliative and, at worst, counterproductive to the advancement of the black group. These critics have argued that all too often counseling activities are irrelevant and changes should be made in society instead. This thrust has resulted in the movement toward social action through community organization and mobilization. It viewed the political, economic, educational, and employment arenas as targets for change. The structure of society was believed to be the causative agent of the problems that beset black persons and communities. Critics emphasized that the problem is not one of personal deficiencies or of personal reactions to social institutions but lies in the system of governance itself, a system which creates barriers to productive living for the majority of black persons in the country. Thus, an exclusive focus on the mental state of the black client, and especially on the worker's own intellectual and emotional problems in relating to racial issues, it was argued, diverts attention from the system or ecological sources of the client's problems and from the possible reasons that the client came to the attention of the social worker in the first place.

Casework services offered to black persons are viewed as suspect, because the theoretical model utilized viewed the person as the problem. In that individualisitc approach, skill acquisition or insight was supposed to assist the black person in the resolution of problems, no matter whether they were caused by an emotional state of distress or an economic issue, such as unemployment. This stance has persisted for a period of years, even though many caseworkers have questioned the usefulness of their individual approach to others. Critics argued that in this way of viewing services the caseworker was not making full use of the range of social work roles available, and they suggested that the caseworker become an advocate for black persons. They urged aggressive and assertive action in the job and housing arenas and in dealings with other social service agencies, particularly those which respond in a slow manner in meeting the black client's resource needs. Advocacy was to become a "programmatic" feature of social agency service structures.

The Black Task Force Report of the Family Service Association of America (Delaney 1979) is illustrative of efforts to meet criticisms of individual intervention based on a psychodynamic theory model. That report stresses an ecological systems perspective, one which "widens the scope of assessment to include the transactions between poor Black individuals and the systems within and outside their neighborhoods" (1979: 12). This perspective does not negate a psychodynamic approach, but broadens the areas of concern to structural factors which impinge on the lives of black persons and which may be determining influences of the problems that first brought the individual or family to the attention of the social agency.

The integration of methods, advocacy, counseling, group work, and family life education thus was seen as necessary to meet the service needs of the black population. Yet a blending of individualistic and group approaches, along with advocacy, even then may not be congruent with the values, lifestyles, and family situation of the black person. Those who have argued that traditional intervention techniques are not always successful with many blacks have suggested that this is so because the techniques employed do not take into account the complexities of life, particularly family and community life, from a black point of view (Thomas and Sillen 1972, Hill 1971). One may argue that group and advocacy intervention may also fail to take into consideration the identical factors that critics of traditional interventions have so clearly indicated as being important.

A second criticism has been that the role of the black family as a source of strength for black persons has been ignored. Years of research and more research dollars than probably can be accounted for have gone into demonstrating the supposed deficiencies of the black family, blaming it as the source of black problems. These studies culminated in the Moynihan report (1965), a document whose influence persists, despite its weaknesses and the criticisms made against it (Rainwater and Yancey 1967). The black family was described there as a "tangle of pathology . . . capable of perpetuating itself without assistance from the white world" (Moynihan 1965: 47). This notion of the black family as the source of its own problems has been attractive to conservative interests, to whom it has been convenient to "blame the victim" (Ryan 1969). But the idea also held appeal for a number of liberal, humanistic, largely white scholars and social workers, who were attracted to the "culture of poverty" idea and who, despite a genuine concern for righting the inequalities of racism, were prone to romanticize pathology and find its causes in the family of the very people who were being victimized. It is now apparent that these deficiency-oriented explanations and the catch phrases associated with them—cultural deprivation, multiple-problem families, the female-centered family—were seriously misleading.

The black community is more diverse than has been recognized; black families and households are often highly flexible and effective in coping with the problems of poverty; and black values centering around children and on the quality of interpersonal relations are much more intense and subtle than outsiders have been willing to recognize. A distinctive black culture exists, but its life-sustaining features have often been ignored. These features are all sources of strength and represent, according to Billingsley, a "bundle of complexity" rather than a "tangle of pathology" (1968). What that cultural complexity means for the effective delivery of social services to black clients is a topic almost untouched in the social work or social science literature.

Staples (1971), in his evaluation of black family sociological research, noted the emphasis on structural features but found little attention being given to the process of black family interactions. This seems particularly true in regard to middle-class black families. The "bundle of complexity" resides within the varieties of black families. A research focus on these transactional patterns may well advance our knowledge of the strengths of the black family, and it may illuminate internal black family processes as they relate to social and environmental conditions experienced by black families. Black families must be viewed as different, and a full understanding of these families must focus not only on structural features but also on the interactional processes of the black family and the black community within which it exists. The perceptual and theoretical screen of white values and standards that derives from a white, middle-class orientation will not aid in this process of discovery.

The third criticism of the social service system that is made by black social workers is the neglect by social work of the indigenous institutions of the black community. It must be recognized that currently many institutions in the black community are externally controlled, and that they have been established with only minimal or no participation by black people. Two institutions, the black church and black family, have remained relatively unaffected by external forces. The black church has served a nurturing function for black people for many years. The religion and the social services provided by the church have been strong supportive elements, which have held out hope for black people in times of crisis. Senior-citizen services, day-care services, credit unions, housing developments, and the education groups in which adults and children learned the social skills needed for survival purposes are just a few of the social service needs provided by the black church. These latent functions would also include, according to Staples (1976), maintaining family solidarity, status conferral, leadership development, release of emotional tensions, and providing sources of social activity and amusements and centers of black social protest activities.

The religious as well as the other functions of the black church have continued to operate whether in store-front operations or in the black affiliates of mainline religions, since before Emancipation. That social work, with its historical roots in modern-day religious thought, has not drawn on the black church experiences of the black people is rather surprising. It may be due, in part, to the fact that white religious institutions practiced institutional racism themselves, practices resulting in the formation and development of the black church as a separate institution. The techniques and the effectiveness of the black church in meeting the social service needs of black people thus are virtually unknown outside of the black community.

It is interesting that the black church has understood emotional catharsis through testifying as a technique of encouraging emotional release of tensions, of encouraging converts, and of maintaining the commitment of its members. "The Black church has been a much stronger force as helping resource than traditional agencies and helping practitioners" (Solomon 1976: 327). A service delivery system that is church-focused is suggested by Solomon as an alternative structure that is capable of meeting the needs of black persons who would not be attracted to traditional agencies.

Nor has the influence of the expressive arts as a black institution been fully appreciated by social workers. Black music, art, and poetry, with few exceptions (Keil 1966), have not been viewed as forming an institutional base for articulating and disseminating a distinctive black world view.

The black church and the black expressive arts contain the "soul" of black institutions, and social workers need to learn more of the background of their clients relative to these two areas. This information may enhance their service effectiveness. It is the challenge of black leaders who are critical of social work's neglect of black clients and indigenous black institutions.

THE FAMILY
AND THE BLACK COMMUNITY

It is important to look briefly at the history of black people in America, not because we are simply concerned with history as such, but because most whites really do not know much about it, and they consequently fail to see why blacks feel as deeply as they do about what has happened to them as a group. In addition, many of the problems currently experienced by the black community, and by black clients, are not new. They derive directly from the past. The failure to resolve problems at an earlier time has meant that they reappear today as costs to this generation. The development of the black family can be appreciated by considering its sources in Africa and by noting the social and political forces that have been important influences on it in this country.

Billingsley (1968) has provided a useful overview of the African past. He notes that in West Africa, from which most of the slaves came, family life had great strength and was complex in ways not appreciated by Europeans. Marriage was not the private affair of individuals, but a community event, in which permanent relations between lineages and between villages were established. Those relations had important economic and political significance for the families involved. Consequently, marriage ceremonies were marked by extensive public rituals. These customs had the authority of centuries of tradition and were linked to highly elaborated theological systems and well-defined principles of family organization. In a lineage system traced through the male line, typical of some groups, a man, his sons, their wives, and their children all shared a living area under the senior male's authority. In lineage systems traced through the female line, as was common in other areas, groups of brothers, their wives, and their offspring all lived together, and the brothers acted collectively in behalf of their lineage. In each system of lineage relationships, a complex series of rules of behavior governed relations between spouses, adults and children, and members of other households. This system of domestic relationships, embedded in larger lineage relationships and ultimately in village and regional linkages, had evolved over many generations. The system was both ancient and rewarding to those who grew up in it. Every individual had a place in the world, based on kinship ties. Citizenship was equivalent to kinship, and large complex kinship networks assured that the physical necessities of daily life, as well as moral support in times of crisis, would always be available.

The organization of the slave trade and of the slave-based plantation economy in North and South America and in the West Indies made it difficult if not impossible for enslaved Africans to maintain an uninterrupted and secure domestic life. There were a variety of reasons for this difficulty. In the slave trade itself, men were enslaved more often than women, because slavery was primarily a labor-supply system; more could be gained by having men rather than women working on plantations. Unlike slavery in Catholic-Hispanic areas such as Brazil, the predominantly Protestant-English areas of settlement placed no value on the slave family. Individuals had the status of chattel property and could be sold individually according to economic need and the sentiments of slave owners. Family relationships were an impediment to efficient plantation operations. The lives of slaves on plantations were short, rarely more than a decade in the early years of slave trading. Where the economic value of slaves was high, or where owners had emotional (and occasionally kinship) interests in their human property, older persons were a liability to an estate, and few were given care in their very short later years.

Given these demographic characteristics of plantation life and the lack of legal standing for marriage relationships, the possibilities of maintaining family life were very limited. The most outstanding characteristic of the slave family was its lack of autonomy. Legal marriage did not exist, and the remembered African marriage rituals that might have been practiced were not tolerated by whites. Whereas some planters encouraged marriage among their slaves, others had little interest in the matter, and none would allow a marriage relationship to interfere with the sale and transfer of slaves where that seemed necessary. Frequently owners simply assigned specific men and women to share a dwelling, with or without a marriage ceremony. This was done in order to minimize time spent on courting activities and to preserve a measure of domestic peace in the slave cabins. When one partner to the relationship died or was sold to settle an owner's debts, another was purchased as a replacement if the financial health of the estate permitted it.

The economic demands of the plantation regime also interfered with people's ability to establish enduring parental roles. Both men and women were expected to work for the estate, not on behalf of their domestic units. Most of that work was in the fields, although some also worked in the houses of the masters as personal servants. While their parents labored, small children were tended by old women or by older children. Some estates even had small huts beside the fields, where children were kept during the day. When the men and women returned from the fields, their children had been fed and tended by others, thus limiting the influence of parents in the rearing of their own children. The fact that slaves were required, on their own time, to work small provision grounds to supplement the food supplied by masters meant that men and women were further separated from their children and from each other. A man's economic role in the domestic unit was limited to supplying whatever he could to his mate and children. It was impossible to protect them from abuse or separation by owners. Women spent what time they could caring for children and in small domestic chores. But, as with men, their work on the estate came first.

Instability in domestic life was inevitable, given the lack of legal sanction for marriage and the fact that estate tasks interfered with the cultivation of parental and marital relationships. Nevertheless, certain patterns did emerge. Men asserted domestic authority when they were able to do so and established close and affectionate ties to their spouses and children within the limits imposed by plantation life. Women were attentive both to their children and to their husbands, and they played important roles in instructing children in the etiquette of race relations and the strategies of survival. Often these supportive functions were carried out within a monogamous nuclear-family unit. Where individual planters permitted, older persons and single adults shared quarters with a family, so that the nuclear family became in some instances an extended one as well. It was the general practice of estate owners to avoid involvement in domestic relations in the slave quarters unless issues of plantation economics were involved. (The important exception, of course, was the sexual license of white men with their female slaves.) Consequently, a limited measure of household control was possible, and men and women could exert authority within this sphere. The degree to which they did so depended on the predisposition of individual planters.

Family autonomy was always threatened by the selling of individuals and the dispersal of persons over many estates. Marriages or stabilized mating relationships were often ended this way. Yet the sense of kin ties and obligation persisted. Vigorous efforts were made by both men and women to be reunited with spouses, children, and other persons regarded as family friends or members. Consequently, kinship linkages and the sentiments of kinship often spanned many plantations. This created a network through which communication and limited economic support could travel. It extended the knowledge of the slaves of the world about them, including the knowledge that in a time of need, help might be available if conditions permitted. Thus the sense of isolation and helplessness that might have existed was moderated by an awareness of a larger community which would be supportive in both an emotional and a moral sense.

The popular white view of black family life as disorganized by slavery overlooks the historical facts, and it is a view that remains one of the most persistent stereotypes of American life. Yet the cultural history of the black population of the United States since slavery suggests a community both active and able in working to meet its own needs. There is now ample evidence that the slaves on the estates were not so demoralized that they were incapable of organizing revolts. Indeed, white fear of revolt is one of the most evident motives in the many laws that were made to regulate slave and master relationships. Revolts on individual estates often spread quickly, and whole regions were placed under martial law when the threat of slave rebellion was imminent.

Following Emancipation, the energy and planning that went into slave uprisings were transferred to efforts to organize the interests of black people throughout the country, North and South. This work took several forms. W. E. B. DuBois, a distinguished black teacher and writer, worked to make higher education available to larger numbers of black persons. In coining the phrase, the "talented tenth," he argued that it was necessary that a tenth of the best minds in the black community have the chance for education and for leadership roles, leadership which he hoped would attack the caste structure of Jim Crow racism. Marcus Garvey, a Jamaican, organized the first mass-based black movement in the United States. He promoted a return to Africa as the only hope of black people, and organized groups throughout the country for that purpose. His United Negro Improvement Association developed a newspaper, owned the Black Star shipping line, and sought to create awareness among black Americans of the similar problems afflicting black people in South America, the Caribbean, and the colonized areas of Africa. Author George Padmore and others developed the concept of Pan-Africanism, a movement of political and intellecutal leaders from all parts of the black world. They sought to give literary and political expression to the black struggle for dignity and to do so in an international perspective.

All of these leaders and their political movements struggled against the disabilities of caste, which isolated the black community from participation in the social and economic benefits available to others. Illiteracy, unemployment, landlessness, and despair were so great that collective self-help efforts were difficult to initiate and maintain. In addition, opposition from the white community was quickly and effectively aroused whenever the success of even modest efforts appeared to challenge white political and economic dominance. Thus, efforts at improving life in the black community were slow, were often blocked, and were always carried out under an implicit or explicit threat to black leaders and participants alike.

The black church, however, provided a setting in which the community could gather relatively undisturbed. The Great Awakening, a religious revival which began in the North during the mid-1700s, sent traveling preachers (usually Methodist and Baptist) throughout the country. They carried their evangelistic message to both blacks and whites and inspired the rise of black preachers on estates and in cities throughout the South. This led to a proliferation of black churches, ranging from large, urban-based congregations to small, more spontaneous gatherings in rural areas. Most whites recognized the potentially dangerous role of blacks in leadership positions, and laws were enacted to control the size of congregations and to assure that whites made administrative decisions related to church activities. Nevertheless, church membership grew rapidly, especially among free blacks, and the desire to control their own congregations led to splits such as that which resulted in the founding of the African Methodist Episcopal Church in 1816.

After Emancipation, the "invisible" churches of the plantations became open and visible and operated alongside the larger denominations. In every area of the country, there was a multitude of independent and enthusiastic congregations. Whether small or large, however, the churches functioned to provide significant services to the black community. Churches were centers of educational activity at a time when schools were either unavailable or closed to black students. Leadership skills were developed in the operation of churches. Ministers enjoyed high prestige not only as spiritual advisors but as highly visible community activists. Mutual aid societies and benevolent associations were established, often within church organizations, in order to provide health and welfare services to those in need. These societies provided a kind of insurance, collecting small donations from members on a regular basis and making funds available to families confronted with the expenses of doctors, funerals, or other crises.

The church remains a central institution in the black community. The forms of religious activity are highly varied, yet all deal with problems of survival in a hostile world. The larger denominations—Catholic, Methodist, and Baptist in particular—have substantial black memberships. But the storefront church remains a healthy and vigorous component of most black communities. Movements based on a charismatic figure, such as Father Divine or Elijah Muhammad, also flourish. It was not by chance that the civil rights movement and groups such as Martin Luther King's Southern Christian Leadership Conference developed out of religious institutions.

Finally, the role of the arts or "expressive culture" must be considered a significant component of the black historical experience. The areas of West Africa in which slave collecting was most intense were rich in musical styles, oral traditions, and fine arts. What Levine (1977: 3) has called the "sacred world of black slaves" was made up of the remembered and preserved traditions of the African homeland. In particular, song styles, folklore, oratory, and musical patterns survived best. These were easily adapted to religious practices—often an amalgam of white Christianity and various African religions—to produce new expressive forms, of which the gospel spiritual is one example. Work songs, blues music, and jazz also represented the creative fusion of African elements to European traditions, resulting in new expressive forms.

One of the most remarkable periods of black artistic creativity occurred just after World War I. Known as the Harlem Renaissance, it was a period of intense interest in the arts and the artists of the black community. Poetry, novels, drama, stage musicals, dance, and graphic arts had all been developing since slavery, but this growth had been slow, due to lack of financial support and public appreciation.

With increasing numbers of blacks migrating to northern cities, the opportunities for collective celebration of the artistic efforts of the black world grew. Whites became aware of an expressive culture tradition that had been largely invisible to them. Blacks discovered both social and financial opportunities, especially in New York, for expanding their interests. The Harlem Renaissance period brought into national prominence black artistic work and legitimized, for both the white and the black communities, the large role of black artistic creativity in American life (Lewis 1981).

As black traditions, artistic and musical efforts fulfill more than simply entertainment functions, as they are also collective representations of the concerns of the black community. Like black ministers, creative artists often embody and articulate values and sentiments that are widely shared among blacks. They are symbols, but they are also spokesmen and spokeswomen. As such, their public statements and private lives are not viewed as ornamental to or separate from the day-to-day realities of black life. They are an exemplification of that life and the struggles that black people have made to survive in a hostile world.

CULTURE AND LIFESTYLES

Because black people have endured a history of caste separation and limited economic and political advantages, the image of the black community for most whites has been a negative one. That image has included notions of poverty, of family and community disorganization, and of deviance from what is assumed to be the accepted cultural patterns of mainstream American life. In social research, as in the social services, this perspective has led to a deficit model as the basis for explaining differences in childrearing, household composition, language, religion, work habits, or other features of the black community. By a deficit model, we mean any principle of explanation which finds the black community itself responsible for the problems it experiences. Popular deficit explanations have included such ideas as the "culture of poverty" or the "female-centered" family.

Deficit interpretations of black life have had a number of damaging effects. First, such explanations have reinforced stereotypes that suggest that all black people conform to the same set of values and living styles. In fact, there is enormous diversity in the black community, as we shall see shortly. Second, in focusing on how blacks appear to "fail," deficit models do not account for the many who succeed in one way or another. The achievements of blacks as individuals, when they are recognized, are viewed as proof that the institutions of the larger society "work" for those willing to minimize their affiliations with a stigmatized culture and community. The social and psychic price of individual achievement is thus unappreciated. Finally, the deficit tradition of explanation ignores the fact that any culture has both strengths and limitations for a people. By dwelling on limitations and failure, the values and behavior that make life endurable and satisfying for people are discounted. Of all the minorities in America, it is the culture of blacks that has been most consistently ignored through reliance on the deficit approaches to analysis and understanding. The need now is to identify those social and cultural themes which are distinctive of the black community and which illustrate the variety of lifestyles. Such a picture confirms Billingsley's (1968) observation, quoted earlier, that black culture represents a "bundle of complexity" that outsiders have yet to appreciate.

There is enormous cultural variation within the American black community, but that variation is not an indicator of deviance or pathology; it is a response to the crippling effects of powerlessness imposed by the larger society and the need to survive many economic and political disabilities (Solomon 1976). In his review of the strengths of black families, Hill (1971) has identified the culture themes which are the bases of survival in the black community and which provide a set of cultural values and social strategies that serve the needs of survival. While these values and strategies are responses to the problem of powerlessness and of caste isolation, they are also themes which underlie the diversity of the black community and give it coherence. Briefly, those themes are:

1. Strong kinship bonds among a variety of households.
2. Strong work orientation in support of family ties.
3. High level of flexibility in family roles.
4. Strong achievement orientation, particularly in the area of occupational and educational aspirations.
5. Strong commitment to religious values and church participation.

Family characteristics which manifest these themes will be described more fully below. What is important to note at this point, however, is that these themes are not those associated with the deficit model of the black community or the stereotypes that come from it. They represent positive values, which contribute to the stability of life and to survivability. For instance, strong kinship bonds have meant that older persons in black families have significant and often powerful roles in decision-making. The merging of households and the informal adoption of children are also reflections of a powerful sense of family obligation. Hill notes that "this feat of self-help among Black families is remarkable when one realizes their precarious economic position" (1971: 7).

Many households maintain their economic positions not through welfare, but due to the fact that in the black community there is a high percentage of husband-and-wife joint wage earners. Grown children are expected to contribute to their parents' household when the need is there. Adolescents who work make their earnings available for family maintenance rather than private needs. This kind of reciprocity within the family also influences relations between adult members, relations which are often egalitarian despite the popular misconception that black families are female-centered or matriarchal. Decision-making and household tasks often are shared between husband and wife, because that is an efficient way of assuring that household chores are completed. In single-parent families, there is heavy reliance on interhousehold kinship networks for the provision of financial help, services, and advice. All of these factors—extensive kinship ties, a strong sense of household and kinship obligation, expectations of reciprocity between households, egalitarianism between adults within households, and a sense of the adaptability of family roles to meet the needs of others in the kinship network—are black culture characteristics that make survival possible in a difficult world.

There is in addition to these themes a value dimension that is more difficult to define. Solomon (1976: 169) has referred to family patterns that "for the most part are more humanistic and have greater validity than the hollow values of middle-class American society." This sense of hope and of humanistic concerns within the family is undoubtedly connected to a strong religious orientation, a value orientation that has evolved parallel to white values in America but without the prevailing influence of the Puritan ethic. If the Puritan work ethic can be defined as a predominating task orientation that is usually motivated by economic achievement to the exclusion of other values, then a contrast to black cultural values is suggested. These values stress person-to-person relationships and their cultivation, in preference to object orientation or the completion of tasks. Very little research has been done to explore the contrast between black and white cultural values in this way. The work of Keil (1966) and Baraka (1973) in the area of black expressive culture—music, dance, written and oral literature—is suggestive. The African tradition provides an alternative to a Northern European Puritan variant of work and family values. In addition, the isolation of the black community has permitted the parallel development of this distinctive system of values and family behavior. The specific components of this broadly humanistic orientation have yet to be fully defined, but the presence of such an orientation needs to be noted, because it indicates another source of personal and community strength.

By themselves, however, these themes do not adequately describe the culture of the black community. There is also great diversity. Concepts of class (for example, upper, middle, lower) or of origins (urban ghetto, rural, suburban) are sometimes used to explain that diversity. Here we will use the concept of lifestyle, because it helps focus attention on the kinds of diversity that social workers can expect to find. We are interested in the behavior of people, not just their class or geographical origins, and the lifestyle approach emphasizes behavior and its various forms within a particular culture.

Within the black community, at least four major lifestyles can be identified. Following the approach of Hannerz (1969) who carried out extensive research in Washington, D.C., we can describe those lifestyles as follows:

1. "Mainstreamers" are those who adhere most closely to mainstream assumptions about American life. These are people for whom standards of respectability as represented by home ownership, employment success, educational achievement, and sometimes religious affiliation are important. Mainstreamers usually are married, often live in nuclear families with stable composition, and for them consensual unions or divorce are rare. Persons attached to the

household may include an aged parent. The physical appearance of mainstreamer homes reflects the comforts available to those with adequate incomes and for whom appearances as a "respected family" are important. Leisure time is spent in family-oriented activities and household maintenance. Such families are composed of individuals who have struggled heroically to achieve what the values of the larger society promise but often withhold. This group, the black middle class, is growing and will continue to do so (McAdoo 1979).

There are important historical precedents for mainstreamers in American society. During slavery, there was always a small but rigorous class of free blacks. They lived in cities and towns and were often skilled tradesmen and merchants. Over the past century, this class has grown, thanks in part to the large number of black colleges in the South, which provided leadership and which were important avenues to social mobility. Some mainstream blacks have moved rapidly into high-paying occupations as professionals and white-collar workers, just as they have begun to move into improved housing areas. Those who remain in ghetto areas have worked to improve the quality of their homes and lives there. Not all mainstreamers have achieved the living standards of the white middle class, but such persons are identifiable by their commitment to middle-class values of home ownership, stable family life, and at least some participation in civic or religious activities.

2. "Swingers" are the children of mainstreamers, young adults who often delay settling into mainstream patterns until their twenties or thirties. They are unmarried and are intensely involved in a variety of social, athletic, or political interests with peers. Their domestic commitments are light. Many people at this stage of their lives are experimenting with various occupations and gaining experience of the world through travel and companionship.

Hannerz notes that "swingers typically spend relatively little of their free time just sitting around at home alone or with the family" (1969: 42). Traveling about, spontaneous gatherings, visiting, and social activities are important. Great emphasis is placed on personal style in clothing, dance, and other expressive activities. One can be poor or well-off and still be a swinger. Economic capability simply governs possibilities, not enthusiasm, for this highly individualistic period of one's life. Marriage and the routines of family life normally mean an end to this period of freedom. But for some, they also present conflicts, because of the need to reconcile the excitement that marked the swinging life with the inevitability of the domestic tasks that infringe on that individualism.

3. "Street families" are childrearing households whose lifestyle is one of the most widely stereotyped of the black community. Street families are usually headed by an adult female, who struggles to keep the unit together. Such families are found in the poorest sections of cities, and contain people usually lacking education and employment skills. Members of these families are forced to be highly mobile in order to take advantage of economic opportunities. Street families are distinguished from mainstreamers in that they are the ones most obviously suffering the debilitating consequences of poverty.

Street families are often parts of larger networks of households, which will be described below, and some of their members are swingers or former swingers. Mainstreamers who may share an apartment building or neighborhood with street families often have strong objections to the street-family lifestyle. They point to the unstable composition of these units, the seeming lack of concern with sexual fidelity, and the public display of family arguments as evidence of disorganization and moral weakness. However, such households perform a variety of services for their economically depressed members: where several adults reside together, babysitting, job hunting, and other tasks can be shared. Income, when it is available, also can be shared. Relatives or friends in need can be housed and fed, and they often contribute to household maintenance. There is a sense in which such families are relatively open and flexible, taking in new members easily. This kind of flexibility is crucial to survival among the very poor.

4. "Street-corner men" make up the lifestyle most visible to outsiders who come into the black community. Men of all ages who are poor, poorly educated, and lacking in either opportunities or skills are characteristic of this particular group. Their lifestyle represents, along with street families, the view most commonly held by whites in regard to the black world. Yet they are often a very small percentage of the black population. Street-corner men have few domestic attachments, living temporarily with street families, with other street-corner men, or alone in cheap hotels. They may or may not have been married, and they may or may not have children. They have difficult relations with the nonblack world—police, judges, employers, unions —and difficult relations within their own community. They are condemned by mainstreamers, particularly for a seeming lack of interest in jobs. They may have been in and out of a number of street families and no longer be welcome there. Some men are in transition from one street family to another and find the company of similarly situated males more congenial than the demands of women with children to maintain. Others have never left the swinger life and pursue it as best they can. Street-corner men are poor, usually unskilled, and so, defenseless. They retreat to the world of all-male gatherings in bars and at other public places. Odd jobs and petty criminal activities provide them with intermittent incomes; the rest of the time they are dependent on each other. There is an appearance of camaraderie at the street-corner gatherings with their drinking, gambling, card playing, and talk. But there is also animosity and sometimes violence. Old insults are remembered, small windfalls are jealously protected, and slights are revenged. For the most part, street-corner life is one of monotonous routine—the same food, drink, and people, endured along with the worst poverty to be found in American cities.

How accurately do these four social categories describe life in a black urban area? Returning to the concept of lifestyle, it is very important to reassert the purpose but also the limitations of the concept. Essentially, the lifestyle approach is an aid to organizing information that would otherwise appear overwhelming, if not chaotic, in its diversity. The value of such an approach is that it simplifies reality so that it may be more understandable. This simplification is necessary as a learning device, but it is also dangerous. It has the potential for contributing to new stereotypes, just as it demonstrates the unsuitability of older ones. This is a risk that is inherent in any typological approach to sorting out sociological data. The risk is justifiable, however, if it is recognized that such labels as "mainstreamer" and "street family" are only approximations. They describe collective, not individual, responses to the problems facing the black community. Therefore the accuracy with which they describe any specific individual is always a matter of degree and of judgment. Stereotyping occurs when that distinction is ignored and when group characterizations, be they positive or negative, are applied to individuals without regard to their specific circumstances. Indeed, if each and every black person were to fit one of these four lifestyles perfectly, we would have a culture unique in all history for its rigidity and simplistic homogeneity.

The lifestyle concept helps us move beyond the previous misconceptions that have obstructed a wider understanding of the complexity of the black community. That complexity, however, must be related to the core cultural values suggested by Hill (1971). Kinship obligation, interpersonal and interhousehold reciprocity, egalitarian relationships between adults, flexibility in family roles, and high value placed on achievement—all within a religious context—are themes which occur in the behavior of individuals in each lifestyle listed. The particular manifestation of those themes varies according to the specific circumstances of individuals and family units. A family that is upwardly mobile in a Northern urban setting will of course cope with problems differently from a family that is well established in a Southern rural county. It is the job of the culturally sensitive social worker to identify those variations within each family and each client, thus individualizing the help that is offered. To do that well, the worker must appreciate core family values and community and lifestyle diversities and also appreciate how households in the black community operate.

HOUSEHOLD AND FAMILY STRUCTURE

If social workers are to be effective helpers with black families, they must try to understand the resources, strengths, needs, and problems of those families in the same way that their clients do. This requires a client-oriented perspective, not one based on models of family organization imposed by outsiders. The majority of clients seen by a social worker will be or will have been members of an extended family network. The existence of that network and the material and emotional support it provides for family members was largely ignored by early research, which focused on the female-dominated, welfare-dependent household or "street family." Female-dominated households were considered almost universal among poor blacks, even when statistics showed that they were not. The thousands of words that have been written exploring the female-centered family model assumed negative effects on family members from this pattern. Part of the underlying problem of that research was its starting point—that a household is the same thing as an independent nuclear family. A household and a family need not be identical social entities. The view that among blacks the nuclear family unit is disorganized or "broken" because households do not contain "complete" families reflects the confusion of many on this issue. The confusion can be eliminated by looking at the network of family relations that binds households together. This provides an altogether different view of black family life.

We derive our approach from the work of Martin and Martin (1978), Stack (1970, 1975), Scanzioni (1977), and others, who have begun a new phase of sociological research, exploring black family patterns from a black rather than a traditional academic perspective. In that view, almost every household in the black community functions as either a "base household" or an "affiliate" or "subunit household" in a complex system of interconnections. Subunit or affiliate households are linked to base households in an extensive mutual aid family network that may encompass as many as 100 members. It is this model of interconnected, extended-family households, not the imagery of broken, female-dominated units, that is essential to understanding black family relationships.

Martin and Martin define the black extended family as:

> a multigenerational, interdependent kinship system which is welded together by a sense of obligation to relatives; is organized around a "family base" household; is generally guided by a "dominant family figure"; extends across geographical boundaries to connect family units to an extended family network; and has a built in mutual aid system for the welfare of its members and the maintenance of the family as a whole. (1978: 1)

Obviously, the importance of these various family components will vary from place to place and with the circumstances of individual family members. But this model of black family organization can make more meaningful the behavior of individuals within their families and can help identify the sources of support to which individuals may turn in times of need.

A typical extended-family network may include five or more households, as shown in the figure entitled "Hypothetical Extended Family Network." This hypothetical example of a family network is centered on the base household, the family "home," where the informally recognized family leader lives. The base household membership varies dramatically, according to the economic conditions of family members. It may include an elder dominant ruling couple or dominant ruling female, typically the grandmother; an unmarried or divorced daughter and her children; a married daughter and her spouse and children; a single adult son; an unmarried son and his mate and their children; the children of another adult son, who is temporarily unemployed; or the children of persons distantly related to the base household leadership. What is important to recognize, however, is that despite the variable composition of the base household, there is a recognized family leader resident there, one who has a powerful voice in the affairs not only of the base household but of the affiliated units as well. That individual provides a sense of centrality for other persons in the network, and it is that position of authority and respect which is an indication that a particular household is also a base household. In our example on the chart, that position of centrality could be held by the husband or the wife or both.

Household membership in affiliate households or subunits of the network is also variable. It may include the base household's grown children, their spouses and children, partners, or same-sex friends, or more distant relatives of the base household leaders. Looking again at our hypothetical example, the affiliate households include (1) a married daughter, her husband, and their children; (2) a married son, his wife, and their children; (3) an unmarried son; and (4) a brother of the

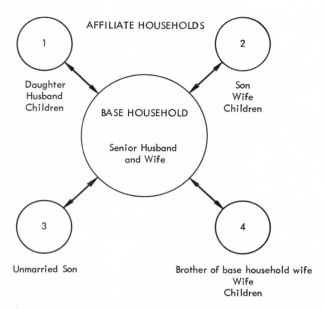

AFFILIATE HOUSEHOLDS

1

2

Daughter
Husband
Children

BASE HOUSEHOLD

Son
Wife
Children

Senior Husband
and Wife

3

4

Unmarried Son

Brother of base household wife
Wife
Children

FIGURE 6-1. Hypothetical Extended Family Network

Adapted from *The Black Extended Family* by E. Martin and J. Martin by permission of The University of Chicago Press. © 1978 by The University of Chicago.

senior woman in the base household, his wife, and their children. Each of these affiliate households may have stronger or weaker links to the other affiliates or to the base, depending upon their circumstances. The affiliated households of the married son or daughter may be in economic distress, or one or both may be upwardly mobile and economically successful. In either case, they may want to share with others in the network more of what they have, or they may choose to loosen their ties in order to focus on their own needs. The household of the senior woman's brother may have come into the network because of a particular household crisis, because of a strong emotional tie to the base household members or to some of the affiliates, or because the senior wife's brother had something special to contribute to ongoing family network maintenance.

Among the poorest "street families," non-kin are sometimes adopted into this network. Sometimes new members will be actively sought. While each new member brings additional problems and needs, each adult member also brings new resources to share—a paycheck; a supply of material goods, such as clothes, furniture, or a car; and knowledge about work opportunities or goods and services that may be needed by family members. Pooled resources thus make it possible for family members to meet basic needs which otherwise would be more difficult to handle. Stack (1975: 6) cites one case of a family of fourteen persons existing on a yearly income of $4,500, with fixed expenditures of $3,500. Clearly, in such a case, contributing members of the network are discouraged from leaving, and contributions of even part-time or seasonal wages to the household may be vital to the entire family's survival. In this instance, Stack notes, when the oldest child received a draft notice, a major family crisis was imminent. The parents petitioned the draft board to excuse the son, because his meager salary was so desperately needed.

Young men, particularly if they are unemployed or in low-paying seasonal work, can survive by pooling resources in the family network. The affiliate household of the unmarried son might be such an example. In a desperate circumstance, he may sleep at one household in the network, eat and store his clothes at other households. His acceptance into a new household depends on how easily its available resources can be stretched to absorb his needs.

The male head of an extended family network typically assumes the role of provider; the female head is responsible for the equitable deployment of pooled resources throughout the network, for maintaining communication among family members, and for some supervision in socializing the young. When the network has both a male and a female head, moral and social discipline of the young is shared. When the dominant figure is incapacitated by illness or is unemployed, his or her authority and moral force in the family decrease. When the father dies, the mother becomes the leader of the family by virtue of her age and authority. Her greatest concerns and responsibilities are in helping family members develop a closeness and a sense of responsibility for one another. She is expected to be strong and to show ingenuity in finding resources to help others in need. A leader is not domineering to the point of control, but advice, guidance, and moral support are given freely. There are few, if any, disputes concerning a leader's authority.

When the dominant figure in an extended network dies or is incapacitated, most families will without hesitation "ready" another to take her or his place. There is no conference or discussion among family members, and, for the most part, most family members may be unaware of the process of transferring power, because it happens informally and by consensus. Even if death comes suddenly, family members will accept without difficulty the chosen leader. The new leader is often the eldest daughter of the preceding dominant head, and she may have been prepared for the position over a period of years by the family head. In some instances, after the death or incapacitation of the dominant figure, when no family member emerges to assume the leader's role, the cooperative mutual aid system of the expanded network gradually disintegrates. At that point, the affiliate households either attach themselves to other base households or form new extended family networks with their own households as the new bases. When an affiliate household has sufficient resources to meet its own basic needs, it may also cease to function as an active participant in the mutual aid system. But participation is seldom cut off entirely. Family dinners and occasional contributions to family members in need usually continue, if on a more limited basis. More recent detailed studies of particular extended family networks show a constant and continuing push by family members to move out of the base household and establish their own self-sufficient homes. When problems overwhelm these attempts, the base household remains available to them—a place of security and emotional and financial support—until they are ready to venture forth again. The base household also serves as a communication center among all affiliate households, a place where family arguments are arbitrated; family resources can be marshaled to meet sudden emergencies faced by individual members; and counsel, comfort, moral direction, socialization, recreation, and acceptance are always available.

The structure of the extended family as it has been described here illustrates Hill's argument that one of the strengths of black families is in the diversity of their kinship roles and the adaptability of those roles. Kinship provides a kind of "social security" when other institutions—economic, educational, social service—may shut people out. Researchers are not agreed as to whether or not strong kinship bonds are necessarily associated with poverty or castelike exclusion from other social and economic resources. Nevertheless, Martin and Martin assert that "extended families have been responsible for providing many Black Americans over the generations with basic economic and emotional security" (1978: 1). Even where more people in the black community achieve affluence comparable to that of others, there remains a substantial number of households which continue the extended family tradition through reciprocity in goods, cash, and services (McAdoo 1979).

EXCHANGE RELATIONSHIPS

Because family income may vary significantly over time, one of the most important activities carried on through the extended family network is the exchange of goods or services. Martin and Martin call this the "mutual aid system" and point out that it operates on the twin assumptions that families should seek security and independence, but that where family integrity is threatened, sharing resources across households is crucial. For instance, family members may need to visit all of the other households in the network to obtain a needed or desired item. What is placed on the table at night for dinner may have been obtained in exchange at several households during the day. Services such as child care, sewing, or household repairs are also used in this swapping activity. Occasionally money is used to purchase an item from another family member. There is a fine line between what is and is not accepted in terms of "exchange." Each family member is seeking to improve his or her lot. When no exchange is offered for a swap, there is liable to be anger and frustration created, which may need to be arbitrated by the family leader. But the daily repetitive swapping of goods and services provides personal and emotional benefits. It is a time for sharing joys and troubles, for gossip, plans, and dreams—a time to give and receive emotional support and to affirm the individual dignity, respect, and acceptance which may be denied by the wider society.

Adult wage earners and welfare or social security recipients have control over the disposal of their own incomes. But each is expected to contribute to the general welfare as much as he or she decides is feasible. In addition, all family network members are expected to accept some responsibility for helping to maintain the base household. Frequent gifts of money or goods may be offered to the family leader as a token of respect, as well as to meet specific emergency needs. Cash may also be given informally among family members to meet emergency needs. News travels rapidly of a member's sudden windfall of money. An individual stands to lose much more than he or she gains by refusing to share. Unexpected income is rapidly dispersed among members of the network to meet pressing immediate needs. Money not eaten up by various emergencies may be rapidly spent to fulfill long-delayed wishes—a television set, new clothing, or furniture. Whites often interpret such behavior as evidence of irresponsibility and "inability to defer gratification." It may also be viewed, however, as a realistic response to the individual's economic situation: cash not spent now on an immediate and obvious need may be drained off by others in the network who have needs and problems of their own. The balance between individual desires and network contributions is a delicate one, which calls for a careful weighing of personal and family interests in virtually every economic transaction.

Practical help is also available to family members in the network. For example, the combined resources of four or five family members may be required to collect money for a health crisis, to find emergency transportation, to deal with the death of a distant relative, or to pay the tuition costs of college-bound children. A new single mother is advised on how to apply for federal aid, and one or more experienced family members may accompany her to the proper agency to guide her successfully through the necessary paperwork and offices.

Problems within the network can develop when an individual decides not to cooperate in the sharing of possessions or participate in group activities. A decision to withhold personal resources from the family may be based on an individual's feeling that others are not contributing their fair shares. Some may feel that they are being held back from completing school or improving their financial position because of the financial obligations created by other family members' crises. The decision to withdraw from the mutual aid network may enable a particular family member to achieve a stable and adequate income level. But it may also lead to a sense of loss among family members still active in and dependent on the network, who must then find a way to survive without that resource. This situation has the potential of splitting apart family members at different economic levels and is one of the strains in the extended-family system.

SOCIALIZATION PATTERNS

Black families and the extended family network serve their members not only as an effective means of supplying basic material and emotional needs but also as the means of socializing children and transmitting cultural values. But, Billingsley points out, for black people, "socialization is doubly challenging, for the family must teach its young members how to be human, but also how to be black in a white society. The requirements are not the same" (1968: 28). The dilemmas of childrearing are those of teaching self-respect in the home, when self-depreciation is taught elsewhere; of urging persistence and patience in pursuit of laudable goals, when the means of reaching those goals are restricted or denied.

Lewis (1975) has tentatively identified some of the cultural characteristics of black childrearing, characteristics implicit and explicit in the current trend toward developing a black-oriented psychology and sociology. She finds that a "high valuation for personal uniqueness is a significant configuration in black culture. Individualism, expectations of idiosyncratic behavior and non-conformance within bounds, are traits which have been well documented" in recent sociological, sociolinguistic, anthropological, and folkloristic studies (1975: 222). This emphasis on individualism as a cultural theme has a number of consequences for black lifestyles and for black childrearing. First, individual attributes often serve as the most important criteria for judging others. This is in preference to ascribed features, such as education or occupation. A sense of personal "style," of one's presentation of self to others, is a notable component of interaction. Second, inhibitions on the expression of one's uniqueness are regarded as undesirable or hurtful, be those inhibitions rigid feeding schedules or discriminatory hiring policies. Third, the individual is viewed as a powerfully self-willed entity, taking an active role in manipulating the environment. Fourth, active involvement with the world is more correctly directed toward involvement with other human beings than with inanimate objects. The implications of these principles are profound, nowhere more than in childrearing patterns.

To dramatize these points, Lewis suggests contrasts between black and white socialization preferences and behavior. Infants are constantly held, cuddled, kissed, talked to, and played with by all adults, male and female, in the black family household. The baby is constantly observed, and each grasp, movement, burp, or cry is interpreted as expressive of the child's own unique personality. (White parents, suggests Lewis, are more inclined to view the infant as an undeveloped personality and the infant's actions and reactions as indicative of growing but immature physical development.) This close, physically intimate, and emotional involvement with the infant continues until age three, and with it the emphasis upon individualism and personal uniqueness in all that the child does.

Children are encouraged, for instance, to see themselves as separate, unique individuals valued for their own special, sometimes idiosyncratic, personality traits. They are encouraged by adults to act on their needs, to be willful, assertive, and even playfully defiant of authority within bounds. The adults' focus on the personality of the infant as assertive and independent is combined with an emphasis almost exclusively on the child's interactions with other persons, rather than things. The child is not often encouraged to explore the physical world of objects. When the child reaches for an object, its attention is usually turned to exploring a face or playing with an adult. Early attempts to crawl or walk are often inhibited by adults, who immediately pick up the child. The result is the development of a child who has a strongly developed sense of self and who is at ease in interpersonal relations, but who may have less familiarity with objects and with manipulating the physical world. "It seems richly suggestive," Lewis argues, that these childrearing practices are linked to a "conceptualization of the nature of the person as an independent, initiating being" (1975: 224).

The infant's treatment up to age three fosters this sense of personal uniqueness and intensity in interpersonal relations. This treatment is the same for both boys and girls. Little differences will be found on the basis of sex in early child-rearing practices, but clear differences can be identified on the basis of age and order of birth. After age three, the child is sometimes placed in the care of a child group, which is led by an older child, male or female. The child group includes all the children in the household, and the oldest child's authority over the group is powerful. The oldest child and all the older children in the group, both male and female, share nurturing responsibilities for the younger members. It is at this stage of the black child's development that the sense of relatedness and of the benefits and responsibilities of kinship are firmly implanted. The strong "I" developed in infancy is brought into the strong "we" of the childhood peer group.

The first-born in a household gets special training for this leadership role in the child group. Lewis cites studies showing that, almost universally among black families, the first-born child receives more mothering and stimulation in infancy than do the children who follow. Defiance of parents and other adults and encouragement to express desires and needs are more carefully nurtured in the first-born. Extra cuddling, talking, and interplay with adults in infancy and early childhood produce a child who is therefore the most competent and self-assured among its siblings. A distinct personality emphasis on assertiveness and leadership is common to black, first-born children, and this is evidence of the highly patterned and selective treatment of the eldest child. Not gender, but age, is the criterion for training for leadership of the childhood peer group.

While no significant differences are noted between the childrearing practices applied to black male and black female children in infancy and early childhood, sex-based differences in socialization patterns do emerge in early adolescence. Adolescent girls are reared to move quickly into adult roles of responsibility. They are encouraged to complete their education, to find work, and to accept family responsibilities. Lewis refers to studies showing that black mothers expect and insist upon more "responsible" behavior from their adolescent daughters than from their adolescent sons. To the resentment of the daughters, young adolescent males are permitted a great deal of freedom, while girls are ordered to study hard, do the family laundry, and participate in household chores. Lewis suggests that the differences in adolescent training for males and females is based "directly on perceived employment opportunities," and that as wider education and employment opportunities for black males are available, this will be reflected in changed role expectations for older boys.

Despite differences in family expectations for adolescent boys and girls, there are few differences attached to preferred male and female personality types. While traditional, European-based cultures emphasize gender identity based on contrasting sets of personality traits—one for males and one for females—black children are usually taught that personality characteristics are equally acceptable for either sex.

Among whites, the personality traits that are popularly viewed as distinctively male include aggressiveness, independence, emotional reserve, and competitiveness. Stereotypic white female personality traits have been seen as the opposites of these: passiveness, dependence, expressiveness, nurturing, and cooperativeness. Black youth are taught that such traits as assertiveness and nurturing are desirable for any individual, regardless of sex. This is consistent with the principle of individualism and uniqueness, where each person is expected to respond to situations as an individual rather than a bearer of a rigid gender identity. Studies of working-class and middle-class black families, for instance, show that nurturing and provider roles in the family are frequently shared equally by husband and wife (TenHouton 1970, Kunkel and Kennard 1971). The degree of authority in the household is closely linked to the degree each member contributes economically to the family, not to sex-linked roles.

Much has been made in past research on the black family of the absence of the father. The assumption of that research is that the absence of a father figure is related to the male adolescent's poor academic performance, inability to defer gratification, and low self-esteem. Further, it has been suggested that the absence of a father encourages preoccupation among young black males with toughness, defiance, excitement, and autonomy—all viewed as efforts to break the dominance of a presumably "emasculating" female figure. Scanzoni (1977) suggests, however, that the real cause of distress among black men is not the negative influence of powerful women in the family, but blocked access to opportunity in the job and economic system. His study of working-class and middle-class blacks, those who had succeeded in entering the opportunity structure, found that 21.8 percent had been raised by the mother, 6 percent by the father, and 13.5 percent by "others," such as kin in a family network. Of the entire sample, only 12.5 percent could not identify males who had played father roles in their upbringings. Those who were raised in households without fathers cited stepfathers, grandfathers, uncles, cousins, and elder brothers as significant in the provider-nurturer-disciplinarian role of father in their upbringings. What this suggests is that not only is the extended family network a highly flexible mechanism for fulfilling socialization functions but that the lack of highly stereotyped, gender-linked personality traits means that many individuals can act to carry out supportive and nurturing roles when necessary.

It is difficult to specify precisely how black childrearing patterns, with their emphasis on individual uniqueness, assertiveness and independence, and avoidance of early gender identity, are linked to larger social institutions, to black history, or to issues of powerlessness in a racially stratified society. It may be that the requirements of survival for black people never permitted the seeming luxury of rigid allocation of tasks to one gender or the other, as has been true for most whites. The emphasis on the person, on native intelligence, ability, and style, rather than on attributes of title, rank, or authority, may be a response to marginality and powerlessness. On the other hand, it may be, as Lewis (1975) argues, a distinctively African way of being in the world. If that is the case, it brings us back to

Billingsley's comment about the dilemma faced by black parents in rearing their children (1968). That dilemma is one of conserving in their families an old tradition that is distinctively person-oriented, one that is flexible in its role expectations, in a society where rewards often go to those who are object-oriented and those who find success in highly structured living and working arrangements. Blacks, like whites, desire their share of the rewards of American affluence. The issue is whether or not fulfillment of that desire would require them to abandon the childrearing practices that have assured their survival and cultural distinctiveness.

EXTERNAL INFLUENCES ON THE FAMILY

The form of the black family is determined by many things, including values, traditions, and origins. But it is also shaped by the character of black-white relations in the larger society. Those relations have been characterized by domination and exploitation, which existed even before the establishment of the United States as a country. It would not seem necessary to restate here the common and immediate problems that many black people face as a consequence of exploitation. It was Michael Harrington in his important book, *The Other America* (1962), who dramatized the fact that poverty and its effects are often invisible in a society with a high level of affluence that is broadly distributed. It is also significant to note that poverty, even where blatantly apparent, does not exist simply because some have worked hard to change their lot in life and others have not. Poverty always serves social purposes. That is, the interests of someone, somewhere, are being met through the disadvantage of others. If those disadvantages are "invisible" because of mass affluence, then the gains of special interests are simply that much more easily assured. Consider, for instance, housing.

Housing shortages, as well as inferior and inadequate housing, remain major problems facing black urban community leaders. The numbers of low-rent or rent-controlled apartments are insufficient, and public housing projects have long waiting lists. Purchasing a home or condominium is a dream out of reach for the thousands who live on the desperate edge of economic survival. Inflated rental prices and the difficulty of obtaining home loans ("red lining") make it virtually impossible for the poor to find adequate housing. The need for repairs in overcrowded and unsafe apartment units is a common problem. When conditions in a living unit become uninhabitable, families are forced to move elsewhere. When a family is unable to pay its rent, eviction is usually the result. Often too many people are forced to live in a small living space, sometimes eight to fifteen adults and children, sharing a two-bedroom unit. Adequate maintenance of the unit becomes difficult if not impossible. Front and back yards of overcrowded apartment buildings housing the poor are cluttered with garbage and discarded refrigerators, cars, and junk. Failure of electrical and plumbing systems and fixtures, which were designed to accommodate far fewer numbers, is a constant problem.

Antiquated heating systems fail. The result is an unhealthy, depressing, and unsafe living environment. Attempts by the occupants to compensate for these problems, as in using an electrical hotplate or open oven to heat their quarters, create fire hazards for the entire building.

Many blacks are forced to live in segregated sections of the city, because of their dependence on public transportation or because housing is too expensive or unavailable elsewhere. Finding vacant houses constitutes a problem for the poor, who must spend an enormous amount of time and energy locating and checking whether apparent vacancies are inhabited or have been condemned. Requirements for references, large security deposits, and cleaning fees place otherwise affordable rental houses out of reach and lengthen the search to find suitable, affordable housing. When a family has been evicted before other housing can be found, an already overcrowded base household may take them in until other quarters can be found. The combined problems of unemployment and poverty hinder the search for a stable living situation.

It is not unreasonable to ask—and the alert social worker should do so—how such conditions, which depress one group, result in benefits to others. It is obviously costly to a city government to provide extensive fire, police, and social services to areas of town occupied by poor people, whose taxes cannot cover those costs. But is it costly to landlords, who pay low taxes and contribute little to the maintenance of their buildings? Is it costly to the banks that collect depositors' money in one branch and make it available for investment through branches in more affluent parts of the city? Is it costly to small businesses, often absentee-owned, whose business volume is dependent on customers with regular welfare checks? Is it costly to suburban residents, who rely on the depressed areas of the city for cheap labor, particularly in service occupations? Poverty—viewed as a network of consequences as well as a condition of life—involves more than its victims. It is a condition of life in which many who live outside the ghettos are implicated.

Even the provision of services to alleviate poverty must be viewed from this critical perspective. Obtaining help from a government agency, such as the social security or welfare system, brings additional stress and problems to many persons. For example, the aged or handicapped may encounter enormous difficulties in traveling long distances on public transportation to report in person as required at a centrally located welfare office. Those applying for aid, who in the past simply asked for help from kin and neighbors, must learn a whole new set of rules, regulations, schedules, and qualifying processes in order to deal successfully with the agency. The poorly educated may have difficulty understanding and following the complex procedures that must be completed to qualify for assistance. Trying to convey to social workers and other agency representatives the seriousness or the nature of the specific problems for which the applicant is seeking help may often be frustrating.

Agency regulations in public welfare programs have also placed the social worker in a role that is perceived as being more punitive than helpful. Caseworkers' visits to their clients' homes are often regarded as spying missions, made to determine whether the recipients are more affluent than was revealed in interviews. The road to improvement in a client's economic condition is threatened by denial of assistance if signs of material improvements are discovered. Additional income that is so discovered may be deducted from the assistance check. Marriage, a boyfriend in the home, or a father's return from a distant job may result in economic disaster if an assistance check is terminated as a consequence. In many clients' minds, therefore, the social worker is part of the organized authority which they fear and which has imposed a measure of control over their lives.

IMPLICATIONS

Implicit in the more recent studies of black lifestyles is the need for a basic re-orientation of services, practices, and attitudes. Mental health services which not only treat those in need of therapeutic resources but also promote preventive strategies need to be developed. Preventive work cannot begin until the natural support systems of communities are recognized and utilized. How, for instance, is conflict handled by leaders of base households? How are individuals counseled by other family members? What goes on in the relationship between a store-front minister and a troubled congregation member? How is trust developed and maintained? Once the needs of survival are met, what are the special needs of the upwardly mobile? How can the cultural values of family sharing be maintained as more people move into professional, business, and trade activities and into previously all-white suburbs? What counseling styles will promote a strong sense of self-understanding and of the freedom of action that Solomon (1976) has called "empowerment"? These are critical issues, to which the ethnically competent worker will want to give serious consideration.

Social workers have a professional responsibility to become familiar with the black press, literature, and music, wherein expression of the main currents of black life is reflected. This background is essential for the social worker in gaining an understanding of the real problems affecting the client. But social workers especially need to understand that there is a great need to develop the intervention techniques that will be helpful with black clients. Cultural sensitivity is simply the first step in that direction. Beyond that, the sensitive worker will want to know how to mobilize a particular client, a family, or an entire family network for work on resolving a problem. Some problems may be treated best by individual therapy, some by group action. When are these options important, and how does the worker utilize them in dealing with critical issues? Cultural sensitivity is a beginning in devising more effective helping techniques for resolving the problems of people in a pluralistic society.

CHAPTER SEVEN
SOCIAL WORK
WITH ASIAN - AND
PACIFIC - AMERICANS
Hideki A. Ishisaka
and Calvin Y. Takagi

INTRODUCTION

The umbrella term, Asian- and Pacific-Americans, emerged during the civil rights and minority protests of the 1960s to refer to members of those nationality groups whose ancestry can be traced to the continent of Asia and to the Pacific Islands.[1]

HIDEKI A. ISHISAKA, Associate Professor, has been with the School of Social Work, University of Washington, since 1971. He received his graduate training at the University of California at Berkeley. His interests include child welfare, human development and clinical methods. He is currently involved in a research project with attempts to identify cultural contributions to counseling process among Pacific-Asian Americans. He is a consultant and staff trainer with the Asian Counseling and Referral Service in Seattle.

CALVIN Y. TAKAGI received his MSW (1952) and Ph.D. (1958) from the School of Social Work, University of Minnesota. His teaching, practice, and research interests are in the areas of mental health, minorities, and human development. He is currently co-director of the Multi-Ethnic Mental Health Training Project funded by the National Institute of Mental Health.

[1] The term commonly includes the following populations: Chinese, Japanese, Korean, and Pilipino Americans (the "old" immigrant groups and their descendants); Samoans, Guamanians, Hawaiians, and other population groups from the Pacific Islands; and the "new" immigrants and refugees from Vietnam, Thailand, Cambodia, Laos, and Indonesia. In some instances, it is broadened to include persons from India, Pakistan, and Ceylon. The distinctions between "old" and "new" immigrants are not clearcut, because many recent immigrants are members of the so-called "old" groups and vice versa. The distinction is made in this chapter because of the differences that exist among groups with respect to the nature of the social problems that each group faces.

The term was essentially a call to members of the numerous, disparate, and relatively self-contained ethnic communities to transcend their historical differences for the purpose of uniting in the common struggle to overcome racial discrimination and oppression in America. As a political strategem it has been successful, and the term has achieved general currency both within and outside these groups. The bringing together of these populations under one designation has helped to call the attention of governmental and civic leaders to the problems and plight of members of these communities far more successfully than would have been the case had each group acted separately. In addition to these political benefits, the psychological value of the term has been to provide individuals with a sense of ethnic identity which is "larger" (hence, more powerful) than the hyphenations then commonly in use—e.g., Chinese-Americans, Japanese-Americans, etc.) with their connotations of numerical insignificance and political powerlessness.

For all its political and psychological usefulness, however, the term, by suggesting a homogeneity among Asian and Pacific communities, serves to obscure important differences among and between them. Just as the term European-American would mask the ethnic and cultural differences between the Swedes and the Italians or the Poles and the English, so too does Asian-American fail to differentiate among the various Asian and Pacific populations with respect to their history, culture, values, and characteristics. It is, therefore, less useful as a descriptive or analytical tool for developing understanding. What is needed to understand an Asian-American client is to view him or her in the context of the appropriate culture, the family within that culture, and the interaction of the individual with his or her own particular family.

The immigration histories of the Asian- and Pacific-American populations have a great deal to do with the composition, age, and present status of the families found in each. Early immigration patterns for each national group were determined largely by restrictive legislation enacted by Congress in response to the ebb and flow of the racist and anti-immigrant sentiment that was endemic generally in the United States, but particularly virulent on the West Coast. Laws enacted between 1882 and 1934 effectively halted or limited the flow of immigrants, first from China, then from Japan, and finally from the Philippines. Unlike other immigrant nationalities, for whom the influx of newcomers to the New World was continuous, the populations of these Asian groups can be divided by age and generational distinctions.

The first, or immigrant, generation was characteristically made up of young adult males, recruited as cheap labor by agricultural, railroading, lumbering, and mining industries. Prohibited from becoming U.S. citizens, given only limited access to occupational opportunities, denied the right to own land, to intermarry, or even to seek redress in the courts for grievances against whites, these first-generation Americans were ready targets for economic exploitation, official acts of discrimination, and mob violence. Women did not enter the country until later. As soon as was possible, however, these new arrivals attempted to marry and to establish normal family lives, even though, particularly in the case of the Chinese and

Pilipinos,[2] the settling-down process was delayed for a number of years. Because new immigration was prohibited, the children born to all of these marriages comprised an age-discrete generation, which remained readily identifiable. Their children and grandchildren, in turn, would be identified as the third and fourth generations. Since 1965 and the liberalization of the immigration laws, immigration from all Asian countries and the Pacific Islands has increased to the extent that the generational characteristics that were once so distinctive may no longer be as relevant. Where as "young" Asians in the past were likely to be third and fourth generation Asian-Americans, for example, they are just as likely now to be recent arrivals.

The "old" immigrants, their descendants, and the more recent arrivals share similar values.[3] Strong emphasis placed on the importance of respect for authority, hard work, diligence, educational success, and loyalty to the community are the cultural legacies of the donor society. Faced with the need to succeed, without recourse to capital, positions of power, powerful kin or friends, the immigrants took the only road open—that is, to persevere with the spirit of the old values while adapting them to new circumstances in the United States.

A useful way of conceptualizing differences among Asian-American groups is to identify family lifestyles in regard to generational differences as reflected in such matters as language, socialization, childrearing practices, religion, cultural values, and family roles. It may be possible to identify three approximate family lifestyle patterns for Asian-Americans: (a) immigrant families—that is, those Chinese-Americans and Japanese-Americans who arrived before the 1924 exclusion act—and Pilipinos, Koreans, and others who came shortly thereafter; (b) American-born, or the descendants of the first generation of immigrants; and (c) new arrivals, that is, recent immigrants, who arrived after the 1965 revision of the national-origins quota. The last category includes political refugees from Indochina. The early immigrant families and the recent arrivals, for the sake of analysis, might be termed "traditional," to the extent that the donor cultures dictate normative lifestyles, including childrearing methods, enculturative content, parent-child roles, sibling interaction, and the like. American-born families tend to be acculturated to American norms, but many continue a bicultural lifestyle.

SOCIAL SERVICE NEEDS

Unitl recently, the prevailing opinion that Asian- and Pacific Island-Americans were a problem-free minority population was seldom challenged. It was generally believed that most Chinese, Japanese, Pilipino, Korean, and other Asian- and

[2] The spelling "Pilipino" has been used to reflect the actual native pronunciation of the word, since there is no soft f sound in the Pilipino language.

[3] Values in a human group manifest the conception in the group of that which is right and wrong, good and bad. Such values provide a set of shared criteria for assigning priorities of meaning and hence of choices. Values are the designs by which an individual's structure of consciousness is raised. One's hopes and aspirations, one's anxieties and fears, one's loves and dislikes, and one's sense of the sacred and profane are products of those values to which humans are reared. Values are patterns of attitudes which guide behavior and which color one's perception.

Pacific-Americans made up a relatively successful and upwardly mobile segment of American society. Statistics concerning educational achievement, occupational, and income status (Petersen 1971: 113-22), as well as low rates of crime and delinquency, divorce, and mental illness were cited as evidence for the "model minority" thesis (Kitano 1969: 257). Later scholars contended that the oft-quoted evidence was misleading and did not accurately portray the true condition of the populations in question nor the extent of need existing in their communities (Kim 1973: 44; Endo 1974: 203). For example, some studies showed that Asians were generally underemployed, that family income figures cited represented the combined earnings of two or more underemployed workers in a household (Kim 1978: 10-11), that the number of delinquency cases was increasing (Abbott and Abbott 1973), and that the low rates of mental illness reflected patterns of underutilization (of mental health services), rather than the actual incidence of illness (Sue and McKinney 1975). Other studies emphasized the problems of overcrowding in substandard housing (Nee and Nee 1974: xxiii-xxiv), the high incidence of disabling diseases and suicide, and the lack of medical care in Asian communities (Lyman 1970: 115). Lyman (ibid.) observes, for example, that San Francisco's Chinatown had the highest rates of tuberculosis and suicide in the nation. Owan found that San Francisco Pilipinos had a tuberculosis rate slightly over four times that of the general population, while the Chinese were two times greater. He also found that Japanese had the highest reported death rate from tuberculosis (Owan 1975: 32). In another report, San Francisco Chinese were said to have a suicide rate considerably higher than the overall rate for the city, which has a rate three times the national average (Murase 1977: 955). Still other writers have called attention to the special problems of the Asian elderly (Cheng 1978: 13-29; Fujii 1976; Ishikawa 1978: 13-30; Peterson 1978: 13-30), and of immigrant children and youth (Lyman 1970: 24-25; Murase 1977: 953).

The existence of these two opposing points of view about the presence or absence of significant problems in Asian-American communities needs to be explained. Historically, these communities had, in fact, developed a remarkable degree of self-sufficiency. Those who emigrated from China, Japan, Korea, and the Philippines in the nineteenth and early twentieth centuries came from countries with strong traditions of local autonomy and regional identification. Upon their arrival in this country, many formed voluntary associations based on common ties of provenance and kinship. These early mutual-aid associations provided a way of alleviating the problems of cultural adjustment. At the same time, self-sufficiency was a necessary defense against the widespread hostility directed toward Asians. Community solidarity, buttressed by strong public opinion and pressure, along with appeals to family and ethnic pride, all helped to maintain social controls over deviant or unacceptable behavior on the part of individuals. When difficulties did arise, they could generally be handled quietly within the community. These cases, in short, did not show up in official statistics. Thus the relative self-sufficiency of Asian communities historically, combined with the belief on the part of the broader society that social problems did not exist or that Asians "take care of their own," have led to serious neglect of the problems and needs of these populations.

The provision of culturally appropriate services to meet the needs of the growing Pacific and Asian population in the United States is dependent, in part, on practitioners who have developed an understanding of Pacific and Asian cultural patterns. The limitations of space prohibit coverage of all the major Pacific-Asian American communities. The authors have chosen the three "oldest" and most populous Pacific-Asian communities for discussion, with the hope that some of the material presented may be useful in considering the other Pacific-Asian communities. In this chapter, selected aspects of the Chinese-, Japanese-, and Pilipino-American communities will be discussed. Their implications for practice will follow.

CHINESE-AMERICANS:
IMMIGRATION HISTORY

The arrival of the first Chinese immigrants to the U.S. was a result of severe conditions in China. In the second half of the nineteenth century, there were floods and famine, with subsequent social unrest in the southeastern coastal provinces (Lyman 1974: 5). In Kwantung Province, the effects of flood and famine were joined by the Tai Ping Revolution of 1850-64 to create massive social upheaval. The discovery of gold in California and other prospects for work and riches drew thousands of Chinese to the New World as sojourners who planned only to stay long enough to amass wealth before returning to China. In the first thirty-year period, the lure of the riches of the New World was strong enough to draw some 300,000 immigrants to the West. Of these, over one half returned to China in the same period. From an early positive reception as industrious and hard-working assets to the labor pool, the Chinese immigrants were increasingly subjected to hostility, as their growing numbers triggered irrational fears among the majority group. Increasing agitation against the Chinese resulted in the 1882 passage of the Chinese Exclusion Act, which effectively halted emigration from China to the U.S. This pattern of initial welcome, followed by increasing hostility, culminating in anti-Asian agitation and exclusion laws, was to be replayed with each group from Asia. Prior to the passage of the Exclusion Act, uncertainty regarding conditions in the West, in conjunction with an ancient pattern of leaving wives with their husbands' lineages when men traveled, resulted in a predominantly male population of Chinese in the U.S. and Hawaii. Although many of the early Chinese immigrants were married before emigrating to the New World, the conjugal and family relationships that were sundered by emigration were never to be regained, and many of the original immigrants died alone in the New World. The radically imbalanced sex ratio in the Chinese community has only recently become nearly equalized. Laws forbidding the immigration of family members to the U.S., coupled with antimiscegenation laws passed in many states, postponed the birth of an American-born second generation until the late 1930s. It was not until 1950 that American-born Chinese came to comprise over one half of the population of Chinese in the U.S. population.

From early on, a hostile environment of angry and suspicious white Americans, the passage of notorious laws restricting labor opportunities, and the availability of traditional organizations in some localities led to the development of segregated Chinese settlements in some areas of the West Coast. That the populations of the early Chinatowns were predominantly male was a reflection of the overall composition of the Chinese population. Denied the opportunity to have their own families join them in the West, the sojourners in the U.S. and Hawaii turned increasingly to community organizations modeled after those in China for aid and mutual assistance. Territorial (district) associations and clan associations, the organizations that provided the immigrants with the majority of needed services, developed quite early in the Chinatowns of the U.S. and Hawaii (Nee and Nee 1974: 60-122). The territorial associations fulfilled a variety of roles to assist new immigrants. The *hui kuan,* as the territorial associations were called, derived from the *t'ung hsian hui,* or same-village associations, which were quite ancient Chinese institutions (Hsu 1971: 44). Originally, the *hui kuan* were composed of persons originating from the same districts in China, but conditions in the U.S. led to the development of *hui kuan* which had language as the shared element. The *hui kuan* sponsored hostelries, provided employment assistance, acted to mitigate disputes within the Chinese community, and served as community representatives to the majority society and its agents. In the Chinatowns, the *hui kuan* were also the sources of much venture capital, which went into underwriting the development of an entrepreneurial class. Personal funds were accumulated under the sponsorship of the *hui kuan* and lent out to members with interest (Kulp 1925: 120). And since the members had little access to the usual sources of capital, due to discriminatory practices, the revolving credit systems developed by the *hui kuan* substituted for banks.

The development of *hui kuan* was simultaneous with the arrival of large numbers of Chinese immigrants. In 1851, Cantonese from the Kwantung districts of Namhoi, Punyu, and Shuntak organized the Sam Yap Company. In the same year, the Sunwui, Sunning, Yamping, and Hoiping district associations organized the Sze Yap Company (Melendy 1972: 71).

Around the same time, the Chung Hua Hui Kuan was developed to coordinate the organization of the various *hui kuan.* Finally, in 1901, the Chung Hua Hui Kuan was incorporated as the Chinese Benevolent Association (Hsu 1971: 45). While originally established as district associations to provide services and assistance to persons originating in the same district of China, the *hui kuan* tended to be flexible about membership in the U.S. and Hawaii. This change was a clear example of the adaptation of an ancient institutional form to meet the changed conditions in the New World.

The clan associations were originally actual clan organizations, whose members traced their descent within a common lineage. In the U.S. and Hawaii, a common surname supplanted lineage membership as the membership consideration, and blood ties with their attendant loyalties and obligations were assumed on the basis of shared surname and membership in the clan association. Similar to the *hui kuan* in function, the clan associations provided shelter, food, and other forms of aid to new immigrants and longer-term residents.

As Chinese communities grew in the U.S., certain clans in different locales developed strong interests and influence in various areas of community life. Clans became highly influential in business, trades, and the services. For example, in San Francisco's Chinatown the Yee and Lee families became dominant in the operation of fashionable restaurants, while the Dear family branched into the candy and fruit-store trade (Lyman 1974: 31). In cities across the U.S., clans have risen to positions of domination in the life of Chinatowns, exemplified by the Lees in Philadelphia, the Toms in New York, the Ongs in Phoenix, and the Moys in Chicago (Lee 1960: 64; Sung 1967: 135). Competition between clans for control of various areas of community life placed the smaller clans at a disadvantage. As a result, in some areas smaller clans merged interests to compete on more equal terms. Thus the Lau, Quan, Cheung, and Chew clans established the Four Families (Kung 1962: 22).

The services provided to the Chinese communities by these early organizations acted in many ways to replace the family, the lineages, and their resources in the New World. While providing these important services, the early development and maintenance of adapted ancient Chinese organizations also functioned to affirm the lifeways and values of the homeland. The community organizations of the early Chinatowns were the structures around which the living communities were built. Acting to reinforce and conserve the values of old China, the organizations of Chinatown helped to maintain traditional culture within the U.S. and Hawaii. The Chinese community in the U.S. at present is highly heterogeneous. Although a small proportion of the total population, some Chinese in certain occupations were able to bring their families to the New World. Thus there is a Chinese-American-born population which has been in the U.S. for several generations. During World War II, a number of Chinese immigrants arrived under the relaxation of immigration restrictions prompted by the alliance of the U.S. and China in their common war against Japan. More recently, with the 1965 change in the immigration laws, entry of Chinese has increased dramatically. In addition to including immigrants who arrived at different times, the Chinese community in the U.S. is also comprised of speakers of several different dialects. The early immigrants, originating in a locale of Kwantung Province, were mostly speakers of Cantonese and Toisanese. The more recent arrivals are largely Cantonese- and Mandarin-speaking. With the arrival of a large number of ethnic Chinese from Southeast Asia, there have arrived a significant number of Fukienese-speaking refugees. Finally, the Chinese community is stratified by differences in education and income. Attempts to characterize the Chinese community in global terms must invariably run the risk of oversimplification and overgeneralization, yet some generalizations may be made.

The following section provides a summary of traditional Chinese values and family patterns. The reader is encouraged to keep in mind that it is a portrait of a system of values, and not necessarily a picture drawn in detail of any Chinese-American individual or family.

CULTURAL VALUES
AND THE CHINESE FAMILY

Traditional Chinese values governing family life have been heavily influenced by Confucian philosophy and ethics. In the philosophy of the Master of Wisdom, the world and the life that people are privileged to live are not necessarily considered the best of worlds or of lives, and yet they are the only ones we have to experience. The quest for spiritual fulfillment was met not through a search for final salvation, but through an effort to achieve harmony in this world, in this life. In the Confucian system, this valued harmony could be achieved and maintained through observing the five basic relationships of society: those between a ruler and his subjects, father and son, husband and wife, elder and younger siblings, and friends (Keys 1977: 195). These five relationships demand loyalty and respect, and also evince a social order based on highly personalistic interrelationships. In Confucian thought, a social order is ordained by Heaven, and its order is maintained by people knowing and fulfilling their given places in life.

The other great philosophical system of Asia, Buddhism, also left its legacy in Chinese folkways. Buddhism teaches compassion, a respect for life and moderation in behavior. Self-discipline, patience, modesty, and friendliness in relationships, as well as selflessness, are qualities which are highly valued in Buddhist canon. Individualism is devalued, with a corresponding emphasis placed on dedication and loyalty to others. The tenets of Confucianism and Buddhism are complementary and have played a major role in shaping the lifeways of the societies touched by their teachings.

Whether represented by lineage membership or, as in the U.S., by the bonds of blood assumed on the basis of common surname, kinship is basic to the definition of the relationships that are important in everyday life and to an individual's prerogatives. The importance of the family in Chinese culture cannot be overemphasized. The family is the institution that provides the individual with his or her basic reference group, the source of personal identity and emotional security throughout life. The family exerts control over its members through a well-defined structure of hierarchical roles and a clear code of interpersonal conduct. The family also provides the mechanism whereby cultural values are transmitted across the generations, and preferred ways of dealing with the world and coping with life's difficulties are taught to new culture carriers. Within the family, filial piety or the respectful love of parents is of paramount importance. The Chinese child is taught to behave only in ways which will not bring shame to his or her parents.

The effect of one's behavior on one's parents and clan must be the major consideration governing action (Ritter et al. 1965: 39). The dominance of elders and males in family and clan life are extensions of the Confucian principle of filial piety. Concern for avoiding situations of family and personal shame, for attending to obligations to others, and reticence regarding personal hurt and discomfort are behavioral patterns acquired through instruction and imitative learning. Individual family members are taught to subordinate their individual needs and goals to those of the family. Toward that end, the expression of complaints and personal concerns is discouraged as a threat to family solidarity. The ideal family is a multigenerational household with patrilineal descent and patrilocal residence. Because the bonds of kinship are considered both to be primary and to last throughout life, great care is taken to ensure that new family members (through marriage, for example) will be assets to the lineage. Selection of a wife involves the evaluation of the candidate regarding her suitability as a daughter-in-law and as a potential mother to the next generation. A marriage is thus a family and clan matter, involving the future of the lineage, and should be negotiated with much family discussion and ultimate decision making by family elders.

In social relationships, friendships should be clearly secondary to the needs of family and other kin relationships. The individual in traditional Chinese culture is enmeshed securely in a wide network of kinship. Relatives, through common domicile or frequent visitation, play important roles in the affairs of family life and in the socialization of children. With emphasis on mature behavior, children are ushered into adulthood and adult responsibilities. Through their presence at adult functions and inclusion in the activities of the family, without the strict demarcation of child and adult activities that is common in Western families, Chinese children have the opportunity to learn through observation the lifeways of their families (Hsu 1971: 25).

While admittedly an idealized view of Chinese families, the foregoing is offered as a generalized pattern, by which the functioning of Chinese families may be better understood. As an idealization, the portrait may not represent in all its detail the actual functioning patterns of every contemporary Chinese-American family. Divergence from the ideal can be expected, but the ideal may continue to be the family goal toward which many strive.

CHANGES IN THE FAMILY

Changes brought about by acculturative pressures and by changing social and economic circumstances have tended to undermine many of the traditional cultural values, especially among second-, third-, and fourth-generation, American-born Chinese. But even in spite of change, traditional values are still potent as manifested in self, family, and community expectations regarding conduct. Ho (1976) suggests the preservation of traditional values across the generations by pointing to ongoing conflicts between traditional and majority American values as a major source of personal dysfunction.

An example of change is the transition from the family as a self-contained and integrated economic unit, with individual goals secondary to the family's welfare, to that of a group of socially interdependent but financially independent nuclear families with neolocal residence. Among the early immigrants and their families, the pooling of wages and sharing of living expenses through common residence in families with many wage earners was an adjustment to the poverty resulting from economic marginality. Often enforced by residential segregation, it was also an expression and a reinforcement of traditional values regarding family life. It is romantic to believe that in every instance the multigenerational extended-family household resulted purely from the force of traditional values. In many instances such a family pattern was a basic concession to hard economic reality. The wretched overcrowding in substandard housing still common today in the Chinatowns of the U.S. must be seen in the light of ongoing prejudice, racism, and institutional neglect, rather than as simply the preferred cultural choice of Chinese families. With increasing acceptance in the labor marketplace and increased educational opportunities, the traditional Chinese family will continue to change toward the more Western form of nuclear households. But the pull of tradition manifests itself in patterns of loyalty and obligation to the family of origin and parental lineage, expressed through frequent visitations and participation in collective activities and family rituals.

The role of traditional Chinese values in the Chinese communities of the U.S. is further complicated by the arrival of increasing numbers of Chinese immigrants. Among American-born Chinese and their families, the influence of Western values, coupled with changing economic circumstances, have led to the emergence of a unique Chinese-American subculture, which is an amalgam of the old and the new. The efforts of third, fourth, and newer generations of Chinese-Americans to identify with, express in behavior, and hence affirm their traditional ethnic heritage, in combination with the assimilation of those values necessary for mobility in the majority society, attests to this change. As examples, the emergence of Chinese-American literature and art forms, the reawakening of interest in Tai Chi, and the widespread popularity of Chinese student associations all point to this cultural revival.

For more recent arrivals from Hong Kong, Taiwan, and the mainland, traditional values exercise considerably more force as determinants of behavior and in governing choices. The maintenance of the extended family system among a fairly substantial number of Chinese families is another example of the continuity of traditional values in conjunction with economic necessity. The actual number of multigenerational extended families may be increasing—a trend that may be explained by the growing numbers of elderly Chinese forced to take up residence with their adult children and their families, and the number of immigrants who establish residence with relatives already settled in the U.S.

The incidence of both divorce and outmarriage, low in comparison to other ethnic groups, probably indicates the continuing influence of strong norms governing family life and a continuing preference for within-group marriage. But among the younger American-born generations, this pattern of intraethnic-group marriage seems to be changing. Increasing rates of outmarriage may signify nothing more than the increased mobility of many Chinese-American families, which has led to settlement in areas peopled largely by members of the dominant group. Movement away from ethnic enclaves has usually meant that the social relationships formed by young people are more racially and ethnically varied, which increases the pool of possible mates available to them. Recent arrivals may have a better understanding of lifeways in an industrialized society, because they have been socialized in societies in which ancient cultural themes have been modernized. The American-born Chinese evince the development of a subculture reflecting both the traditional culture of their immigrant forebears and mainstream white America. There continues to be a need, therefore, to understand the differences that do remain between the Chinese and the dominant communities. The need for understanding these differences to permit adequate cross-cultural service delivery will be clarified in a later section of this chapter.

JAPANESE-AMERICANS:
IMMIGRATION HISTORY

In contrast to the Chinese and Pilipino communities, the Japanese-American community has not experienced a dramatic increase in population due to continuing immigration to the U.S. While immigration from Japan to the U.S. has continued over the years—with some periods of increased immigration, such as the large number of "war brides" brought to the U.S. by returning U.S. servicemen—the overall contribution of immigration to the population of Japanese in the U.S. has been small, numbering some 5,000 per year. More so than the other groups, the Japanese-American population is made up in large part of the survivors and descendents of the original Japanese immigrants. Japanese-Americans commonly utilize a generational system of labeling to identify the generational status of individuals. The original immigrants, who were born and reared in Japan and emigrated to the U.S. and Hawaii between 1885 and 1924, are referred to as "Issei" or first generation. The American-born children of the "Issei" are called "Nisei" or second generation, while the third generation are styled "Sansei." In Hawaii and in some areas of the mainland, there are fourth-generation "Yonsei" members of the Japanese-American community. The term "Kibei" refers to "Nisei" who were sent to Japan, often at an early age, to be educated. Kibei, as a consequence, tend to be more culturally conservative than their Nisei counterparts, and maintain fluency in the Japanese language. Coming into more common usage is the term "Nikkei," referring to any Japanese-American, regardless of generation or status.

The original emigration of Japanese from their homes to the New World was a result of an economic crisis in Japan, coupled with the belief, engendered by the labor contractors in Hawaii and the U.S., in unlimited opportunities to be found in the West. The attempt on the part of the Meiji oligarchy to industrialize and catch up with the Western powers in the late 1800s was followed by a period of high inflation and subsequent deflation of currency. Resulting unemployment and social unrest motivated many poor farmers, fisherfolk, and others to seek or re-establish their fortunes overseas. The majority of Japanese immigrants originated in the highly conservative rural prefectures (counties) of southwestern Japan, which were historically overpopulated (Melendy 1972: 90). Although poor, the immigrants were in large part members of an honored social class in Japan. Japanese society was hierarchically divided into several social classes during the Tokugawa Shogunate. This social system survived into the Meiji era (1868-1912), a period of major immigration to the U.S. and Hawaii. In the rigidly structured social hierarchy of Japan, the farmer class was located just below that of the warrior aristocracy in status. To some extent the Japanese immigrants, faced with economic uncertainty in Japan, were downwardly mobile and highly motivated to recoup the economic and social status of their families and lineages. The Issei emigrants were socialized with traditional values, both through the agency of training in their homes and through education. The Issei were fairly well educated, and the majority were literate. The Senate Immigration Commission of 1911 found that some 98 percent of males and 72 percent of the females could read and write Japanese (Senate Immigration Commission 1911). The high level of educational attainment reflected an emphasis on education during the Tokugawa Shogunate that was greatly expanded throughout the Meiji period. Public education, focused on literacy and other basic intellectual skills, was coupled with moral instruction, which taught proper attitudes of individuals toward the family and the state. Education was provided through the *terakoya,* or parish schools, and the *gōguku,* or country schools. In addition, there were a number of private schools *(shizuku),* which provided education to the children of the privileged classes. In 1872, four years of compulsory education was instituted for children between the ages of six and ten years. With the passage of the National Immigration Bill in Japan, a large number of young Japanese men, moderately well educated, emigrated to the U.S. and Hawaii between 1890 and 1924. With adjustment for differences in the pace and content of education, it has been estimated that the majority of Issei had the equivalent of a tenth-grade education in American terms (Kitano 1969: 10).

DEVELOPMENT OF ORGANIZATIONS

With increasing numbers of Issei immigrants arriving in the U.S. and Hawaii, the initial positive reception accorded the Japanese altered through fears of economic competition in the labor marketplace, and irrational anxiety over the growing numbers of persons increasingly perceived to be unassimilable. Because the largest group of Issei worked in agriculture, some of the first organizations to develop were those involving agricultural workers. Developed by the Issei, these unions organized labor stoppages and boycotts to gain economic leverage. The unions served to coordinate efforts for the demand for improved wages and farmworker housing. The early union and labor associations also served as a liaison between new arrivals and non-Japanese employers. As the Issei were able to save capital and to lease their own farms, farm organizations developed which assisted the Issei in finding properties, setting payment levels for workers, and coordinating crop planting and marketing. The farm organizations also provided the important service of gathering and disseminating information and advice regarding agricultural and horticultural practices (Iwata 1962). Through such organizations of farming and through pioneering in specialty crops, the Issei came to dominate the retail distribution of fruits and vegetables in California and much of the West Coast.

Although the majority of Issei found employment in agriculture, the remainder worked in a variety of industries. At one time, some 10,000 Japanese immigrants were working on the railroads, and others were employed in the mining, lumbering, and canning industries.

Another form of organization served the function of a lending institution in the Issei community. With uncertain legal status and faced by hostile and distrustful attitudes on the part of the majority group, the Issei, like other immigrant groups, had little access to capital. There developed in response to this need a Japanese form of revolving credit association called *tanomoshi (Kō)*. The *tanomoshi* aggregated capital from members to be lent out with interest. The very term *"tanomoshi,"* derived from the verb *tanomu,* "to depend," suggests a spirit of understood mutual dependency, which was the basis for this form of banking. The *tanomoshi* provided the venture capital for many Issei businesses, which formed the entrepreneurial foundation for the subsequent development of Japanese communities in the U.S. (Petersen 1971: 56; Masuda 1937).

Another form of organization in the early Japanese communities was that of *kenjin-kai,* or prefectural organizations, which were similar in function and structure to the *hui kuan* of the early Chinese immigrants. *Kenjin-kai* were the mechanisms that allowed the Issei to congregate on the basis of similarities and geographical origins, and with the further benefit of providing the locus for the establishment of relationships among people who were fluent in provincial dialects. The *kenjin-kai* acted to maintain traditional cultural values and served as mechnisms for community solidarity. These organizations also served as employment bureaus and as sources for legal assistance, and they provided mutual assistance and information about conditions in the U.S.

In later years the *kenjin-kai* became member organizations of the Japanese Associations that developed on the West Coast. The Japanese Associations acted as intermediaries among the Issei, their families, and the dominant community (Petersen 1971: 57). In 1900, the Japanese Association of America was founded in San Francisco; by 1921, three others were established in other regions of the West Coast. The Japanese Associations provided education to newcomers about conditions in the U.S. and translated and disseminated information to the Issei regarding laws enacted to harass the Japanese, including the notorious Alien Land Laws. These organizations also provided translation services and advice in family matters and in agricultural technology (Melendy 1972: 147). The development of regional Japanese Associations culminated in the establishment of the Japanese American Citizen's League in Seattle, Washington, in 1930. The JACL inherited many of the functions of the earlier Japanese Associations, and to this day it is a major representative of the national Japanese community.

Japanese language schools developed early in the Japantowns of Hawaii and the West Coast. These schools taught both Japanese language and culture and trained pupils in correct Japanese behavior, with a heavy emphasis of filial piety.

As is true of China, both Confucianism and Buddhism were enormously influential in the development of Japanese culture and values. The traditional values brought to the New World by the Meiji-era immigrants placed great emphasis on the hierarchical relationship between superiors and inferiors, and this was generalized to most interpersonal relationships among the Japanese. Differences in status are expressed not only through deferential conduct but also through the use of the highly complex honorific system in the Japanese language. In this system, differences in status are recognized through the use of different linguistic forms, depending on the status of the speaker in relationship to his or her audience.

In general, there are four distinct language forms that are used to denote differing degrees of respect: the honorific, the polite, the ordinary, and the humble. An example from the work of Yamigawa (Yamigawa 1965: 205-06) will clarify the appropriate use of these varying forms. When a young man is speaking to a peer, the construction *"Ore ga iku"* ("I will go") may be used, with both the ordinary form of the first-person singular *(ore)* and the verb *(iku)* used to indicate the equality of status between speaker and listener. The same young man speaking to his father would be likely to use the polite construction. Thus, *"Ore ga iku"* becomes *"Boku ga ikimasu."* *Boku* is the polite form of the first-person singular, and the suffix *-imasu* added to the verb stem shows respect to the listener. The same young man talking to a friend about a respected person, for example a teacher, would use the construction *"Sensei ga irrassharu"* ("The teacher is going"). In this construction, the honorific verb form *irrassharu* replaces the ordinary *iku*, thus indicating respect for the subject of the sentence. Finally, if the same young man is speaking to the teacher's wife, the construction *"Sensei ga irrashaimasu"* would be used, with the addition of the *-imasu* suffix indicating respect to the listener. In a like manner, the form of the noun used may reflect important degrees of respect. Thus "my husband" could be stated using the noun form *shujin* for husband, but "your husband" would be designated by using the formal *go-shujin*, in which *go-* indicates honorable.

Of paramount importance in traditional Japanese culture is the patrilineage *(ie)*, or the family extended through time and space. The maintenance of a good reputation for the *ie* in the community is a responsibility to the predecessors within the lineage and to its current members. It is also a cherished patrimony, to be deeded to future generations. The *ie* is thus the collectivity of the descendants of some identifiable ancestor and is the basic unit of society. As the Emperor would expect loyalty from his subjects, and a prefectural baron from his feudal vassals, so too would a lineage patriarch expect loyalty and obedience from his family. The legacy of the Confucian philosophy of social order is manifested in ways similar to those that are common in Chinese families. The head of the family is accorded the respect due his position. In general, males are accorded prerogatives and status superior to those accorded women. In traditional Japan, this system of vertically structured roles was exemplified in the *chōnan* system of primogeniture. Although not always adhered to, the rule of primogeniture involved the eldest son's succeeding to his father's position as family head, inheriting both family properties and the traditional occupation. Younger siblings were expected to behave toward the eldest, the *chōnan,* with appropriate respect (Yanagisako 1975; Watanabe 1977; 10-15). In this system, younger brothers and their children were accorded special status as *shinrui* or *shinseki,* terms roughly corresponding to the English "relative," but defined by custom to include a higher degree of loyalty and respect to obligation than is expected in the Western concept of the family. The Japanese individual develops in a complex web of relationships, finding personal identity and security within the bonds of family and extended kin network.

Some of the traditional values brought to the U.S. by the Issei have been preserved by later generations of Japanese-Americans and reinforced by more recent immigrants from Japan. Because of this fact, it is necessary that service providers have an understanding of the system of values of the Japanese-American subculture and of how these values influence behavior.

Strong prescriptive values provide guides to intrafamilial behavior, and these will be enumerated below. Filial piety, with its extensions to all situations involving the relationship of a superior to an inferior, was a major value governing family life. Filial piety is the cornerstone of morality and is expressed in a variety of forms. *Oya-koko,* or filial piety to parents, requires a child to be sensitive to his or her obligations to parents, to evince unquestionable loyalty to lineage and parents, and to be aware of his or her duties to both. One of the criteria used to assess different *ie* is their ability to rear children who consistently display *oya-koko* in their behavior. Behavior deviant from that expected and sanctioned would reflect on the *ie* and diminish its respectability and acceptance in the community.

A closely related value is that of *oyabun-kobun,* which prescribes the proper weighting of respect, awareness of obligation, and dependence that should be reflected in any relationship between a superior and a subordinate, whether parent-child, teacher-student, or employer-employee. The unique pattern of dependency on superiors, with the prototype of the child's dependency on its parents in which relationship the customary obligations and duties accrue to both, is called *amae.* *Amae,* a need to be cherished and held in special esteem by selected others, is an extremely complex form of culturally sanctioned dependency that has been suggested as a major mechanism underlying the behavior of the Japanese (Doi 1962).

In traditional Japanese culture, those values that are reflected in family patterns are extended to extrafamilial realtionships. In a similar manner, values governing interpersonal ethics add to and reinforce family values. Among the important cultural values that influence general interpersonal relationships is that of *giri,* or the honoring of obligations. Sensitivity to one's obligations and awareness of debts incurred through complex reciprocity patterns demand that such debts be met automatically and voluntarily, without the need for a demand for "repayment" by the debtee. In family life, the parallel value is called *ōn,* which prescribes the behaviors that can be expected by parents of their children for the love, nurturance, and support provided them. Another expression of *giri* is the pattern of reciprocity in social obligations, or *kosai*. In Johnson's (1973: 306) study of *kosai,* the author describes the role of gift-giving in the definition, maintenance, and strengthening of relationships among Japanese. One example of *kosai* is the offering of incense money, or *go koden,* in the form of a funeral donation to the bereaved family. While meeting a variety of needs, the *go koden* systems provides tangible evidence of the widespread network of people who, through offering their donations, identify themselves as close to the bereaved family and willing to offer assistance during a time of emotional hardship. The *go koden* system also is a form of insurance, which defrays the financial cost incurred through death and its attendant, customary rituals. Over the course of years, families will give and receive donations with a resulting heightened sense of community solidarity.

Another cultural value prescribes and proscribes behaviors toward the goal of reducing possible sources of interpersonal conflict and disharmony. The value *enryo* requires that an individual maintain modesty in his or her behavior, be humble in expectations, and show appropriate hesitation and unwillingness to intrude on another's time, energy, or resources. Blatant intrusiveness, self-centered assertion, and personal arrogance would be violations of the spirit of this enormously influential value. Related to the value of *enryo* is that of *gaman.* To *gaman* is to evince stoicism, patience, and uncomplainingness in the face of adversity and to display tolerance for life's often painful vicissitudes. *Gambatte* is a closely related value regarding one's attitudes and motivation, which calls for untiring and patient effort as an end in itself. To maintain the struggle toward an important goal is in itself honorable, regardless of eventual success.

Finally, *kenshin* demands devotion to group purposes, an abnegation of selfish desires in favor of common interests. In its most general form, *kenshin* is a commitment to and a concern for the whole community.

The influence of Confucianism and Buddhism on Japanese cultural values pertinent to family functioning should be obvious. Reflected in these values is a highly hierarchical, stratified society, which is shown by the primacy of groups, lineages, and families over individuals. This interdependence of individuals and families is reflected in the values that govern reciprocity and obligations. For harmonious relationships to be established and maintained, conflict must be avoided or controlled through common subscription to shared values stressing sincere other-orientedness.

The Japanese family, in a sense, is a microcosm of the larger society that is represented in the traditional constellation of values. A strong emphasis is placed on a complex set of interdependent roles, with an elaborate code of conduct influencing behavior. The Japanese family ideal is that of a smoothly operating hierarchy of roles with the code of $\overline{o}n$ and $ko\text{-}\overline{o}n$ determining intrafamilial relationships. Enmeshed in a tightly intergrated community, the Japanese family is both an extension and a perpetrator of the traditions of that community.

CHANGES IN THE FAMILY

In the U.S. there have been and there continues to be changes in the patterns of family functioning, with changes away from the archetypal patterns that have been described above. There is a shift from a more traditional, sociocentric (group-centered) orientation to one with increased legitimation of individualism (Kiefer 1974: 185). A major influence on the family patterns of the Japanese in the U.S. was the wartime concentration camp experience. Prior to the war, many Issei had been able to accumulate sufficient capital to establish family businesses, including family-operated farms. The need to cooperate in family businesses acted to reinforce traditional family values. With the evacuation, family-managed businesses ceased in large part to operate on the West Coast. With the end of the war, the Nisei began in increasing numbers to seek employment outside the family (Watanabe 1977: 16). The Nisei veterans of the war were able to utilize the G.I. Bill of Rights to obtain college and graduate-level education, with a resultant rise in the number of skilled employable persons. With the change there occurred a general decrease in the size of households, as young adults established their own families and careers. Increasing opportunities for varied employment and social mobility among the Nisei have tended to alter the traditional, lineage-derived authority structure of the Japanese family. Family roles and the complex code of conduct prescribing interpersonal relationships have yielded somewhat to Western forms, through the pressures of adjustment to the dominant society. Yet it would be incorrect to assume that with such adaptive changes there has occurred a wholesale abandonment of traditional culture and lifeways. Examples of the survival of customary norms of social behavior among more recent generations of Japanese-Americans include sensitivity toward and recognition of positions in a hierarchical structure, brevity of speech, a tendency not to give opinions in direct conversations, and an attitude of self-effacement and modesty (Johnson et al. 1974: 581-82). Behind this general pattern of self-presentation and management of countenance, however, there are likely to be strong feelings and opinions, so that there may in fact be some truth to the lingering stereotype of oriented inscrutability. The continuing importance of avoiding situations of possible shame, whether in personal life, at work, or in school, is another example of the preservation of traditional values. In the face of widespread loss of facility in the Japanese language among Nisei, Sansei, and subsequent generations, the survival of traditional values as reflected in behavior may seem puzzling. Yet a consideration of the role of social learning through modeling, as a primary means by which children acquire behavioral patterns, may provide the key to understanding how cultural patterns in behavior are transmitted across the generations.

PILIPINO-AMERICANS: IMMIGRATION HISTORY

The immigration of Pilipinos to the U.S. has occurred in three major waves. The years 1900 to 1934 marked the period of initial immigration, when, in response to a call for laborers from the U.S. and Hawaii, a large number of mostly young male

138

laborers emigrated from their home province in the Philippines. Represented among the early immigrants were two different types of emigrés: those who were contracted under the Sacada system of indentured labor, a system which lasted until the passage of the 1934 Exclusion Act, establishing an annual quota of 150 from the Philippines; and the Pensionados, or government-subsidized students and workers. The latter were sent to the U.S. as students to learn skills needed in the development of the Philippines. Because of the territorial status of their homeland, Pilipinos were awarded fairly liberal immigration rights, even though not permitted citizenship. With the 1934 Exclusion Act, only 150 immigrants per year were admitted.

Following Philippine Independence in 1946, a small quota of Pilipinos was established, but, to all intents and purposes, they became subject to the same restrictions then in effect for other Asian groups. However, in the 1940s and 1950s, many Pilipinos were recruited into the armed forces of the U.S. Through this means, thousands were able to acquire U.S. citizenship and to enter the country. Thus a second wave of immigration can be said to have occurred roughly between 1940 and 1960, when the population increased from 98,000 to 176,000. Unlike the first wave, this second group was composed primarily of family units, and it has been the parent generation for the majority of American-born Pilipinos. The families of veterans were permitted to join their husbands and fathers in the U.S.

Beginning in the 1950s, and greatly increasing during the 1960s and 1970s, was the last great wave of Pilipino immigration. Sometimes referred to as the "brain drain," this most recent phase of immigration continues unabated and has included a large proportion of highly skilled and well-educated emigrés. Physicians, scientists, nurses, lawyers, and engineers are examples of the professionals represented. Another major subgroup of this recent immigration has been made up of women, usually in their late twenties and early thirties, a number of whom were joining much older husbands, survivors of the first group of immigrants who were establishing families late in life.

Currently, immigration from the Philippines numbers between 25,000 and 30,000 a year. At this rate, the Pilipino population will soon number among the largest of the Pacific-Asian subpopulations in the U.S. Because of the relatively small numbers of American-born Pilipinos in the Pilipino population in the U.S., the majority are and will continue to be those who are foreign-born. The Pilipino community, like the Chinese, is an extremely varied community, with complex generational, regional, and dialect differences in evidence.

As a consequence of restrictive legislation, and through the influence of traditional culture which discouraged the migration of women, the majority of early immigrants were male. Unable to marry, due both to a variety of restrictive laws prohibiting miscegenation and the relative absence of Pilipino women in the U.S., many of the survivors of the Scada system today are elderly single men. As mentioned, it is only recently that many survivors of this earlier period have returned to the Philippines to find wives. The establishment of a Pilipino-American community in the U.S., with attendant family stability, was impossible for the first generation. The legal status of the first immigrants was paradoxical. They were considered nationals, neither foreigners nor citizens. Accorded some of the rights and privileges of citizenship, they were denied the right of franchise, property ownership, or the freedom to marry whom they chose. According to Lott (1976) Pilipinos were thus not able to assimilate into American society. In their powerless position, the early immigrants found their sojourner status reinforced by external constraints against any meaningful form of assimilation. Subject to housing and employment discrimination, many of them were forced into marginal neighborhoods and jobs, especially those of seasonal agricultural and canning industry workers. The more recent arrivals from the Philippines face the considerable legacy of anti-Asian prejudice that is still extant in American society. Many of those considered to be part of the "brain drain" have been denied positions commensurate with their training, because American professional bodies have refused to recognize their educational preparation. Like their predecessors, they often lack or are perceived as lacking proficiency in English, and they also face discrimination in employment.

The varied regional identifications and languages found among early Pilipino settlers militated against the development of strong pan-Pilipino community organizations. Factionalism, directly traceable to the divide-and-conquer tactics of oppressive colonial rulers over several centuries of domination by Spain and the United States, prevented the establishment of a national identity among the colonized peoples. Given this history of factionalism, it is not surprising that immigrants to the New World found it difficult to establish unified organizations based upon a national consciousness. Employment in occupations involving considerable mobility as migrant laborers, the scarcity of well-established families, and the lack of a settled permanent community were further obstacles to such organizational development. Finally, in a community of young men who had been culturally socialized to defer to the wishes of elders, the growth of organizations may have been retarded by the absence of such sanctioned community leaders. Although a number of district and fraternal groups were organized from time to time, many of which are still functioning in the Pilipino community, none of them emerged as powerful centers of Pilipino community life (Cordova 1973).

An exception to this pattern was the early emergence of labor organizations among the Pilipino immigrants. Faced with predatory and unethical labor contractors and employed under conditions of extreme hardship, the immigrants made several attempts to organize themselves into labor associations to demand improved working conditions and wages.

Because of the recency of the first wave of immigration to the U.S. and Hawaii, there continues to be a fairly large number of survivors who represent in their behavior the values of their Old World upbringing. This first generation of immigrants today is a community in need of many social and health services. The second and third waves of immigrants, although representing varied subgroups, reflect strong subscription to traditional cultural values and norms of conduct. Among their American-born progeny, there is a considerable range of behavior, evidence of the acculturative processes that operate in American society. But tradition is still a potent measure by which the behavior of the American-born generations is reckoned.

CULTURAL VALUES
AND FAMILY FUNCTIONING

The majority of early emigrants from the Philippines came from rural regions that were characterized by strong traditional social organizations based on the extended family, village, and barrio memberships. The patterns of settlement in somewhat isolated, self-sufficient communities probably engendered a strong sense of local loyalty and identification, which was retained by the immigrants and carried over to the new country. The tradition of cooperation among families and villagers around the need for pooled labor evolved into a complex set of social values based on reciprocity and the avoidance of conflict within the group. The priority placed on social acceptance coupled with an avoidance of situations of shaming, humiliation, and embarrassment to and by others is one expression of traditional values (Lynch 1964: 5-7). The enormous emphasis placed on getting along with others, of evincing appropriate sensitivity to interpersonal needs, and the use of indirection in speech to avoid potential conflict and embarrassment all point to the ultimate priority placed on harmonious relationships and the importance of maintaining group memberships.

Traditional Pilipino society, like that of the Chinese and the Japanese, is strongly family-centered. The interests of the individual are secondary to those of family welfare, and the reputation of families and their members is to be watchfully maintained through circumspect behavior on the part of family members. In return, the family can be expected to meet the basic needs of the individual. Trust, aid in times of need, acceptance, and the right to share in the good name of one's family are some of the personal benefits that are derived from family membership. The priority of social and family values operating can be expressed by a quotation from the work of Nydegger and Nydegger (1966: 103-4): "To strengthen and extend the bonds of neighborliness, and to make them secure, to establish a family of which one may be justifiably proud, to improve one's socioeconomic position if possible, largely as a legacy to the next generation. . . ." Reflecting the priorities of social life found in the Ilocos areas of the Philippines, a major donor region of early immigrants, this quotation makes clear the great value placed on family, its continuity, and the importance of strong extrafamilial social bonds. Indeed, the motivations resulting in immigration to the U.S. reflected such values as the strong desire to improve the fortunes of family.

Among Pilipinos, kinship relationships extend beyond the set of relations generally suggested by the concept of an extended family among Asian groups. Rather than reckoning family membership only by patrilineal descent, Pilipino families tend toward bilateral equality in family relationships, with the relatives of both parents being incorporated into the extended family. Relatives acquired by marriage play roles of importance equal to those related by blood ties. An additional source of members is the *"compadrazgo"* system, in which trusted friends and allies can be recruited to serve as godparents to children. Thus incorporated into the family network, the godparent also assumes the responsibilities and obligations attendant to the role.

Within the family, great respect and deference is due to elders and the family head. Among children, deference to any older person is both desired and enforced. All persons involved in rearing and teaching children are entitled to the love and respect usually accorded to one's parents. Deference toward and recognition of people with special relationships to the family are expressed through language and in general interpersonal behavior. The Pilipino child is reared within a complex system of interdependent and highly defined social roles and relationships, and receives a great deal of love and protection from older siblings and adults. The ideal child should be respectful and submissive toward those in authority and in superior statuses, and should also be reticent with adults (Bulatao 1962).

In the Pilipino family, marriage is considered to be an alliance between kin networks. Each family is involved in determining the appropriateness of the marriage, through consideration of such factors as the reputations and social statuses of the respective families and the personal suitability of the individuals concerned. Formal negotiations involve the use of a go-between, since the negotiations could be potentially embarrassing or contentious for family members. While the traditional family pattern continues as a culturally endowed ideal, there is continual adaptation to the majority culture. The trend toward establishment of nuclear families living and working in separate locations inevitably diminishes the amount of interaction among family members. The complex of obligations involving reciprocity has been simplified, and nuclear families are autonomous but part of a still powerful, larger extended kin group. The ideal family is still thought to be a multigenerational system, with grown children and their families sharing the parental residence or established in nearby homes of their own.

The values brought to this country by the first Pilipino immigrants have been maintained in the community and supplemented and reinforced by later arrivals. Perhaps the most important traditional value is that of *pakikisama,* which in general suggests a willingness to comply, to go along with, to follow another's lead, and to accept the will of the group (Lynch 1964: 8-9). This value prescribes the behaviors deemed requisite for social acceptance, which include a sense of sympathy to the will and needs of others, courtesy, and humility. An individual who insists on his or her point of view or remonstrates for special consideration by the group can be called *walang pakikisama* (without *pakikisama*), a term of severe censure. A closely related value is that of *bayanihan,* which is the spirit by which individuals, families, or other groups cooperate toward a common goal. To pull together toward the common good, whether in houseraising or in labor organizing, is an example of *bayanihan.* Much of the group effort which assisted the early immigrants in their long struggle to establish themselves in a largely hostile and discriminatory new environment was founded on the basis of a willingness to work together to improve the common lot. Both *pakikisama* and *bayanihan* involve patience, tact, and a willingness to place self secondary to group needs and goals. To be *pakikisama,* an individual must avoid unpleasantness in interpersonal relationships, with euphemism and indirection providing critical mechanisms for minimizing the potentially destructive effects of differences (Lynch 1964: 9-11). The statement, *"siguro nga"* ("I guess so") evinces the rule that a minimized form of agreement is preferable to open disagreement. The necessary delicacy in handling matters of potential conflict or disgrace often requires the use of a go-between or negotiator, who can protect both parties from embarrassment or unpleasantness by skillful diplomacy. Shame is often rendered synonymous with the Tagalog word, *hiya.* Yet *hiya* encompasses much more than is commonly implied in the word *shame. Hiya* is the sense of discomfort, of anxiety, that is tied to an individual's perception of being in an unacceptable situation. Thus being in a situation perceived as socially awkward can result in *hiya.* An individual who remains silent when asked a direct question may be expressing the fear of *hiya* by avoiding the possibility of censure through giving an inappropriate response. *Hiya* is a condition, an experience which is sufficiently aversive to motivate both escape and avoidance behaviors and is a powerful determinant of behavior. The statement, *"nahihiya ako sa iyo"* can be roughly translated as, "I am ashamed *to* you" in an interaction with a superior. A more meaningful rendition in English suggests: "Because I have behaved in a way I define as inappropriate in light of your superior status, I am in a situation of experiencing *hiya." Hiya* is an experience which can accrue not only to individuals but also to family, friends, or other social groups to which one belongs. The strong sense of interdependence among group members, with the group accepting responsibility for the actions of its members, results in individual behavior which must be guided by the will of the group (Lynch 1964: 16-17; Bulatoa 1962).

An individual who is aware of social ethics involving *hiya,* but who transgresses in spite of such knowledge, is *walang hiya* (without *hiya*), another form of severe opprobrium. Such a person would be perceived as acting shamelessly. *Utang na loob* is the sense of inner debt, or a debt felt deeply, hence of gratitude. *Utang na loob* is also the awareness that an individual has displayed of his or her obligations to others and the quality that summarizes the individual's record of establishing and maintaining relationships based on mutual reciprocity. Failure to reciprocate or to express gratitude is to deny *utang na loob* and to be open to extreme criticism and loss of reputation.

Finally, among the major Pilipino values is that of *amor propio,* or pride in oneself and one's personal integrity. An individual must maintain an understanding of and a respect for his or her own strengths and virtues. An individual must respond with appropriate emotion to an affront that is perceived as a challenge to his or her core role. A man might respond with humor if chided as a worker, but with outrage if criticized as a father. As Lynch suggests (1964: 17) *amor propio* can serve as a personal defense, guarding the individual's best claims to the respect of others and to their social acceptance. If an individual demonstrates strong commitment to a position or belief, it is assumed to be an expression of his or her *amor propio,* and others will take pains to respect that commitment.

The value system described portrays a society of highly interdependent social units, in which priority is placed on the establishment and maintenance of conflict-free relationships. Whether in the context of family life, with its demands for intra-familial respect, or in other spheres of behavior, proper Pilipino conduct requires exquisite sensitivity to others and a willingness to yield self-interest to the needs of the group. But as is true of any community, subscription to the values governing appropriate social behavior carries the promise of acceptance and respect awarded by one's family and peers. Markedly deviant behavior can be controlled through censure, community gossip, the threat of denial of reciprocity, or, finally, through community ostracism.

While cultural values can be viewed as generalized within an ethnic community, it should be clear that subscription to traditional values will vary across individuals and subgroups. The Pilipino community, like the Chinese and Japanese communities, includes a variety of family patterns and speech preferences and capabilities. The overall delay in beginning family life in many first-generation families has resulted in a sizable age difference between husbands and wives. Many second- and third-generation individuals, while fluent in English, may lack fluency in their parental languages, thus rendering intergenerational communication difficult. The first generation of immigrants largely maintains its ancestral languages while achieving varying degrees of proficiency in English; among more recent immigrants, many may tend to rely exclusively on their native languages, although there are some who have acquired relative fluency in English.

As has been shown, the Pilipino community is highly complex and heterogeneous. Regional differences, the time of migration to the U.S., subsequent acculturation experiences, and socioeconomic status have all contributed to this diversity. Underlying the heterogeneity are unique cultural patterns that are general to the Pilipino community, many of which survive to this day. Service providers need to develop an understanding of and a sensitivity to these cultural patterns if they are to succeed in delivering effective services to the Pilipino community.

IMPLICATIONS FOR PRACTICE

The Pacific-Asian communities in the U.S. represent very complex subcultures among the ethnic minority groups of America. Attempts to generalize about Pacific-Asian communities must be informed by the profound differences that exist within each, as well as among the several ethnic groups usually included under the rubric of Pacific-Asian. Within the communities there exist differences both in time of arrival of the immigrants in th U.S. and in generational status among the American-born. Mass suggests that the problems of each group are distinct enough to require different approaches (Mass 1976: 161). The Chinese and Pilipino communities are further complicated by the number of different languages spoken within each. For example, among the Chinese in the U.S. there are three major dialects spoken: Cantonese, Toisanese, and Mandarin. In the Pilipino community, the Tagalog, Ilocano, Cebuano, Hiligaynon, Bicol, Waray, Kapampangan, and Pangasinan languages predominate. The long isolation of Japan has resulted in both ethnic and linguistic homogeneity, reflected in the shared language and ethnic values (Beardsley 1965: 358). The Chinese, Japanese, and Pilipino communities are stratified in regard to income and occupational statuses, and are further subdivided by differences in education, site of education, and English-speaking ability. Finally, among the major differences is that of acculturation. American-born generations of Pacific-Asians may reflect considerable acculturation to American values and norms, in addition to widespread loss of or decreasing facility in their parental languages.

However tempting it might be to view Pacific-Asian communities as monolithic cultural and behavioral entities, such a view would serve only to mask the critical differences that must be considered for an informed understanding of community, group, family, and individual functioning. Too often, stereotyped views of the functioning patterns of ethnic minorities have clouded the vision of service providers, to the detriment of both the minority and the professional communities. Yet some generalizations must be made in this presentation. For ease of presentation, commonalities between groups will be emphasized in the following section. The limitations of space preclude discussion of specific ethnic groups.

For each of the Pacific-Asian groups being considered, the population can be demarcated into two major subgroupings. The early immigrant individuals and families and the recent arrivals may be termed traditional, to the extent that it is likely that the donor societies provide the major normative system for determining behavior. The American-born of any generation are more likely to display acculturated behaviors that reflect their socialization in the U.S., although many function as bicultural individuals. The basic normative configuration influencing behavior within and among groups has important implications for informed service provision. In this comparative approach, each group represents a different and a unique environmental context for social service delivery and usage. Among traditional families and individuals, the availability of extended family networks, coupled with only marginal assimilation into the lifeways and practices of American society, often results in a tendency to seek help within the family and the ethnic community. Only in dire circumstances will help be sought from the "outside." American-born individuals, who may both possess the knowledge of majority systems and also have no reason to distrust such services, may be more inclined to use existing agencies.

In addition to length of stay and country of origin, help seeking may be influenced by socioeconomic status and facility in English. At the time of intake, requests for service tend to vary with financial circumstances and English-language competency. Recent arrivals and more long-term residents who lack English language and salable work skills often are unemployed or are employed in marginal and low-paying positions. Initial requests for service tend to be predominantly requests for information and referral, advocacy, and such other concrete services as English-language instruction, legal aid, and child care (Kim 1978: 233). Additional requests for service may arise with an increased understanding of helping possibilities on the part of clients and increasing trust in their workers. Those who are

American-born or of long residence in the U.S. are more likely to seek help for personal matters or difficulties at the time of first intake than are recent arrivals. For many, if not the majority of Pacific—Asians, meeting the daily demands of survival, including the need for shelter, food, and work, must often take priority over other forms of help seeking for less concrete needs. It may be useful to illustrate this point through a schematic repesentation.

In Figure 7-1, the base of the pyramid represents the relatively large number of individuals and families who seek assistance in the forms of concrete services and information or referral assistance. There are significantly fewer persons who seek counseling and treatment at the time of intake. The latter are more likely to be of upper- or middle-income status. American-born, and fluent in English. Exceptions to the pattern indicated include the number of clients referred for service from other systems, such as mental hospitals. But the tendencies that are represented illustrate one way of conceptualizing the interaction between certain characteristics within Pacific-Asian communities and help-seeking behavior.

Pacific-Asian communities require a broad range of services to meet their existing needs. Service needs include the development of culturally syntonic and community-situated service agencies and the recruitment of bilingual and bicultural Pacific-Asian providers into existing service agencies and community education and prevention programs. Service providers must be aware of the history and events that have shaped the Pacific-Asian communities of contemporary America. Some of the social difficulties encountered today in the Chinese, Japanese, and Pilipino communities are direct results of the immigration history of each group and the collective experience of the groups in their struggles to survive in the New World. The large number of single, elderly, poverty-stricken Pilipino men residing in slum areas is a case in point. Denied the right to family life by various restrictive laws, and enduring decades of job and housing discrimination, many Pacific-Asians face their declining years still denied the comforts, services, and basic security that a lifetime of labor should have ensured. Driven inward from years of enforced segregation, job discrimination, and other forms of hostility, the Chinese, Japanese, and Pilipino communities have founded upon ancient cultural traditions subsocieties which are in many ways outside of and parallel to the majority society. Within these subsocieties are a variety of institutions which have traditionally provided assistance to community members. Part of the reluctance of Pacific-Asians to seek help in majority agencies may result from the years in which this population was virtually

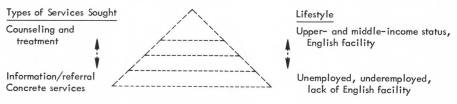

FIGURE 7-1   Mental Health and Social Service Requests for Help
              by Asian-American Families

ignored by the service systems of the larger society. No meaningful or culturally appropriate help was available on the outside, and this reality has reinforced the tendency to seek help from within the communities. In many instances, the early forms of organizations, which did so much to protect, succor, and guide the first immigrants, have fallen victim to changing times and needs.

But there are a host of surviving organizations and a variety of newer forms which provide many of the services needed in the community. Practitioners involved in the development of social policies targeted on the Pacific-Asian communities and those involved in community organization activities would be well advised to study the models and principles of organization to be found in the organizations currently providing services within the communities. An agency which includes the provision of mental health services among its range of service offerings may stress its ability to provide social and advocacy services. Such an approach to community services lessens the chance that the Pacific-Asian clients who feel stigmatized by the need for mental health treatment will avoid any agency that is primarily identified as a mental health facility. The ability to offer a range of services, such as can be found in some multiservice centers within Pacific-Asian communities, is critical both for meeting emergent survival needs and for providing an experience with help seeking to clients who are unfamiliar with such practice. It also has the potential for short-term and relatively immediate client benefit (Ho 1976). Through the trust and confidence engendered by such an experience, a Pacific-Asian client of social services may choose to seek help for other, more personal, matters when and if it is needed. The benefits to be gained from the use of the multiservice model in Pacific-Asian communities in increasing community usage of services is in contrast to the tendency toward increasingly specialized and compartmentalized services in the dominant society.

Community sanction gained through legitimation by community and organizational leaders is essential to the success of new service organizations operating within Pacific-Asian communities. Sponsorship by or affiliation with existing organizations may be a critical start-up step in the development of service agencies and other organizations. Such integration into the community, with broad representation on governing boards, has been suggested as a critical factor in predicting the effectiveness of organizations (Murase 1977: 958). Organizations which have developed and followed the model suggested have met with success in reducing the typical underutilization pattern found in Pacific-Asian communities (Sue and McKinney 1975; Homma-True, Chen, Ow-ling, and Louie 1976).

Policymakers and the implementers of social policy must be aware of the continuing legacy of distrust and suspiciousness that has resulted from the years of oppression and enforced marginality experienced by Pacific-Asian people (Ho 1976; Murase 1977: 953-54). In many instances, this historical experience has reinforced and provided external reason for the strong survival of certain traditional behavior patterns. The reticence that is culturally normative may be transformed into extreme reticence or distrustful silence because of a history of punishment for speaking out. Attempts to solicit testimony at public hearings geared to the development of policy or in decision making are more likely to be successful if handled through existing community organizations and agencies that have developed the trust of community members. Appeals for testimony or opinion which meet with little response do not imply that there are no important community opinions. Rather, such generalized requests ignore both history and the widespread cultural tendency not to give responses until some indication of how they might be received has been given.

Another form of policy implementation shaped to fit cultural patterns is illustrated by the following case. To meet the emergency nutrition needs of the elderly Pacific-Asians living in an ethnic enclave of a city, the city administrators, in keeping with established policy, planned to start a congregate-meals program. Community people, on the other hand, believed that a meal-voucher program, instituted with the cooperation of local restaurateurs, was more appropriate. In time, the city officials were persuaded to begin a meal-voucher instead of a congregate-meals program. This program has proved successful, and the reasons for its success can be related to a number of considerations. Not the least of these is that it enables the elderly to purchase meals of their own preference, in restaurants of their choice, and according to their own schedule. More importantly, it ensures a degree of privacy to people. Congregate meals tend to be highly visible, thus exposing individual participants to possible public humiliation, insofar as they may be viewed as having been abandoned by their families or as not having planned adequately for their own later years. Under the voucher system, men and women also have opportunity to treat their children or grandchildren to lunch or dinner by saving their vouchers. In this way, they are helped to behave in a manner consistent with their own views of appropriate role behavior, as well as to maintain a general sense of well-being and competence.

Finally, the development of organizations geared to rectifying the problem of inadequate services within and available to Pacific-Asian communities can be facilitated by building early organizational affiliations with existing informal, non-Western, service networks. Churches of various denominations, priests, and practitioners of ancient healing sciences are some example. As will be seen, appropriate services to Pacific-Asian communities must reflect a good grasp not only of history and cultural differences but also of how the traditional is combined with the modern.

THE VALUES APPROACH

The discussion of traditional cultural values in the earlier sections of this chapter is not meant to imply that such values, taken in their aggregate, constitute lifeways followed by all members of the Chinese, Japanese, and Pilipino communities. An understanding of the sociocultural complexity of each Pacific-Asian group also demands the recognition that subscription to culturally traditional values will vary among families and individuals. Yet these broad value themes are well represented among the survivors of the first generation of immigrants, recent arrivals, and, to a lesser but important extent, the American-born. For the service provider working with the foreign-born who attained adulthood in their homelands, or among those who were American-born but sent to the parents' homeland for education, an understanding of the lifeways characterized by traditional values can serve as an important guide to an exploration of views of the world that are often quite unique. In working with the American-born and American-reared, the continued influence of traditional values should be understood for their effects on bicultural functioning. Even among those whose behavior is highly Westernized, the influence exerted by the value patterns that were acquired throughout childhood is often considerable (Jung 1976; Mass 1976; Sue and Kirk 1972).

The bicultural model does not assume that cultural replacement occurs with acculturation, but that individuals will tend to show unique syntheses of traditional and Western values in their behavior. Some specific behaviors may be in response to traditional values, but in other instances the individual might well respond in ways similar to his or her majority peers. This point of view provides additional complications for providers. While it would be convenient to place people on a simple continuum, from traditional to modern, and to assume that increasing acculturation to American values and norms leads to a proportionate decrease in the influence of traditional values, such a view does not adequately describe the vagaries of human learning nor the number of individuals who function well in several, often contradictory, cultural environments. For instance, the individual might behave according to traditional values while in the minority community and according to modern values in the majority community. The behavior would be quite different in each situation, but appropriate to each. On the other hand, an individual might appear to have successfully amalgamated elements from two cultures in his or her behavior patterns, but be unable to fit comfortably in either community. The latter individual, not fully accepted by either group, cannot accurately be described as being bicultural. In any case, the provision of appropriate services of high quality to Pacific-Asian people requires an understanding of traditional culture.

One of the major problems of cross-cultural service delivery lies with the fit between the conceptions of psychiatric illness and appropriate treatment that are shared by members of a cultural community and the often divergent conceptions that undergird the thinking of the help givers. It is clearly desirable that the explanations offered by providers regarding the etiology of dysfunction be both acceptable and culturally sensible to the client. The client's orientation to the process of help seeking and the fit between traditional paradigms and those utilized by providers may be critical to successful process and outcome. (Tseng and McDermott 1975). The intrapsychic etiological systems underlying so much of Western service provision, especially in the mental health area, are of relatively recent origin in the West, and relatively unknown in the East.[4] Seeking intrapsychic dynamics to

---

[4] See, for example, Lapuz 1973 for a discussion of orientations to emotional dysfunction that are found in the Philippines.

account for difficulties may be meaningless or even insulting to a non-Western client (Lapuz 1973: 72-73). Similarly, incautious use of environmental theories that stress the contributive role of significant others, especially family members, may create problems for clients who have been socialized to the value of filial piety.

For many centuries, the ancient civilizations of Asia and the Pacific have developed and refined theories regarding the origins of behavioral dysfunction. Among the most common theories of dysfunction with logically derived prescriptions for treatment are those that implicate social, moral, and organic origins. A brief description of each follows. Social explanations may be used when an individual is perceived as having experienced some traumatic or disorienting event. Such experiences include the illness or death of a loved one, the loss of a job, or ongoing family or conjugal conflict. In this approach, the individual is seen as a victim of some unfortunate but uncontrollable circumstance that may have involved some personal complicity but that is, in the final analysis, a result of nonpersonal determinants. Traditional prescriptions for such difficulties reflect the strong sense of mutual obligation and love that characterizes the Pacific-Asian family and friendship networks. The individual might be encouraged to seek advice from family elders or other persons considered to be wise. From his or her family, the troubled person might expect to receive nonjudgmental sympathy, understanding, and support and might also receive permission to abdicate certain duties and responsibilities temporarily—to take a vacation or simply to have time for solace. The Chinese, Japanese, and Pilipino cultures all have developed an acute awareness of the interrelationships between people, their feelings, and their environments. In this sense, social explanations are the closest analog to the Western emphasis on psychological factors. Although an environment-individual perspective has existed and continues to exist in traditional cultures, there is a major difference in the mechanisms whereby such influence is thought to occur. Traditional Pacific-Asian social theories tend to underplay personal culpability. Difficulties may be attributed to bad luck or to some other form of general misfortune, rather than to the individual, whose dignity is thus maintained. Prolonged mourning may be seen both as a highly respectable conformity to tradition and also as a sign of deep emotional attachment to the departed that extends beyond death. There is no tendency to view such behavior as neurotic, even if there is some interference with functioning. The statements *"Bahala na"* ("What God wills"), in Tagalog, and *"Shikata ga nai"* ("It can't be helped"), in Japanese, indicate the prevailing attitude that many of life's failings and hurts are beyond human control.

Moral explanations involve the presumed violation of values held sacred by members of the cultural community. Dysfunction is seen as a punishment or a direct result of such moral failure. Among Japanese, the expression *bachi ga ataru* implies some cosmic retribution for misbehavior, especially when such transgressions verge on or violate the value of filial piety. Similarly, the assumed violation of filial piety among Chinese traditionalists may be held accountable for an individual's suffering. In the Pilipino community, the widespread influence of Christianity results in the belief that an unexpiated sin may result in personal grief, misfortune, or mental illness. Like the social theories, moral approaches to the explanation of personal dysfunction must be seen in the unique contexts in which they operate. In the Chinese and Japanese communities, guilt does not result from a violation of a value-based prescription for behavior that is derived from super-natural sources, but rather from transgressions of the interpersonal duties and loyal-ties that are derived from the traditional culture (Beardsley 1965: 369-70; Norbeck and DeVos 1972: 27). These cultures place enormous value on the sensitivity of individuals to the opinions and expectations of others regarding conduct. Exter-nally derived evaluations become a part of one's system of self and form a signifi-cant basis for one's view of self (Norbeck and DeVos 1972). Violation of prescribed conduct carries with it the threat of rejection by or disownment from the family. As a consequence, the forms of moral infractions that are implicated in the moral theories are those involving transgressions not against scripture but against inter-personal duties. In a more cosmological sense, individuals may be punished for the "sins" of their fathers. In some instances, the misconduct of one's forebears is cited as the cause of one's misfortunes. In all three communities, traditional prescription may involve the intercession of priests, community elders, or family members who might be expected to exhort the individual to improve his or her behavior or to engage in rituals of expiation.

Organic explanations for personal dysfunction are the most common in all three cultures and can range from the simple to the complex. The latter are exemplified by those based on the Chinese model of *yin* and *yang,* which suggests an imbalance between the two basic life forces as being the source of difficulty in physical or emotional functioning. The popularity of these somatic explanations can probably be accounted for by two major themes found in traditional cultures. First, they have a long history in the traditional medicine of all three cultures. Con-cepts of holistic medicine, emerging into prominence fairly recently in Western perspectives on health care, have long been part of the belief systems of all three cultures. Never having embraced the Western dichotomy of body and mind, psyche and soma, the traditional cultures have for centuries been accustomed to linking physical with emotional functioning. Thus with the authority of such longstanding tradition, the Pacific-Asian client might understandably insist that there is an organic basis for a problem that Western service providers might attribute to psychological causes. Second, cultural values that equate personal maturity with the ability to suppress emotions, to suffer silently (for example, *gaman*), and to be pleasant toward others may result in a high incidence of somatization of anxiety arising from self-doubt or interpersonal conflicts (Chang 1965; Lapuz 1973: 107).

Organic explanations may serve other cultural purposes as well. All three cultures traditionally hold the whole family accountable for the behavior of its members. The degree of responsibility is extensive. Families are expected to protect and guide members so as to avoid impious behavior and to provide sufficient guardianship so that family members can be preserved even from the powers of fate. The preference for "impersonal" physical origins of illness can be understood in light of the fact that since physical illness can befall anyone, there is no imputa-tion of moral failure to the individual, nor need there be any question raised about the family's ability to protect and guide the victim or provide adequate nurturance.

The individual is simply ill physically, and no one can be blamed. The stigma traditionally associated with the more severe forms of emotional and psychiatric breakdown adds another dimension to this pattern. No family can be held responsible for a member's physical illness, and an organic explanation obviates the threat that the use of the theories of inherited insanity, family moral failure, or faulty rearing that are implicit in purely psychological or emotional explanations would entail. Finally, within this context, somatic complaints may persist and be resistant to change, because they result in a variety of secondary gains accruing to the patient whose needs for nurturance and care are catered to.

It should be noted that within any one family several theories of dysfunction may exist. Depending upon education, general socialization, age, generational status, or simply idiosyncratic preferences, different family members may offer different explanations for illness.

When individual behavioral difficulties persist, despite the use of a variety of treatment attempts within the family, help may be sought from the outside. The pathway to such help seeking involves several different phases. The family attempts to help the individual by:

1.   Using its own members and resources.
2.   Soliciting the help of selected extended family members or trusted friends.
3.   Consulting such professionals as teachers, ministers/priests, physicians, or mental health professionals.
4.   Agreeing to hospitalization for the individual. Often this is accompanied by labeling the patient.
5.   Accepting the patient home, if discharged, with renewed efforts on the part of the family to cope with and assist the individual.
6.   Increasing sense of despair and family failure if the individual requires rehospitalization.
7.   Blaming and rejection of the individual.
     (Lin et al 1978; Lin and Lin 1978)

The course described above involves the exhaustion of family resources before other sources of assistance are considered. In large part, this pattern of delayed help seeking from extrafamilial sources indicates the strong values placed on intrafamilial help and dedication that are evident, for example, in the principles of *ōn* and *oya koko* among the Japanese. Another contributing factor may be fear of what might happen to the individual if his or her problem were brought to the attention of outside authority. A powerful third factor that must be considered in the pattern of help seeking is that of shame. To admit to the family's inability to deal with a member's difficulty is an admission of failure of deep-seated obligations and, at the same time, a tacit admission regarding the seriousness of the disturbance for which help is being sought. Because of the strong sense of family responsibility, such admissions may be considered shameful, thus stimulating the experience of *haja* (shame) among Japanese, *hiya* among Pilipinos, and a failure of *men tz* among Chinese (Murase 1977). It is of utmost importance that providers who are unfamilar with the particular cultural systems should appreciate the profound nature of these values. In their own realms, they are as strongly prohibitive as is, for instance, the incest taboo. These values, in short, are extremely powerful in their capacity to govern behavior.

For culturally sensitive service provision to occur, it is of paramount importance that help givers have some inkling of the human dramas represented in the lives of their clients. When seen against the backdrop of his or her unique cultural and experiential history, it can be better understood that for the Pacific-Asian client the very act of seeking help may be humiliating, implying as it does the loss of personal and family face. Sensitivity in one's approach to Pacific-Asian clients is critical to their continuing in treatment and their eventual improvement. Untoward haste in problem identification, gathering of family data, and attribution of blame are all very likely to result in the client's dropping out of treatment. Not only is the therapeutic situation itself often novel to Pacific-Asian clients but the behaviors themselves that are expected of clients may also be distasteful or even prohibited to Pacific-Asian persons. For example, the value placed on direct self-disclosure in treatment is antithetical to the traditional cultural values, which demand stoical repression (for example, *gaman* in Japanese). Similarly, the tendency toward certain "professional" behaviors on the part of service providers, including an attitude of detached objectivity, minimal emotional exchange with clients, and a careful observance of interpersonal boundaries, may appear to the Pacific-Asian client as evidence of lack of interest or caring, personal dislike, or, at worst, hostility.

Clients who have had little or no previous experience with counseling are likely to want information about what they can expect in the situation. A clear, nonpatronizing explanation from the counselor regarding the role of the therapist, the agency policies, the principle of confidentiality, and the therapeutic process can be of enormous early assistance in establishing an effective relationship. For example, sharing some illustrative material which suggests how confidentiality has been maintained in other cases can help to relieve the client's concern about his or her privacy. Recognizing the client's discomfort, by generalizing about the difficulties people commonly have in coming to seek help or by making particular reference to ethnic group sensitivities, may serve to indicate to the client that the counselor both understands and is accepting of such difficulties.

Counselors who are aware of the elaborate protocol governing interpersonal relationships in most Pacific-Asian cultures have learned not to move too hastily or too abruptly into delicate areas. Speaking in quiet tones that convey a sense of respect and caring, these counselors favor general "feelers"[5] over direct and intrusive questions, and they pay attention to the willingness of the client to address

---

[5] "Feelers" are information-seeking questons, but they do not take the form of direct questions. They are similar to indirect questions and are statements which introduce the issue to be discussed in a noninterrogating manner. Examples are: (a) "It must take a lot of patience to cope with such a situation," in contrast to the direct, "How do you cope with such a situation?" Such a feeler may be especially appropriate for use with a person who was raised to believe in stoical suffering. (b) "You must have many thoughts about being arrested," in contrast to, "What are your feelings about your arrest?"

sensitive areas. Clients who respond in vague, euphemistic, or circumlocutory terms may sometimes be engaging in testing behavior for signs of counselor attitude, and it is important for counselors to monitor themselves so as to avoid expressions of surprise, distaste, or impatience. Other clients may respond to questions with answers that they believe are expected or desired by the counselor. In a sense, such responses are predictable, given such cultural values as *pakikisama* among Pilipinos, which demand a willingness to go along with others and to try to gain the approval of persons in positions of authority. Such responses should not be perceived as hypocritical or dishonest, but rather as expressions both of respect for the role of the helping person and of unfailing courtesy to others in accordance with ancient forms of etiquette.

In the United States, the role of the professional helper is substantiated by the culture and is authenticated by his or her clientele (Nelson 1965). For Pacific-Asians, the role itself may be a novel one, and clients might well relate to the counselor as they would have behaved toward persons in analogous roles in their homelands. Albeit unwillingly, counselors and other help providers will tend to be perceived as authority figures, who require highly deferential treatment. The power that accrues to such authority figures must be wielded gently, with attention to culturally-derived areas of sensitivity. Knowledge of the importance of the family to an individual and of his or her loyalty to it should warn the counselor against imprudent use of the causal explanations that place blame on family members or onto the client directly. For example, awareness of *amor propio* among Pilipinos should deter counselors from insisting that clients accept personal responsibility if doing so is perceived as a threat to his or her core role. Deep intrapsychic probing may strike the client as being rude and even irrelevant. Thus great care must be taken to give explanations of the client's difficulty that permit logically related treatment methods and also do not do violence to the client's major loyalties and obligations. Therapeutic approaches should be based upon a view of the family as an interdependent whole, whose functioning requires assistance toward strengthening ties among its members. To the extent that the family is a major source of personal identity and gratification, to be rejected by one's family is, in many instances, tantamount to social death. Thus the attitudes toward family that might suggest infantile or neurotic dependence in Western society may actually be expressions of filial piety or, as in the case of the Japanese, culturally sanctioned forms of dependency on others *(amae)*. Whenever possible, family treatment with recognition of the interdependence of family members is desirable.

Similar manifestations of client dependency may be seen in relation to the counselor who is turned to for guidance or help in decision making. It is not unusual for Pacific-Asian clients to define the counselor as a generalized "expert," an authority figure who can be reliably depended on. Although sometimes onerous to the counselor, such dependency, when understood and met, can be extremely valuable in work with Pacific-Asian clients. Socialized in subcultures with strong affiliative patterns, these clients may express considerable interest in the personal history and life of the counselor. It would be a mistake to assume that such over-tures or apparent dependency patterns necessarily indicate transference or other difficulties. Given the interpersonal complexity of traditional cultures, establishing relationships that mirror those found in family groups or in friendship networks may be helpful to the client as a means of guiding the interpersonal process with the counselor. One of the authors was recently working with an Asian gentleman on his family problems and was fairly successful in assisting the client toward improve-ment in his family life. Although considerably older, the client clearly trusted and in many ways was quite dependent on the counselor. In other areas, the client played the role expected of a senior person, freely giving advice on a variety of mat-ters, lavishing praise on the counselor for his efforts, and inquiring after the welfare of the counselor's family. The point is that in any interpersonal system, the actors must have a mutual understanding of their own positions in relation to others, so that social intercourse can proceed according to mutually shared norms. In the case cited, the worker assumed direction and authority in areas legitimized by the client and understood by him to represent areas of special expertise. In other areas, the client was able to maintain his personal dignity and sense of worth by assuming a superior role appropriate to his age. Nonjudgmental acceptance of the social etiquette displayed by clients and comfortably matching the protocol suggested by client behavior can be very useful in forwarding therapeutic progress.

Attention to interpersonal grace with warm expressions of acceptance, both verbal and nonverbal, is critical to work with Pacific-Asian clients. For instance, asking about the client's health, offering a cup of tea, suggesting the need to remove a coat, or indicating a more comfortable chair can serve to convey genuine concern and can add greatly to beginning and maintaining a relationship. Continued atten-tion to the niceties of etiquette consistent with the client's behaviors will some-times result in a relationship that carries over into other areas. The counselor might be invited to family gatherings or other social events, be introduced to potential clients by a grateful client, or be the recipient of gifts which express the gratitude of the client. Such gratitude is consistent with the value of *utang no loob* and of *giri* and should be accepted in the same spirit. Among American-born Pacific-Asian clients, some of the behavior patterns described in the foregoing may be seen, but are most often a synthesis of traditional and American values.

For both types of clients, structured and goal-directed work, with clear and concrete objectives, is preferable to less closely targeted work, focused on emotional clarification (Murase and Johnson 1974). This is not to say that highly personalized work focused on emotional areas is not appropriate. The issue is one of timing. In the beginning phases of work with Pacific-Asian clients, more con-crete, focused therapeutic process is indicated. Over time, within the framework of developing trust and comfort, other forms of treatment become possible. In all instances, however, when the client displays unfamiliarity with the theories or methods that are being discussed, a detailed explanation, with multiple examples, may be necessary.

SUMMARY

The foregoing section has attempted to identify some of the means by which knowledge of cultural systems can be incorporated into cross-cultural practice with Pacific-Asian peoples. While the discussion has been primarily of clinical application, it must be pointed out that many of the difficulties encountered in Pacific-Asian communities are societal in origin. The type of neurotic maladjustments found by Onoda (1977) among Sansei are reflective of the continuing difficulties in the relationship between majority and minority. Differential prestige and legitimation accorded to minority cultures and lifeways in relation to those of the majority point to the subtle but often devastating influence of ongoing cultural imperialism. On a more concrete level, the numbers of poor Pacific-Asian individuals and families who are struggling to meet basic survival needs in the United States point to the continued and pervasive existence of racism and discrimination.

CHAPTER EIGHT
SOCIAL WORK SERVICES
TO URBAN INDIANS
Nancy Brown Miller

The cultural diversity of American Indians is so broad that any generalizations about cultural traits immediately conjure up countless exceptions. There are more than 400 Indian tribes in the United States today, and approximately 280 reservations. About half of the more than one million Indians live in urban areas. Many Indians are highly traditional, live in isolated rural areas on reservations, and know little English; many others have been raised in urban areas and have had little or no contact with their Indian heritage. Many have integrated the values of the dominant society into their lives while retaining pride and identification with their Indian background; while others experience continual conflict in attempting to achieve a balance between their Indian values and those of the dominant society.

The purpose of this chapter and of the research presented in it is to explore some of the cultural traits that have been attributed to "urban Indians," to describe the experiences of Indian people in cities with social and medical services, and to assess the influence of cultural traits in transcultural interactions with professionals.

NANCY BROWN MILLER received her MSW from Michigan State University in 1965 and her Ph.D. in Anthropology from the University of California, Los Angeles in 1978. Her clinical and research interests include handicapped children and their families, parent training, and cultural awareness in the health and mental health professions. She is Assistant Professor in Residence with the Child Development Division, University of California, Los Angeles Department of Pediatrics, where she is Social Work and Clinical Research Coordinator for the UCLA Intervention Program for Developmentally Handicapped Infants and Children.

While it may not be possible to generalize the findings of this research to all American Indian people living in urban areas, these findings do raise questions about the dangers in seeking short-cut knowledge about the cultural values and behavior of other people, as well as pointing up the need for increased sensitivity and skills by the professionals who provide services to people of different cultural backgrounds.

This chapter also demonstrates the values of an interdisciplinary approach in transcultural social work, through the blending of anthropological theory and research with social work knowledge and practice. Anthropologists, often with good reason, have become notorious for their endless studies of Indian life and have frequently been considered the Indians' worst enemy (Deloria 1969). Yet anthropologists have made the challenge of developing models for transcultural social work an easier one by providing theoretical bases for the study of culture and culture change. The integration of anthropology and social work can provide the knowledge and skills required for effective service delivery in our pluralistic society.

OVERVIEW

In contrast to other minority groups in our society, American Indians are not immigrants, who have incurred injustices, high unemployment, or intolerable living conditions in a foreign country. At the time Columbus "discovered" America there were between two and three million Indian people living here whose ancestors had begun migrating to this continent more than 20,000 years ago. As the European settlers pushed their way westward, claiming and changing the land to meet their needs, Indian peoples were pushed out of their homelands. The Indian tribes invaded by European settlers and armies have usually been depicted as fierce warriors with a savage mentality, who provided continuous threats to the safety and well-being of the Europeans. In reality, the Indian tribes of colonial times were not a homogeneous group of people, but represented a wide range of lifestyles and temperaments, varying from highly organized urban living to that of hunters and gatherers. But Europeans had been "given" the land, and they saw Indians as intruders to be feared because they could not be understood and did not share the same value system. Through deliberate policies of exclusion and extermination and the introduction of illnesses, firearms, and alcohol, the Indian population suffered great losses and had decreased to about 200,000 by 1910.

During the middle 1800s, the United States government established reservations—often in hostile, barren, undesirable land—to offer Indian people protection and stability in order to preserve what was left of their cultures. The reservation system also gave the dominant society control over Indian people, as the government had sole control over educational, medical, social service, land management, and other programs in accordance with the dominant society value system and needs. The government even legislated the "definition" of the Indian, which continues even today to have legal, social, and educational implications for Indian people. The reservation system began a process that Linton (1972) has called directed culture change:

Directed culture change can only operate in those contact situations in which there is dominance and submission. . . . All attempts to direct culture change are really efforts on the part of the dominant group to modify and control its own environment. The subject group is always an important part of this environment, with potentialities for furthering or impeding the aims of the dominators. . . . It will also contribute to the peace of mind of members of the dominant group if the inferior one gives up practices which the dominant group finds repugnant. (Linton 1972: 7-8)

The fact of over 100 years of Indian dependence on the dominant society cannot be minimized in considering the effects on Indian personality development and identity. Even though the Indian Reorganization Act of 1934 ostensibly gave Indian tribes more self-determination in their lives, the reality was that most programs for Indians continued to be planned and implemented by primarily non-Indian bureaucracies.

Following World War II, the unemployment rate for Indians returning to their reservations soared. In 1952 the Bureau of Indian Affairs sought to relieve the high unemployment problem by finding jobs for Indians in urban areas. Under that program, interested men and women and their nuclear families were brought to cities and placed in job training programs, with the BIA providing funds for housing, clothing, and medical care for the first year. After that the family was on its own.

Many people have criticized this program as yet another attempt to destroy the Indian culture by encouraging assimilation into the urban environment, rather than attempting to strengthen Indian ways of life by developing more work opportunities on reservations. As Farris (1973: 84) states: "The Indian should have freedom and assistance to live in an environment that provides the optimum conditions for social and economic growth. He should not be forced off the reservation and into complete assimilation just so he can lead a decent life."

Many Indian people who have migrated to cities for economic reasons deplore the loss of family ties and cultural traditions, but see no way of returning to the reservation. Their sense of loss, the lack of jobs, and their ambivalence about urban living is often expressed by frequent moves back and forth. Today, of the approximately one million American Indians in our society, it is estimated that about one-third live permanently on reservations, one-third in urban areas, and one-third move back and forth from city to reservation. About half of the Indian population lives in urban areas at any one given time.

The statistics for income, education, mental health, and crime among urban Indians depict a bleak picture. In many studies (Fogleman 1972, Graves 1970, White and Chadwick 1972) Indians represent the most economically deprived ethnic group in a number of cities; arrest rates for Indians are higher than for any other ethnic group; drinking and related arrests are a major problem; unemployment is higher than for any other group, and the education level is about five years lower than the national average. Urban Indians are the poorest, least educated, and most highly unemployed group of people in our society (Chadwick and Strauss 1975).

The children of these families are being raised with fewer contacts with traditional life, and what they observe most of all is the frustrated hopes of their parents. The choices for many of these Indian children may be even more limited than those of their parents: reservation life is unknown to them, and they may eventually become members of the urban underclass. Their peers are often non-Indian, and they increasingly grow up to marry non-Indians, diluting the cultural heritage they will teach their children (Price 1972).

An intensive study of 120 Indian families living in the San Francisco Bay area found that the majority of mothers wanted their children to learn about their heritage and to retain their cultural identity and practices (Bowman et al. 1975). Unfortunately, many of the mothers felt unequipped to carry out their child rearing roles successfully because of several factors: none of the mothers had been raised in cities themselves, and they had few effective coping skills to teach their children; many had attended boarding schools, and wound up with subsequent feelings of ambivalence about authority and education; their contacts with other Indians did not occur naturally, but had to be actively sought out; and their children were continually exposed to competing value systems.

Most of the publicized statistics about urban Indians portray a highly negative picture. The problems exist and must not be minimized, not only because of the enormity of problems, which are apparent, but also because of their circular effect on the stereotypes and expectations that result. The media, including television, movies, and popular literature, continue to perpetuate the image of the American Indian either as a romantic, mystical figure of the past, with a primitive and savage temperament, or as a displaced, drunken individual. These stereotypes are seen by Indians as well as non-Indians, confusing the development of self-esteem and identity (Wise and Miller 1981).

Indians are consistently portrayed as a homogeneous group, and this portrayal has even carried over into the categorization of "urban Indians" as a distinct group. Many of the Indians who migrated to cities had never had contact with anyone outside their own tribes. Yet tribal distinctions are important to Indian people and reflect their diversity in many areas, such as religion, family structure, their traditional economic livelihoods, and political structure. An analogy would be to use the rubric "European" to identify as homogeneous all Italians, French, German, and English. What Indians do have in common include ethnicity, poverty, discrimination of varying degrees, media stereotypes, and dependence on the federal government. As they arrive in cities and attempt to maintain their tribal identity, they often find that there is great strength in numbers. They may know only a handful of people from their own tribe, but find more camaraderie among other Indians from various tribes than with non-Indians. Thus, Pan-Indian movements have begun, both for social reasons and for strengthening legal and public relations efforts to raise the awareness of the general public about the needs of Indian people, both in urban areas and on reservations.

THE LOS ANGELES OUTREACH PROJECT

Los Angeles has an American Indian population of about 70,000 with some estimates ranging as high as 150,000. In 1977 there were 4,500 identified Indian children in the Los Angeles City Schools, with only 21 in any kind of special education program. In the Regional Centers for the Developmentally Disabled (the primary agency for registration and service for the developmentally disabled) there were no American Indian children or adults registered. Given the available knowledge about the prevalence of developmental disabilities in the total society, it appeared evident that Indian people with developmental disabilities were underutilizing the available services.

In July 1976, the Indian Free Clinic in Huntington Park (Los Angeles County), California, received a grant from the State Department of Health to conduct a case-finding project in the Los Angeles area for American Indians with developmental disabilities. A major purpose of the project was to locate and identify individuals with disabilities and to assist them in obtaining any needed services by referrals, counseling, and providing transportation for appointments (Indian Free Clinic 1978).

Over 400 families were contacted and interviewed by the Indian outreach workers. Of the 400 families—representing approximately 2,000 individuals—33 persons, in 29 families, were identified as probably developmentally disabled (about 1.7 percent of the people contacted). Of these 33 people, only 6 had received any services prior to the Indian Free Clinic contact. All but one of the families expressed an awareness of a problem and accepted offers of help. Appointments were made for evaluations or other services, with transportation provided by the outreach workers.

Twenty of the families were subsequently involved in a combined service-research project with the author. A series of interviews was held with the families in their homes, and the author provided developmental screening exams, referrals, counseling, and advocacy for the families as they obtained, or attempted to obtain, services. There were 24 developmentally disabled individuals in the 20 families. Eighteen had 1, two families had 3 each. There were 15 females and 9 males with an age range of 1½ to 42 years. Six were preschool age, 12 were school age, and 6 were 18 years or older.

The diagnoses were categorized as organic or functional. Within the organic category were 8 females and 3 males, including 3 with chromosome disorders, 1 with mental retardation following meningitis, 4 seizure disorders, 1 deaf, 1 short stature, and 1 birth injury. There were 7 females and 6 males with functional disorders: 6 mildly retarded, 4 moderately retarded, 2 with learning disabilities, and 1 stutterer.

An example of the types of problems that were found included a family with 10 children. There were twin girls, age 8, who were moderately retarded, with very little speech and many stereotypic behaviors. The mother had not consulted a physician about their delays, because they were in good physical health. She had taken them to school at the age of 5 to enroll them and was told that there was no class for them. She went back a year later and the psychologist said that they were "untestable" and to keep them at home until the school called. A year and a half later, she was still waiting. During the course of the study it was learned that their 14-year-old daughter was in a class for the mildly retarded and that the mother was unaware of it, although she remembered signing some papers several years before, so that her daughter could get extra help.

CULTURAL ORIENTATION OF FAMILIES

A Cultural Index was developed, in an attempt to quantify Indian cultural identity in two areas: the extent of traditional Indian practices and preferences, and tribal vs. pan-Indian practices and preferences. A total of 35 questions were formulated, in consultation with the Director and the outreach workers in the Indian Free Clinic Developmental Disabilities Project. The Index consisted of two subscales, an Activity Scale, with 17 questions; and a Preference Scale, with 18 questions. The questions were weighted for "yes" or "no" responses or for scoring on a 3-point scale of "high," "medium," or "low." The highest possible score on the Index was 61, including 32 points on the Activity Scale and 29 points on the Preference Scale. The questions which comprised the Index were organized into the interview schedule, with responses coded from verbal statements made by the caretakers.[1]

Cultural Index scores for the 20 families in the study ranged from 9 to 37 points (x = 21.5; s.d. = 8.5), which was the sum of the scores on the Activity Scale and the Preference Scale. The distribution of scores are summarized in Table 8-1.

TABLE 8-1   Scores for Indian Families on Activity Scale, Preference Scale, and Total Cultural Index

SCORE	ACTIVITY SCALE	+	PREFERENCE SCALE	=	TOTAL SCORE
Highest Possible Score	32		29		61
Range of Scores	3-23		3-17		9-37
Mean Scores	11.9		9.6		21.5
Standard Deviation	6.2		8.5		8.5

The Activity Scale included four general categories: activities in Los Angeles, knowledge and use of an Indian language, visits to either parent's reservation or home community, and evidence of Indian culture in the home.

Activities in Los Angeles included frequency of attendance at Indian events, reading Indian newspapers, listening to Indian programs on the radio, friendships, customs carried out in the home, Indian events celebrated, serving of Indian foods, and use of Indian services.

Three families were active in Indian organizations and attended many events, while 6 never attended any. Reasons given for occasional or no attendance included lack of transportation, "too much trouble to take the kids," lack of interest by spouse, and lack of knowledge of when they occurred. One caretaker reported not liking Indian group activities. Twelve families reported reading the *Talking Leaf* newspaper regularly or occasionally, and 4 families also subscribed to tribal newspapers. Eight families did not know there were Indian programs on the radio.

---

[1] *Caretaker* denotes the person with primary responsibility for the developmentally disabled family member. In most instances, this was the mother, but also included sisters, grandparents, and self.

Thirteen families reported that more than half of their friends were non-Indian; none of them reported having mostly Indian friends. The primary Indian service utilized by families was the Tribal American Children's Center, which provided preschool and tutoring programs, with transportation.

In the observance of traditional Indian customs, 4 families reported the use of an Indian language, at least occasionally, and one caretaker reported using herbal medicines regularly. Three families had returned to their reservations for traditional naming ceremonies for their children and for healing ceremonies for their handicapped children.

Eight caretakers reported serving a few Indian dishes in the home, such as fry bread and beans; three who served none said they would like to learn how to cook Indian foods.

Eight fathers knew their native language fluently and tended to retain fluency in the language longer than mothers. Six mothers could speak their native language fluently. Of the two couples who had married within the same tribe, one couple spoke the language fluently and used it with their children regularly. Five families reported using their Indian language in the home, but only when friends or relatives visited. Very few children had any knowledge of their traditional language.

Twelve families had visited at least one of the parents' home communities within the past year; 3 had visited two to five years ago, and 5 had not visited a home community for more than five years. Children in 6 of the families had spent time in the home community living with relatives without their parents, while another 12 families took their children with them for visits.

Evidence of Indian culture in the home was based on the investigator's observation of any objects on display in the home which were representative of the family's Indian culture. Fourteen of the families had no Indian objects or one or two objects on display. Six families had a very large number and a wide variety of objects, including rugs, pottery, wall hangings, photographs, and other items.

Items on the Preference Scale were constructed to elicit tribal vs. pan-Indian preferences in relation to friends, neighbors, the people whom their children played with and married, and their identity to others. Other items related to ties with their home communities, their preferences regarding their children learning an Indian language, and their use of Indian services in the city.

Tribal preferences were not strongly expressed in this study. One caretaker reported she would like to meet someone from her tribe, to maintain some contact, and one mother stated she hoped her children would marry within her tribe, although this preference was stated less strongly than her desire that they marry other Indians. Eleven caretakers reported a strong desire for others, both Indians and non-Indians, to ask the name of their tribes. Many of the respondents who wanted people to know they were Indian were frequently misidentified as Mexican, and several individuals reported wearing Indian jewelry in public to avoid having people expect them to speak Spanish. One caretaker did not care whether people knew she was an Indian, and one reported she did not like to be asked her tribe. This caretaker also stated she did not want her children to marry within her tribe.

The caretakers repeatedly stressed the quality of the individual, regardless of ethnicity, when stating their preferences regarding friends, neighbors, their children's friends, and whom their children married. Pan-Indian preferences were stronger than tribal preferences, but even those were secondary to the quality of individual behavior and attitudes.

Most of the families stated a desire to visit their home communities more often; 5 stated a strong preference, and a plan, to live there in the future. Two families stated they would return home now if there were services for their handicapped children. Other reasons for not wanting to live in the home community of either parent were lack of jobs, lack of housing, and lack of relatives still living there.

Five caretakers reported a strong desire for their children to learn their Indian language, and that their children were involved in learning the language from them or other relatives. Eight caretakers reported they would like it, but that either their children were not interested, or there was no one to teach them the language. Six caretakers were neutral, saying it would be up to the children to decide, and one caretaker deliberately avoided the use of her language with the child, because he had a severe language deficit, and she was afraid that the use of two languages would result in greater difficulty for the child.

One caretaker expressed a strong preference for Indian services, as she felt Indians were easier to talk to and went out of their way to help. Eleven reported they preferred some Indian services, particularly the Tribal American Children's Center, and one of the medical clinics for medical and dental services, primarily because they provided transportation. However, they also complained about lack of staff and long waits for various services. Several reported that when you went to get help from other Indians, the whole community found out about it. Eight reflected total dissatisfaction with Indian services and preferred to deal with other agencies.

INDIAN CULTURAL TRAITS AND SOCIAL SERVICES

Nine cultural traits, which previous studies have described as characteristic of urban Indians, were selected and operationally defined.[2] The selection of nine traits from the many that have been described was based on both their frequency of appearance in the literature and their assumed relevance to the study. Many of the traits had been described by non-Indian researchers, primarily anthropologists, and none had been operationally defined in previous studies.

Attempts to measure the traits in specific behavioral terms proved largely unsuccessful, for several reasons. First, the traits were defined from an Anglo perspective and were evaluated in terms of how these traits were manifested in Indian-Anglo interactions, including interactions with the author and with professionals

---

[2]Operational definitions are not included here. The definitions and a more detailed description of the research can be found in Miller (1978).

with whom the families had contact. The traits that are manifested to an "outsider" may be quite different from those which are evident in the presence of Indians. Some Indian people may engage in what Farris (1975) calls an "ethnic game" and relate to the expectations of non-Indians as they perceive them.

A second problems was related to the great variability within individuals, as people would often say one thing and do another, or contradict themselves within one interview or between interviews. It would be easy to take statements out of context and report that they confirm or deny a given trait. It is also possible that examples of any of these traits can be found in non-Indian populations and that they may relate more to social class or minority status in general. The author preferred to err on the side of conservatism and to utilize descriptive data to provide some qualitative understanding of these very complex traits. The assessment of the presence of the specified traits was based on verbal statements and on observations of nonverbal behavior. The focus was on the manifestation of traits in relation to utilization of services, knowledge and beliefs about developmental disabilities, and interactions during the interviews.

Suspicion and Distrust
of White Professionals
and Institutions:

Any statement implying perceived discrimination on the basis of Indian ethnicity. If there is a pan-Indian attitude of suspicion and a distrust of white professionals and institutions, it may follow that urban Indians are reluctant to reach out to such services, because of the expectation that they will not receive adequate service.

Only one of the respondents made strong, consistent statements that would substantiate this trait, stating that she felt Indians understood their problems better than non-Indians, and expressing high dissatisfaction with other services received. Another mother felt embarrassed about the child's behavior during several professional contacts and stated that she thought an Indian would have been more understanding and tolerant. Two mothers reported feeling very happy to have the outreach workers accompany them to appointments because they were Indian; others were pleased with the workers' presence, but stated it was primarily because they knew them and not necessarily because they were Indian. Another caretaker stated that she had felt discrimination from teachers of her children because they were Indian, and two caretakers had felt that physicians had discriminated against them. Most families reported having no contact with the police, but several stated they had heard that police treated Indian people worse because they considered them all to be "drunken Indians."

Most of the caretakers reported that quality of service and personal concern on the part of the service provider were the most important considerations, and while some instances of discrimination were related, they were in the minority. There were strong positive feelings from all but one caretaker regarding the Tribal

American Children's Center, because of the emphasis the school placed on the teaching and maintenance of Indian culture. One caretaker did not like the program, because there were too many Indians there causing her children to be "too shy when they started to public school."

Many of the families complained about the discrimination toward non-Indians at several Indian-run clinics, and one family did not like Indian clinics because they were for "poor Indians."

A trait of suspicion and distrust of white professionals and institutions was confirmed in only one respondent, although instances of these feelings were observed in about half of the respondents. It is important to note, however, that the investigator was white and had contacts with these families both as a social worker, representing the Indian Free Clinic and UCLA, and as a researcher. It is possible, therefore, that some of the respondnents had feelings of distrust but did not want to share them, or that during the time of the study had more positive feelings because of the investigator's relationship with them and assistance to them in obtaining help for their developmentally disabled family members.

Generally Passive Nature, Avoiding or Withdrawing From Situations That May Require Assertive or Aggressive Action:

Any statement indicating that the Indian respondent could have taken an action which might have resulted in increased service utilization or satisfaction but did not take that action, or any statement that reflected a deficit in problem-solving skills related to service utilization. If there is a pan-Indian trait of passivity and lack of assertiveness, it may follow that urban Indians will not initiate contacts to agencies, or will easily give up if the nature of services are unclear or not immediately available. If Indians receive information or advice with which they disagree or which they do not understand, they may terminate service-seeking activities.

Five of the caretakers made no statements and manifested no characteristics a passive nature. While they had not all shown a high degree of initiative in seeking services prior to contact, they demonstrated good problem-solving skills for finding services after contact, and they showed no tendency to withdraw from situations that required them to be assertive in getting help.

Fifteen of the caretakers made statements, substantiated by the investigator's observations, to indicate that their primary patterns for interacting with professionals were to wait and not aggressively seek action. During the course of the project, eleven families had to wait for periods of two to seven months to have service provided. None of the families contacted the agencies in the interim to find out reasons for the delays. Several of the mothers mentioned the delays, and their feelings of frustration, to the outreach workers and the investigators, and they were very willing for the workers or investigator to call the agencies. It is possible that their reluctance to call was based on lack of knowledge about how to approach the agencies. With specific instructions and modeling, four of the caretakers began to call for information and appointments independently.

An example of this trait (which may also reflect a trait of shyness) was a mother who needed to enroll her son in the neighborhood public school. The inestigator called her and gave her the necessary information. After a long pause, the mother stated, "I don't know where the school is." She was asked if she had any neighbors with children who went to school. She said, "Yes, but I don't know any of them." I asked if she would like me to find out the name of the school and she said she would. She then said, "I will need a ride, because I won't know how to get there," and a ride was provided.

Several mothers had received letters from agencies telling them to wait for services, and they did so without question. Several had phone numbers of agencies to contact for specific purposes, but had not called, thereby delaying service.

In the investigator's contacts with the caretakers, fifteen exhibited a passive nature in the sense of showing a manner of resignation and a lack of urgency in following through with getting service or following recommendations.

It is important to note that passivity is an Anglo concept and describes a pattern of behavior which is different from the dominant society middle-class norm of showing considerable affect, being concerned with time and deadlines, and being more comfortable in situations which required talking and assertive action. It became increasingly clear to the investigator that passivity has a negative connotation, is highly related to Anglo perceptions, and needs to be more clearly defined. Thus, to other Indian people, the trait of passivity may be defined and judged very differently.

The characteristics that have been defined here as passivity do present problems for the caretakers in getting services, and a major concern in the present study was the interaction between Indian clients and the professionals who represent the dominant culture. A cycle develops and becomes reinforced, as with one mother who stated that she had waited and waited and had given up on anything ever happening. Her feelings of powerlessness and resignation, and possibly her expectation that she would not get good service anyway, were strengthened, and, without help, she is likely to enter her next professional interaction with increased feelings of estrangement and hopelessness.

As another mother stated: "The problem with Indians is they never go out and try to find help. They just wait for help to come to them."

**Shyness and Sensitivity, Particularly
with Strangers, Often Manifested
in a Low Rate of Verbal Behavior
and a Reluctance to Share Personal Problems:**

Any statement which reflected a self-imposed social distance from others. If shyness and sensitivity are pan-Indian traits, it may follow that even if Indians do make contract with an agency, they will find the rapid, personal probings of professionals to be an affront to their dignity and may withdraw.

For purposes of this study, shyness was defined as a low rate of verbal behavior, a soft-spoken voice, the use of few gestures, and little spontaneous talking or leading of the conversation during interviews.

Six of the caretakers manifested a high degree of shyness in initial interviews and maintained some degreee of shyness throughout contacts. In spite of the shyness, the respondents openly discussed not only personal problems that were related to the developmentally disabled family member but also marital problems, problems with relatives on the reservation, and other problems of highly personal nature. These problems were described by the respondents without probing from the interviewer, often the purpose of asking for resources, but often just to have someone to share their concerns with.

Seven of the caretakers manifested initial shyness, which diminished almost totally by the end of the first interview or during the second interview. They were observed to become increasingly comfortable—increasing their verbal interactions, having more relaxed body postures, and engaging in joking.

Seven of the caretakers manifested none of the characteristics of shyness as defined for this study.

Five of the six respondents manifesting high degrees of shyness were fullblood Indians; all seven of those with medium degrees of shyness were fullblood Indians, and three of the seven who exhibited no shyness were fullblood Indians. Two of these reported having grown up in a predominantly Anglo environment.

Thus, shyness as defined from an Anglo perspective was exhibited more by fullblood Indian respondents. There was no association, however, between shyness and a reluctance to share personal problems, nor was shyness correlated to any of the demographic variables, such as length of time in the city, education, age, or income level.

Short-Term Future Orientation, Reflected in Lack of Long-Term Planning and Goals:

Any statement reflecting differentiation in compliance with short-term vs. long-term recommendations or treatments, or reflecting lack of concern about long-term prognoses of problems. If a short-term future orientation is a pan-Indian trait, Indians may see no value in extended "evaluations" of their children or in counseling sessions that have no immediate results. A parent may not be concerned with the long-term prognosis for a child with a developmental disability, but may tend to view the child on a daily or short-term basis.

Several mothers reported that they did not "see the point" in long-term evaluations or in repeated contacts with a professional, but that reaction could be related to lack of information from the professional regarding the purposes for the contacts. Five mothers had their children involved in long-term treatment programs and expressed no reluctance or questions about the programs.

Four caretakers reported inconsistencies in administering medication of a preventive nature to their developmentally disabled family members; three had seizure disorders and one had hormonal problems.

There was no strong evidence of this trait in relation to following through on other recommendations. While many mothers had not made phone calls which would result in obtaining information or services, reporting that they planned to but hadn't got around to it yet, it is difficult to assess the motivation behind this behavior, and it may have been more strongly related to passivity, shyness, or lack of knowledge about the purpose than to short-term future orientation.

Fatalistic View of Life, With Little Feeling of Control Over One's Life:

Any statement reflecting feeling that the primary caretaker or any professional intervention could have little effect on the problem. If there is a pan-Indian belief of fatalism, it may follow that a parent feels that there is nothing that can be done for a condition such as mental retardation, and therefore has no motivation or reason to seek help or to follow through with recommendations.

Only one mother made a direct statement reflecting this attitude. She commented that she had no opinion about professional services, because "What will happen will happen, regardless of how you're treated." The other caretakers all indicated by both statements and actual behavior their beliefs that they thought, or hoped, that interventions would be helpful, particularly special schools or training.

Respect for Individuality, Reflected in Child-Rearing Practices Where Discipline is Not Focused on Attempting to Control the Child's Behavior or Force Him or Her into Choices:

Any statement which expressed a low level of concern for deviant or delayed development. If respect for individuality is a pan-Indian value, families may be less motivated to seek help after learning that there is nothing critical about the child's condition and may not express a high level of concern or anxiety about the child's problem.

One mother reported that she did not think she would take her mentally retarded child for testing because she had asked the child, and he had indicated that he did not want to go. Another mother did not arrange for follow-up appointments after learning that the child's problem was not serious. There were no other indications of this trait in relation to service utilization.

Several caretakers expressed their beliefs that their children who had no language were just lazy and would start talking when they were ready; both children were older than five years. The parents of five children had not become concerned about language delay until they were three to four years old.

In relation to childrearing practices, six mothers were observed to place few limits on their children's disruptive behavior, meeting all of the children's demands. Five caretakers showed some tendency toward laissez-faire discipline, but this was not consistent. They appeared uncomfortable, and their behavior may have been influenced by the investigator's presence.

Nine of the mothers were highly concerned with discipline and with training of their children, and were highly concerned with the children's developmental lags. Only one caretaker seemed relatively unconcerned with the child's deviant development.

In general, while there were isolated examples of the characteristics described, none of the caretakers manifested a consistent trait of this nature, but exhibited concern about their children's symptoms and the possible causes of their problems.

Time Orientation That is Not
"Clock Oriented"; Casual Sense of Time
Reflected in Lack of "Punctuality":

Any statement which reflected a low level of concern about being on time for appointments. If a non-"clock-oriented" time orientation is a pan-Indian trait, urban Indians may be late for, or break, appointments to the degree where services become unavailable because of agency policies.

In relation to the investigator's contacts with the families, every respondent who was contacted for an interview wanted to know the specific time the investigator wanted to come. On six occasions, with six different families, no one was at home at the designated time, and they subsequently stated they had forgotten. Later appointments were all kept. Nine families commented when the investigator arrived more than ten minutes late.

Because many of the families (sixteen) were dependent on the Indian Free Clinic for transportation, they had little control over their promptness for interviews. Outreach workers reported occasionally having to wait for mothers to get ready, and a number of late appointments were due to transportation being late and also to traffic and parking problems. Two mothers who provided their own transportation were always on time. One complained about always having to wait for the professional.

Most families were observed to be "clock-oriented" in their daily lives, in getting children ready for school, planning activities, and being ready for rides. One mother commented that she was occasionally late for appointments because she always left home one-half hour before an appointment, regardless of where the appointment was.

In summary, this trait could not be confirmed or denied with the Indian subjects in this study, primarily because of their dependence on the Indian Free Clinic for transportation to appointments.

Strong Family and Extended Family Relationships;
Family Obligations and Interests are Primary:

Any statement which demonstrated that family activities or obligations had a negative effect on service utilization or compliance. If family relationships take precedence over other obligations, and this is a pan-Indian trait, it may follow that services would not be utilized if they interfered with family activities or responsibilities.

Only three of the families had extended family members in the area. While several others had relatives from out of state come to visit for varying lengths of time, there was no evidence that these visits interfered with service utilization or compliance. Three families made extended trips to their reservations during the process of evaluations, causing the evaluations to be delayed, but all three reestablished contact when they returned.

Several mothers broke appointments when their children were ill and they had no alternative child-care resources.

It is, of course, possible that this trait was not manifested because there were no family crises or obligations that arose to make an adequate assessment possible. Based on the available information from the caretakers, however, family obligations did not interfere with service utilization or compliance during the course of the project.

Noninterference in the Lives of Others; Direct Advice and Suggestions Are Viewed as Inappropriate Attempts to Control the Behavior of Others:

Any statement which reflected acceptance of others not giving advice (input), or any statement which reflected the attitude that advice should not be given to others (output). If a philosophy of noninterference is a pan-Indian trait, it follows that friends and relatives may not give advice regarding a child with a problem, and that caretakers would be reluctant to ask for specific advice from family, friends, or professionals.

Two families reported that they would not like to live on their reservations, because "everyone is always minding your business and telling you what to do." Two other families reported that they had not been concerned about their children until relatives had told them they thought something was wrong and they should get some help. One caretaker reported that her relatives kept trying to persuade her to have a traditional ceremony performed for the child, and that they criticized her for taking the child to a doctor.

Four caretakers reported that they were told by their parents that the causes of their children's problems were the results of something the mothers had done while pregnant, and several caretakers reported that their friends frequently gave them advice. Several caretakers, however, reported that other Indians never say anything about their children; they just mind their own business.

Almost all of the females respondents were observed giving advice to spouses and to children regarding doing chores and running errands. Several mothers reported that they never told their husbands what to do, because they did what they wanted to anyway, but that did not mean that they did not try.

There did not seem to be any reluctance on the part of any of the caretakers to receiving advice from professionals, and, in fact, they wanted specific suggestions and answers.

In general, a trait of noninterference did not seem to exist for any of the caretakers or, in most instances, for their relatives.

In summary, the primary finding of this area of the present study was that traits which reflect values and attitudes are difficult to define and measure. Where these traits have been described in the literature, they have not been operationally defined and thus have often resulted in generalizations and stereotypes, which were not easily discernible in this study. A beginning attempt was made to operationalize cultural traits; it is evident that greater refinement is needed and that definitions should be developed that have reliability for both Indians and non-Indians. The measurement of these traits is more difficult. As Steele states:

> . . . identity is not a static state but an ongoing process, particularly in a society undergoing constant change. . . . Certain behavioral characteristics can be isolated as denoting traditional Indianness. . . . But some of these alleged norms, values and traits are merely given lip service, others are deeply meaningful to most Indians, while many others are espoused by some people and dismissed by some. . . .
> A comprehensive assessment of this complex of attitudes and orientations would require prolonged, systematic research. . . . I suspect that the result might still be unsatisfactory, in light of the fluidity that characterizes cultural considerations. (Steele 1973: 105-06)

A comprehensive analysis of these traits was not within the scope of this study; the focus was on the manifestation of the specified traits in relation to service utilization and compliance, knowledge and beliefs about developmental disabilities, and observed interactions with the investigator. Two of the traits were assessed to be highly evident: passivity, particularly in relation to seeking services; and shyness in relation to interactions with the investigator and with other professionals.

Each trait was described in isolation, yet all of the traits interact and overlap in complex, subtle ways. Each individual is more than a sum of traits, just as Indian identity is more than a sum of scores on a Cultural Index with arbitrary categories.

Two of the cultural traits described, passivity and shyness, can also be defined as personality traits. While culture is the primary determinant for personality development through socialization practices and the shaping of behavior through group values and sanctions, each individual within the culture responds in a unique manner, based on a variety of factors, such as sex, rank in the family, temperament, and intelligence. This continuous interaction of culture and personality has been described by LeVine (1973) as the "two-systems" view of culture and personality theory.

American Indians who move to an urban area have unique personalities and have been shaped and reinforced to accommodate to a set of cultural norms and values, which are, in most instances, drastically different from and often incompatible with the norms and values that are predominant in an urban area such as Los Angeles. Based on the individual's personality, including his or her psychological needs, adaptation to urban living will occur at different rates and to different degrees for each person, and will be influenced by a complex interaction of economic, social, and other factors.

In this study, the term "urban Indian" does not describe or predict the values, practices, and preferences of any one Indian family or individual, as they manifested a wide variety of personality traits, cultural practices, and lifestyles.

UTILIZATION OF SERVICES

In examining the use of services by these urban Indian families, several factors were considered: their knowledge of special education programs in the schools prior to contact by the outreach project; their use of other services prior to contact; the number of appointments kept after contact; their compliance with recommendations made by professionals; their satisfaction with services; and the institutional barriers that impeded utilization.

Nine of the twenty caretakers knew that special education programs existed in the schools. Indeed, five of the nine had had direct contact with such programs. The extent of knowledge ranged from knowing someone in a "special class" to seeing a bus with handicapped children pass by every day. Eleven reported having no knowledge that special education existed. One caretaker stated she thought "school was only for normal children." Of the five who had had direct contact with special education programs, three had children in special education programs (two educable mentally retarded and one deaf), one had been approved and was waiting for funding (educationally handicapped), and one placement (educable mentally retarded) had been rejected by the parents.

In the use of other services prior to contact by the outreach project, one family had sought an evaluation and subsequent treatment for their child. Three had regular contact with physicians regarding some aspect of their children's problems, while the others had sought medical or other services only in times of crisis, not following through with recommendations for further help. It should be noted that ten of the eleven individuals with organic disorders had been diagnosed prior to contact by the project, as well as one of the thirteen functionally disordered. Only one parent, with a deaf child, appeared to have clear and adequate information regarding the disorder.

Following contact by the project, four families showed a high degree of initiative in making their own appointments and keeping them. Eight showed inconsistent behavior in making and keeping appointments, and the other eight repeatedly lost telephone numbers, forgot to call for appointments, and failed to keep appointments (usually without notification).

Compliance with recommendations was generally higher than appointment keeping, with only six families consistently failing to follow through on recommendations such as obtaining or giving medication, making subsequent appointments, or handling a behavior in a different way. But compliance is problematical in its definition. For example, one mother of a profoundly retarded twelve-year-old girl had totally complied with the pediatrician who had told her ten years before to "keep the child at home and treat her as normally as possible."

Satisfaction with services received appeared to be correlated with utilization and compliance. Four families were highly satisfied with all services received, and six showed some dissatisfaction with rushed interviews, lengthy travel time, and other factors, but were generally satisfied overall. Half of the families reported great dissatisfaction, stating that they felt their problems were misunderstood, and that they had not received what they expected or what the agencies promised. Most complained about the excessively long delays in receiving help.

Half of the families had limited knowledge of their children's disabilities and had utilized few if any services prior to contact by the project. During the project, families were provided transportation and other assistance in attempting to obtain help. Many had difficulty in following through and utilizing help, and most of them were dissatisfied with the services they did receive.

It is difficult to know all of the reasons why the majority of families had difficulty following through. Prior experiences, poverty, other priorities of problems in the family—all of these factors and more may have contributed. But before a judgment of resistance, lack of motivation, or cultural factors can be made, it is necessary to examine the role played by agencies in setting up barriers to the effective use of services by urban Indians or any other group of individuals in our society.

INSTITUTIONAL BARRIERS

Families were asked about thirteen kinds of agency policies and procedures and whether they presented any problems in accessibility for the families.

The greatest barrier cited was financial, which included not only direct costs to agency or doctors but also secondary costs, such as transportation (bus fare, parking, or gasoline), babysitters, and lunches away from home. Frequently the problem related to fear of costs, whether actual or perceived, which the family budget could not bear.

The second highest barrier was a lack of a clear understanding of the agency's procedures. Family members frequently had appointments with social workers, psychologists, or other professionals, but did not know the purpose of the meetings and, therefore, frequently did not consider them important. They were often unclear about whom to contact in various agencies, especially as their cases were frequently transferred or unassigned or in transit between an intake worker and someone else.

Transportation was an additional problem. While the clinic outreach workers assisted for many appointments, there were many others for which the families had no help. Most of them did not know how to use public transportation, were fearful of going far from home, or could not manage their children on buses. Attempts by the projects to locate transportation resources were futile, and very few agencies or professionals would make home visits.

The lack of child care services in agencies became distressingly apparent: most agencies which reputedly served children had no provisions for child care or even toys in their waiting rooms. Mothers frequently had no access to baby sitters and had to take their children with them. One mother reported trying to hold her overly active child on her lap while attempting to answer questions from the social worker. She was anxious about providing good answers and was also very much embarrassed by her child's behavior.

Waiting time between appointments, as well as waiting at the agency for appointiments to begin, provided another source of frustration, especially for mothers with several young children who became tired and hungry. Families often waited months to get services. One mother stated, "If they would just call you once in a while to let you know they care about you, it would help a lot."

Another problem was one of general discomfort related to feelings of being rushed, feeling embarrassment, and receiving impersonal interaction. One strong complaint was of professionals who would take phone calls during their interviews. Another mother stated: "All they asked about was my child . . . no one asked me any questions about how the rest of my family was." Several mothers felt embarrassed because they could not remember details about developmental milestones— and one mother was asked the same questions by eight professionals in three different agencies. Most of the mothers stated that they felt pressured to talk, and that they never knew what to say.

Contacts which were described as helpful and satisfactory were those in which the professional was sincere, had a good sense of humor, took plenty of time, and did not appear to be "judging" the mother.

Other barriers included distances to agencies and the limited hours during which the agency was open. Two factors presented major problems for only two families: size of the agency and paperwork. Most of them felt that those were things that could not be changed anyway.

The families were asked whether any questions were asked about their Indian backgrounds. Only two mothers reported that this was discussed at length, and five reported that they were asked about their tribes and where they were from. It is unlikely that the majority of professionals were unaware of their ethnicity.

The results of this research indicated that families who continued to use their traditional language and those who had frequent contact with the mother's reservation community showed lower initiative in utilizing services prior to contact by the outreach project. The only two cultural traits which received support were those of passivity and shyness, and these were related to lower utilization of services. These traits must be considered with great caution, however, as they may just as easily reflect socioeconomic status and the phenomenon of being a member of any minority group in our society.

PROFESSIONAL RESPONSES

In the past decade, there has been a steadily increasing number of books and articles written both for professional service-providers and for the general public about the cultural beliefs and behaviors of the many subcultures within our society. Many of these are written with ardent political fervor, many are highly personal autobiographies, and a few approximate scientific validity. Within the social work, medical, nursing, and psychology literature, a number of articles have appeared which attempt to explain the cultural values of particular groups and which usually include brief suggestions for intervention (Chen 1973, Good Tracks 1973, Kadushin 1972, Morales 1971). In all of the literature concerned with transcultural service delivery, there is agreement that mental health professionals do not currently have adequate knowledge for consistently sensitive and effective transcultural interactions with clients.

A major problem in effective transcultural service delivery may relate to the difference between culture and subculture in this society. The United States has been described both as "the great melting pot" and a "multicultural, pluralistic society." Many service providers may be ambivalent about whether to help clients "adapt" to the cultural values of the dominant group, by taking on white, middle-class values (for example, adopting the work ethic, striving to rise above poverty, glorifying youth), or whether to help clients strengthen and maintain their cultural uniqueness, especially when that uniqueness may be in conflict with the values of the larger society (and of the service providers who represent the larger society).

The current trend in mental health professionals is toward cultural pluralism. In order for transcultural service delivery to be effectve, professionals must develop the attitude that the United States is a society of many subcultures, and that effective interventions with individuals must be related to a thorough understanding of one's own values and the client's cultural values and attitudes, with the client's behavior considered both within that context and within the context of the conflicts between those cultural values and the values of the larger society.

In the present study, the knowledge and perceptions of the professionals who provided services to the Indian families were emphasized, to enable us to begin to understand the degree to which lack of knowledge of cultural factors or transcultural professional-client interactions may serve as a barrier to service utilization.

Mental health, educational, and medical service providers have not traditionally received training in transcultural service delivery, and they may even question how to utilize cultural variables in professional interactions. In order to obtain a more thorough understanding of Indian responses to professionals and to services provided, these issues were explored from the perspective of the professionals who interacted with the Indian families.

Questionnaires were sent to thirty-two professionals, who had contacts with ten of the families. Twenty-six questionnaires, from twenty professionals, were returned, representing contacts with seven caretakers. The disciplines of the professionals included social work, psychology, nursing, pediatrics, and psychiatry.

The twenty professionals had a total of ninety-five person-to-person contacts with seven caretakers. The number of contacts ranged from one to twenty, with a mean of four contacts. Six professionals had only one contact with a caretaker; the one professional who had twenty contacts was the only one to have more than eight contacts. Excluding that professional, the mean number of contacts was three. Eight of the respondents indicated that this was their first professional contact with an American Indian. (None of the professionals was Indian.) Seven reported having had contact with more than ten American Indian clients. Seven of the contacts were for intake interviews, twelve for evaluation, three for combined evaluation and treatment, two for treatment, and two for information sharing.

Twelve of the responses indicated that the families kept all scheduled appointments, nine reported that about 75 percent of appointments were kept, four reported 50 percent, and one less than 50 percent. For appointments not kept, six called ahead of time and rescheduled, five did not come but called at a later time, seven did not come or call. One of the families who kept all appointments was seen in their home.

Sixteen of the responses indicated that the caretakers were on time for all appointments kept. Six reported 75 percent of appointments were kept on time, one 50 percent, and four less than 50 percent. Reasons that the professionals understood for late appointments or cancellations included twelve who had transportation delays, three who had other family problems, two who forgot the appointment, and one who was misinformed about the time.

Professionals were asked what institutional barriers they felt presented problems for the families in using services—including transportation, cost, hours of the agency, size of the agency, paperwork, waiting time, location of the agency, and child care. They were also asked if lack of motivation, confusion or lack of knowledge about procedures, or family problems interfered with use of services. Twenty of the responses indicated that transportation was a problem, ten location of the agency, eight confusion or lack of knowledge about agency procedures, six family problems, five child-care arrangements, two hours of agency, and one lack of motivation. Cost, size of agency, paperwork, and waiting time were all considered to present no problems. Four "other" reasons were stated: one family moved, and three respondents related to the caretakers' shyness, reluctance to share problems, and confusion about the nature of the problem.

In comparing these responses to the Indian sample, a major difference is apparent. The professionals did not perceive cost of any problem at all (many of the services were free; others covered by insurance or medical), while cost was considered the major barrier by the families—primarily the secondary costs related to keeping appointments, such as bus fare, gas, parking, and babysitters.

The professionals reported giving a total of thirty-six recommendations to the caretakers. Seventeen were reported to have been followed through to a "high" degree, seven "medium," five "low," and seven unknown.

When asked the reasons they felt follow-through was a problem, nine responded transportation, eight confusion or lack of knowledge about agency procedures, six family problems, three location of agency, three child-care problems, two paperwork, one waiting time, and one because of passivity. None of the respondents felt that cost, hours of agency, or size of the agency were problems.

The professionals were asked to rate the caretakers on a five-point scale, from "high" to "low" on the following items: comfort in interview, concern about child's problem, awareness of child's problem, ability to communicate effectively, assertiveness, motivation for help, ability to seek out additional services on her own, shyness, and satisfaction with services. A summary of the ratings is shown in Table 8-2.

Comfort in interview scores indicate that most of the caretakers were seen as relatively comfortable during the interviews, with only one viewed as very uncomfortable and four as highly comfortable.

All but one of the caretakers were seen as concerned about their children's problems, with seventeen rated as highly concerned. Only two caretakers rated high on awareness of the problem, and one as low on awareness, with the others having some awareness from the professional's perspective.

Eleven of the twenty-six respondents rated the caretakers low on ability to communicate effectively, and six as high. These ratings indicate that this lack of ability may create problems for the caretakers in utilizing services, as assertiveness and shyness are often related to communication skills. Most of the caretakers were viewed as nonassertive, which may also be considered as passivity from a professional perspective. There were no clear patterns for shyness, with nine caretakers rated low and twelve rated high.

TABLE 8-2   Professionals' Ratings of Caretakers During Interviews

	RATING					
CARETAKER BEHAVIOR	HIGH		MEDIUM		LOW	NO RESPONSE
Comfort in interview	4	7	5		8	1	1
Concern about child's problem	17	8	0		1	0	0
Awareness of child's problem	2	10	7		6	1	0
Ability to communicate effectively	1	5	9		8	3	0
Assertiveness	0	3	5		10	8	0
Motivation for help	2	10	6		7	1	0
Ability to seek out additional services on own	0	2	5		8	9	2
Shyness	4	8	5		2	7	0
Satisfaction with services	2	10	4		2	0	8

Twenty-three responses rated the caretakers in the middle range of motivation for seeking help, but were generally viewed as unable to seek out additional help on their own.

Satisfaction with services was viewed as mainly slightly above average, although there were eight missing responses, possibly indicating that the professionals did not know whether the caretakers were satisfied.

In summary, the professional respondents generally viewed the caretakers as highly concerned about their children's problems, somewhat motivated for help, and generally satisfied with services. Ratings on comfort, communication skills, and awareness of the problem were generally average. The caretakers were also viewed as nonassertive and unable to seek services on their own, and most of the mothers were seen as somewhat shy.

The perception of the professionals tend to substantiate the cultural traits of passivity—both within the interview and in seeking additional services—and shyness. In spite of these traits, the caretakers' concern and motivation for help were clearly evident. The caretakers' lack of initiative in seeking services does not appear to be related to feelings that nothing can be done or to failure to perceive the disability as a problem, but may reflect a skill deficit in interactions with professionals and agencies.

CULTURAL FACTORS
IN CLIENT-PROFESSIONAL
INTERACTION

Seventeen of the responses indicated that there was no discussion during interviews that was related to the family's Indian background and culture. Seven reported there was some discussion, including asking the mother's tribe and how long she had been in Los Angeles. One reported discussing how her child-care practices were related to how she was raised. Two reported asking about life on the reservation, and one reported discussing Indian activities in Los Angeles.

Of the seventeen who stated that nothing was discussed, the following reasons were given: thirteen reported that it did not seem relevant to the purpose of the contact, two did not consider it important, two reported not wanting to overstress ethnic factors, one was unaware the caretaker was Indian, and one did not know what to ask. Three gave additional reasons, which included: "One parent is white . . . in reporting child's disability the ethnicity was not important." "Mother was very guarded and a trusting relationship has not yet been established." "I try to meet all ethnic groups on an equal basis."

"Did the mother say anything in your contacts that you think may have been related to her Indian cultural background and beliefs?" There were thirteen "no" response to this question, which represtened half of the sample. Five replied that the clients were passive or stoic, four commented about family interactions: leniency in disciplining the child, using beating as discipline, lack of concern about

play skills, and lack of involvement of the father. Two referred to mothers' comments about moving from the reservation, and one mentioned the art work in the home.

"Did the mother say or do anything that made you feel she was not comfortable in any of your contacts?" Eleven respondents answered "no" to this question. Eight described the mothers as reserved, nervous, withdrawn, ashamed, shy, depressed, and fidgety. Only two professionals described the mothers as comfortable.

"Do you think that knowing the family was Indian caused you to do or say anything different than you ordinarily would?" There were eighteen "no" responses to this question, which has several possible interpretations. Professionals may not behave differently because they do not feel culture or ethnicity require different behaviors; they may want to behave differently but feel that to do so may be misinterpreted as discriminatory or racist; they may behave differently without being aware of it; or they may behave differently but not want to admit it. Three professionals reported slowing down the pace; three stated they tried to be sensitive to the possibility of distrust of white agencies; one reported an awareness that "WASP standards do not always apply"; and one focused on their "expectations and beliefs within the structure of the relationship."

"Did you feel it necessary to consider any cultural factors in making recommendations or writing up the contact?" There were sixteen "no" responses to this question, and five indicated "yes" without giving any details. The five who gave detailed answers reported consideration of being raised on a reservation and attending a boarding school, recommendation of contacting other Indian mothers for support, and "the way their culture deals with affect." One professional commented: "With her lack of assertiveness I was not sure if the services offered were what she wanted" and, in a similar vein, another stated, "I felt the mother was not aggressive enough in seeking help for herself and her child."

"Were there any areas in which you felt you needed more knowledge of American Indian people and culture in order to have been more effective?" There were four "no" responses to this question. The other responses implied that even though cultural factors were not discussed, there was a perceived need on the part of the professionals to have more knowledge to better understand these families. Four professionals indicated a need or more knowledge about child-rearing practices, three about family dynamics. Other needs included attitudes toward bureaucracies, concepts of time, religion, problems of urban Indians as compared to the traditional perspective, and assessing emotional needs.

The professionals were aware of the need for more information; it is possible that they did not know how much weight to place on cultural variables and were either unaware at the time that these should be considered or were uncomfortable about how to gather information without appearing to overemphasize ethnicity or without making the mothers feel more uncomfortable.

"How was this mother like or unlike other American Indians you have worked with or know about?" Seven respondents did not answer this question;

eight had indicated this was their first professional contact with an American Indian. The others responded that this client was like other American Indians in passivity and difficulty in establishing rapport, having much tolerance with children, quiet and nonassertive, "stoically accepting the child's extreme behavior problems," and "poor and somewhat accepting of environmental circumstances as 'the way things are'."

The mothers who were reported to be unlike other American Indians were viewed as less involved, and as more cooperative and involved than expected.

In summary, the major theme in these transcultural interactions was one of discomfort on the part of the professionals and passivity or nonassertiveness on the part of the clients. None of the professionals reflected a sense of confidence or skill in the interviews. The discomfort of the professionals may have affected the clients and contributed to the perception of passivity.

The responses by the professionals relate to only seven of the caretakers, and may reflect only these limited experiences. The information from the other thirteen caretakers, however, was consistent with the reports of the seven represented here. There were no differences in the professionals by professional discipline, indicating a need for training in transcultural interactions for all disciplines that provide services to different cultures. There is both a need for specific content related to particular cultural groups—such as American Indians—and, perhaps more importantly, a need for strategies for knowing what areas to explore, how to ask questions to elicit information without making clients feel uncomfortable, and how to utilize cultural information in the assessment of a particular problem, such as developmental disabilities. Cultural factors need to be assessed with as much weight as psychological and social variables.

CULTURAL ASSESSMENT STRATEGIES

The identification of culturally relevant material is a difficult task, and cannot be easily distinguished from social and psychological factors. Our increased awareness of the importance of culture has led to considerable confusion in our practice of social work. It is impossible to have a thorough knowledge of the cultural values and patterns of behavior of every group with whom we have contact. In most cases, knowledge about one aspect of a culture, such as child-rearing practices, cannot be thoroughly understood without knowledge of all of the other aspects of the culture that interact with child-rearing, including sex roles, status, religion, marriage, health, and so on. There are the additional issues of the rapidly changing values of each succeeding generation and the changes in values and behavior depending on the area of residence, familiarity with traditional customs and language, contacts with other members of the same group, desires to assimilate, and other equally important factors. To understand traditional Navajo Indian culture, for example, may tell you very little about how to work with a family in which the mother is Navajo, the father half Sioux and half Apache, and the children born and raised in a city, with few reservation contacts and no knowledge of either parent's language.

This author's position is that, instead of focusing on the specific areas of Indian culture that the social work practitioner should know in order to be more ethnically competent, the critical task is to identify those common elements among American Indians—and other ethnic groups in our society—which need to be considered in the delivery of service. This is not to minimize the importance to the worker of familiarity with the values and customs of a particular people. But this knowledge must be used with caution and sensitivity for the individual client who is seeking help.

The following strategies for cultural assessment are offered as guidelines for social workers, and they apply to all transcultural interactions.

1. Consider all clients as individuals first, as members of minority status, and then as members of a specific ethnic group.

2. Never assume that a person's ethnic identity tells you anything about his or her cultural values or patterns of behavior.

3. Treat all "facts" you have ever heard or read about cultural values and traits as hypotheses, to be tested anew with each client. Turn facts into questions.

4. Remember that *all* minority group people in this society are bicultural, at least. The percentage may be 90-10 in either direction, but they still have had the task of integrating two value systems that are often in conflict. The conflicts involved in being bicultural may override any specific cultural content.

5. Some aspects of a client's cultural history, values, and lifestyle are relevant to your work with the client. Others may be simply interesting to you as a professional. Do not prejudge what areas are relevant.

6. Identify strengths in the client's cultural orientation which can be built upon. Assist the client in identifying areas that create social or psychological conflict related to bi-culturalism and seek to reduce dissonance in those areas.

7. Know your own attitudes about cultural pluralism, and whether you tend to promote assimilation into the dominant society values or to stress the maintenance of traditional cultural beliefs and practices.

8. Engage your client actively in the process of learning what cultural content should be considered.

9. Keep in mind that there are no substitutes for good clinical skills, empathy, caring, and a sense of humor.

Cultural traits describing subcultures in our society are profuse in the professional literature. This study is one attempt to question the basis for making generalized statements which are then universally applied. In this age of rapid change and acutely heightened awareness of the need to be culturally sensitive in work with clients, there is a dangerous tendency to look for instant, short cut knowledge. This tendency includes the desire to understand other cultures quickly and easily. But it is probable that no one individual will manifest all of the cultural traits described of a given group; caution must be taken that those who deviate from the assumed norm for that group are not viewed as pathological. Every individual presents a complex blend of cultural values, personality traits, personal history, and externally imposed social status.

> Professionals must be cautious about the attributions given to people based on assumed cultural traits. Clients must be considered as individuals first, sharing the same feelings and needs of all people seeking help such as embarrassment, shame, and feelings of inadequacy, and possible fears of discrimination. The interaction of culture and personality is complex and difficult to differentiate, and our task must be to resist looking for simple cultural categories to explain behavior. (Miller 1980: 56)

CHAPTER NINE
THE CHICANO FAMILIA
IN SOCIAL WORK
Theresa Aragon de Valdez
and Joseph Gallegos

The traditional relationship of the Hispanic community to the social work profession has mirrored that of Chicanos and the total society. What is reflected in this relationship is at worst a perpetuation of racism, and at best benign neglect. That social work, a helping profession that articulates humanistic values, has participated in maintaining Chicano powerlessness is ironic but nonetheless informative. It raises the question as to whether social work as a profession will continue to define the Chicanos as an outcast group with little claim to human respect and individual dignity.

Given that social work as a profession is a reflection of the dominant society, it is not surprising that Chicano perceptions of the profession are largely negative. Historically, social workers were representatives of agencies which sought to deport Chicanos, whether they were citizens or not. To a large extent social workers were

JOSEPH GALLEGOS received his Ph.D. from the University of Denver in 1978. His interests include cross-cultural mental health research in social policy and direct services. He is currently the co-director of the Multi-Ethnic Mental Health Training Project at the University of Washington School of Social Work and Chair of the Council on Social Work Commission on Minority Groups.

THERESA ARAGON DE VALDEZ is on the faculty of the School of Social Work at the University of Washington. Previously, she served as Vice Provost for Special Programs and is a member of the political science faculty, also at the University of Washington. Originally from New Mexico, she received her BA from Seattle University, her MA from the University of New Mexico, and her Ph.D. in political science from the University of Washington. She is active in the Chicago community nationally and locally.

perceived as enforcement agents of the dominant society, rather than as helping persons. The "aid" that Chicanos received from the profession was perceived by Chicanos as assistance in getting deported, denial of welfare checks, loss of children to courts and jails, and even the sterilization of many Chicanas.

~ Prior to the 1960s, social work as a profession had not addressed itself in a positive way to providing for the needs of Chicano constituencies. As noted, the "service" provided was in the nature of enforcement for agencies of control and was not addressed to Chicano needs. Chicanos had not been identified as a constituency; they had been identified as a problem. Research oriented toward developing a basic understanding of Chicanos was not undertaken. As a profession, social work was historically, culturally, and linguistically ignorant of the Chicano, and as such was unable to address itself to their needs.

Given the lack of research and the behavior evidenced by social workers in relation to Chicanos, one can assume that the profession, when it did address itself to Chicanos, did so on the basis of stereotypes supported by dated social science research and derived from popular opinion. That is, they proceeded on the assumption that Chicanos were aliens representing an inferior culture and that this, not their relationship to the larger society, was the cause of their problems.

The socioeconomic and political climate of the 1960s, created in part by minorities, provided a receptive climate for Chicanos and other minority persons in · the U.S. to act on their grievances. Although minorities had to do so through force, conflict, and confrontation, the message was clear. It said, "Ya basta...," "Enough, already!"

The fact that as a result of this struggle minorities were able to gain recognition of their American citizenship, at least at the federal level, gave them clout in dealing with the institutions of the dominant society. For instance, Chicanos demanded full and equal access to necessary social services, including health and mental health services. They insisted that delivery of these services be accomplished in ways cognizant of the Chicano's linguistic and cultural distinctiveness. This had enormous implications for staffing, as well as for the development of new programs to provide relevant services. These services included assistance in organizing communities and in planning ways to facilitate self-determination for those communities.

The Hispanic community was also demanding representation of its members among the student bodies and faculties of schools of social work. Within these schools, demands were being made for the incorporation of Chicano content into the curriculum, for research that focused on developing culturally and linguistically valid approaches for working with Chicanos, and for programs and training placements that would directly involve the Chicano community. Although these demands may have seemed severe and strident at the time, we must remember that they were made within the context of a long history of neglect by service agencies and the necessity for responding to the grievances of citizens of the United States whose needs had been previously ignored by the social service profession.

Although Chicano citizenship rights were recognized at the federal level during the late 1960s, there remained the difficult struggle of exercising that citizenship at the local level—within the communities, the social service agencies, and the mental health clinics. This struggle, which manifests itself in a variety of ways, continues to this day. For instance, administrative policies on eligibility for income assistance (public assistance, food stamps, Supplemental Security Income) have consistently discriminated against Chicanos. In some instances, the inability of the profession to provide relevant services resulted in ignoring the needs of Chicanos, placing them at the end of the line, or putting them in the hands of bilingual clerical staff members who could relate to them but could not provide the services they needed.

In the area of health care, Chicanos have been able to obtain funding for farmworker clinics. However, they are staffed primarily by monolingual, Anglo professionals; the struggle to increase Chicano representatives among those training and receiving training in the health profession continues. Federal and state health assistance in the form of Medicaid for Chicanos is often cancelled by hospital policies that refuse to accept these coupons from Chicanos.

Another facet of this struggle is the profession's need to understand the Chicano family and culture if it is to be effective in the delivery of social services. It is not sufficient to grant the right to social services. Access to social services which are not matched to Chicano needs as those needs are perceived by Chicanos cannot have a meaningful impact on the problem. Although some would argue against the necessity of providing culturally relevant services, research clearly suggests that the examination of patient cultures as a source of information be considered in the total helping process, particularly in its diagnostic phase.

The need for cross-cultural social work has been well documented in the introductory chapters of this text. A dynamic model, incorporating a transactional concept of ethnicity and culturally based patterns of help-seeking behavior, focuses on the relationships between social work and minority groups and on the programmatic consequences of these relationships. The ability to utilize this model requires, at a minimum, some understanding of the history of a minority group and of how that history reflects on the contemporary social service needs of the group.

HISTORICAL BACKGROUND

The American Indian and the Chicano were the only minorities in this country who were annexed by conquest and whose rights were supposed to be guarded by the provisions of treaties with the United States. The history of these two groups in the United States could have been foretold by the fact that the treaties were more often honored in the breach than in the promise. The Treaty of Guadalupe Hidalgo (1848) signaled the end of the war with Mexico and the beginning of Chicano history in the United States. There had been a long history of conflict between the United States and Mexico prior to the Mexican-American War. The Mexicans were justifiably suspicious of the imperialistic tendencies of northern neighbors who predicted that "it would be the destiny of their country to extend its beneficent rule over the entire continent" (Duran and Bernard 1973: 75). There were numerous incidents along the border, and particularly developments in the Mexican territory known as Texas, that resulted in the war. Several offers had been made to buy Texas from Mexico, beginning with those made by John Quincy Adams. These offers were refused by Mexico. Finally, in 1835, the Texans declared their secession from Mexico, and Austin gave the call to arms. The Texas war has been summarized by Harriet Martineau, who called it the "most high-handed theft of modern times" (Acuna 1972: 11). The ensuing battles, especially those of the Alamo and San Jacinto, generated hatred that was to last well beyond the end of the war.

The United States, guided by the doctrine of Manifest Destiny and directed by Polk, a president with an expansionist mandate, annexed Texas in 1845 and moved troops into the area. Mexico moved troops across the Rio Grande to protect her territory, and Polk sent a war message to Congress. Congress declared war on May 13, 1846. Polk justified the war by accusing Mexico of being the aggressor. The rationalization for this accusation was based on and excused by the doctrine of Manifest Destiny, that is, the presumed right of the government to spread democracy and Christianity to those considered less fortunate.

However, these rationalizations overlooked the fact that the war was provoked and executed by the United States for a number of political and economic reasons, not the least of which had to do with the question of slavery in the land of freedom and equality (Ruiz 1963: 168-69). The war culminated in the Treaty of Guadalupe Hidalgo, which was ratified by the U.S. Senate on March 10, 1848. Mexico ceded Texas and California and the vast expanse of land between them (which total represented more than half of Mexico's land), and was to receive $50,000,000, plus the cancellation of unpaid claims (approximately $2,000,000) against its government from the United States (Duran and Bernard 1973: 175). However, even given the amount of land lost, "nothing was more galling to the Mexican officials who negotiated than the fact that they were compelled to assign, as it were, a large number of their countrymen to the Yankees" (McWilliams 1968: 101).

It was because of the strength of these feelings that the Mexican negotiators saw to it that the treaty contained explicit provisions for the rights of these people. Articles 1 through 11 of the treaty addressed protection of the rights of the individuals remaining in the land ceded to the United States. These articles guaranteed the full right of U.S. citizenship, the protection of all property belonging to Mexicans—including all land held by Mexicans prior to 1846—and freedom of religion.

It could be said that the Anglo-Americans deprived the Chicanos of all rights of citizenship, but it would be more appropriate to say that these rights were never granted. The guarantees of the treaty were ignored. The Anglo-Americans made every effort to impose their culture and language on the Chicanos. The establishment of Anglo dominance followed a similar pattern throughout the Southwest. The pattern of establishing dominance was facilitated by the fact that Anglo-Americans were given political control over the territories from the outset. In addition. Chicanos were not considered to be citizens; rather, they were still considered to be enemies and were so treated.

The Anglo-Americans used their control of the government and public offices to facilitate the takeover of the land belonging to the Chicanos in the Southwest. Because they controlled both the legislative mechanisms and the economic resources, such as the banks, they were able in many instances to take over the Chicanos' land in a "legal" fashion. An example of such a "legal" procedure—one that was repeated throughout the Southwest—was that of placing exorbitant tax assessments on lands owned by the Chicanos, inadequately publicizing the fact that they had to be paid by a given date, and then having the land sold off at auction when the Chicanos were unable to pay or did not know that a deadline had passed. As soon as the lands were sold to Anglo-Americans, the tax assessments were lowered considerably.

The blatant injustices were such as to prompt one writer to note that:

> Not only were the Mexicans bamboozled by the political factions; but they were victimized by the law. One law applied to them and another, far less rigorous, to the political leaders and to the prominent Americans. The Mexicans suffered not only in their persons but in their property. The old land-owning Mexican families found their titles in jeopardy and if they did not lose in the court, they lost to their American lawyers. The humble Mexican doubted a government that would not protect their person, and the higher classes distrusted one that would not safeguard their property. (Walter Prescott Webb, quoted in McWilliams 1968: 101)

The Anglo-Americans used notions of cultural and racial superiority and of Manifest Destiny to rationalize and justify encroachment on Mexico before the war and on Chicanos after the war. Such justifications were apparently more palatable and acceptable to the Anglos than was a straightforward recognition of their real motivations of economics and profit. By the end of the nineteenth-century, Anglo-Americans controlled economic and political structures and procedures in such a way as to ensure that Chicanos would remain powerless. The internal colonialization of the Chicano in the United States had been established.

The immigration of substantial numbers of Mexicans to the U.S. began in the early 1900s and greatly augmented the existing Chicano population, especially in the Southwest. The history of both legal and illegal Mexican immigration in this country has been discussed and documented in a number of sources, as have the experiences of the immigrants in this country (Acuna 1972; Meier and Rivera 1972; Grebler et al. 1970; Garlarza 1969; Gamio 1930, 1931).

Although the increased numbers of Mexicans in the U.S. may have represented a threat to the racial sensitivity of many Anglo-Americans, they were not felt to represent a threat in any substantive terms. The increase in the number of Chicanos and Mexicans represented no threat of a change in the existing balances and in the established relationships, because the structures and procedures of dependencies were already well-established, and the mechanisms to reinforce the dependent relationship were already available to Anglo-Americans.

During the first quarter of the century, agribusiness was able to recruit labor in Mexico whenever it was needed. Agribusiness was quick to develop networks with coyotes (labor smugglers) and *engachadores* (contractors) to attract, transport, sell, and exploit Mexican labor. The railroads also relied heavily on Mexican labor, with roughly 90 percent of their section and maintenance crews in the Southwest being made up of Mexicans by 1910. The railroads also were instrumental in providing Mexican labor for urban industries in the Midwest.

The Immigration Act of 1917 sought to put some restrictions on Mexican immigration by placing a head tax ($8.00) on Mexicans and applying the literacy provisions of the Act to them. These laws were ignored by those who were profiting from Mexican labor. Shortly afterward, the exigencies of an impending war were used as justification for waiving the head tax and literacy provisions for Mexicans and opening up the free flow of labor across the border. The interests that profited from Mexican labor were able to prevail in all the congressional debates on legislation that sought to put restriction on Mexican immigration. They were also able to get the legislation enacted that began a *bracero* (contract labor) program that lasted until 1963. (Galarza 1969).

The exploitation of Mexican laborers through the *bracero* program was aided by local governments that were friendly to the interests of agribusiness. The growers established associations, through which they contracted for labor. These associations, in combination with local and federal agencies, controlled the supply, distribution, and wages of the Mexican workers. The individual worker had no recourse to redress grievances, had no rights, and was expendable.

The subordinate status of the Chicano, the Mexican immigrant, and the Mexican *bracero* is well evidenced by what happened during the period of economic depression and recession in the United Stated. During the depression of the 1930s, Chicanos and Mexicans were "repatriated" en masse. Their rights to public assistance were completely denied. Local governments decided that it was cheaper to repatriate Mexicans (they did not distinguish between citizens and noncitizens— they all looked like foreigners) than to subsidize them with public funds (Grebler et al. 1970).

Although Operation Wetback in the 1950s was supposed to be a diligent enforcement effort to deport undocumented workers, it is interesting that a concern for enforcement should have come about in a period of economic recession. Here again, it made little difference for those Chicanos who were citizens. If they did not have their papers with them they were boarded onto trains and sent off to Mexico. Similar concerns with enforcement regarding undocumented workers have occurred in the past few years, again in a period of economic recession.

It is important to note that the Chicanos' struggles to obtain and exercise their rights as citizens in the United States did not begin with the civil rights movement of the 1960s. The history of the Chicanos' struggles for equality to exercise the rights guaranteed them by the constitution of the United States began with the signing of the Treaty of Guadalupe Hidalgo. The resistance to Anglo control prior to the twentieth century took the form primarily of violence, for which there was massive retaliation and reprisals, with the Chicanos suffering the major losses.

Many of the Chicanos who struggled for the liberation of their people during this time were labeled by the dominant society as outlaws and *banditos,* and by Chicanos as heroes.

The period of 1900 to 1945 is important, because during this time a number of the strategies that would be utilized during the Chicano movement in the 1960s were developed and used. The issues that would be highlighted during the movement were articulated and addressed. Further, the major themes of the ideology governing the Chicano movement of the late 1960s and 1970s were delineated for the first time during this period. These themes included political representation and participation, access to equal bilingual and bicultural education, access to equal economic opportunities, opposition to institutional racism and discrimination, the need for adequate social services, and the need for political unity and maintenance of cultural integrity. These concerns were first addressed at El Primer Congreso Mexicanista de 1911, but not until the 1960s were they translated into large-scale activism.

The consequences of racial discrimination and economic exploitation forced the Chicanos to depend on themselves for survival in the United States. The organizations that had been supportive and of assistance to other immigrants, such as churches, schools, and unions, provided little if any assistance to the Chicano and his immigrant brother. Government agencies with the responsibility of providing assistance to U.S. citizens and immigrants to this country found it easier to deport or repatriate the Chicanos (Grebler et al. 1970, Moore and Cuellar 1970).

Chicanos formed a number of mutual aid societies, known generally as *mutualista* organizations, for the purpose of providing fundamental social and economic support for their members. There were also a number of social action organizations established after the 1920s. These organizations generally followed an ideology of adaptation and accommodation to the Anglo-American society. They took a defensive posture, and their major strategy was one of instructing the membership in the arts of good citizenship and in the English language. Several of these organizations still exist today, including LULAC (League of United Latin American Citizens) and the G.I. Forum, which are found in all areas that have even a minimum Chicano population.

During this period, Chicanos also became involved in the labor movement, especially in the Southwest, where they initiated much of their own union activity. Chicanos organized in an effort to increase their wages, but they also found organization necessary for protection against discrimination (Valdez 1978). The first attempt to form a union of agricultural workers in the United States was spearheaded by Chicanos led by Juan Gomez, who called a strike in the Texas Panhandle in 1883 (Valdez 1978). Chicano miners were instrumental in initiating strike activity in Arizona as early as 1903 (Acuna 1972). But because of the nonacceptance of Chicanos in the more conservative labor unions, Chicanos were forced to organize their own unions or to align with extreme radical groups. Their association with radical labor and with the anarchist syndicalists soon resulted in Chicanos being branded as radicals and "dirty Reds." The fact that Chicanos were discriminated against by majority labor created a vacuum that was readily filled by the Communist Party and its affiliated organizations, such as the Cannery and Agricultural Workers Industrial Union (CAWIU). Chicanos were active in and supported by the International Workers of the World (IWW) and initially by the Congress of Industrial Organizations (CIO) (Acuna 1972).

The chronology of unions and strike activity by Chicanos in an effort to improve their wages and working conditions between 1900 and 1945 is a long one. However, none of their efforts could be judged successful in terms of their immediate objectives. Their efforts toward "self-organization were crushed—with violence and gross brutality, with mass arrests, deportations, and repatriations" (Valdez 1978: 51).

The mechanisms that had set in place to ensure Chicano subjugation prior to the turn of the century were used throughout these forty-five years to keep Chicanos "in their place." Law enforcement and other government agencies worked hand-in-hand with employers to provide the Chicanos with their "second defeat" in this country (McWilliams 1968). The second defeat was climaxed by the Zoot Suit Riots, which took place in Los Angeles during the summer of 1943. These riots represented a full-scale offensive against the Chicano minority (Turner and Surace 1956, Tuck 1943). The Zoot Suit Riots began on June 3, 1943. Members of the armed forces prepared to fight for democracy abroad by harassing, undressing, and beating Mexican-American youths in the streets of Los Angeles. The law enforcement agencies of the area welcomed this form of assistance for ridding themselves of the Mexican-American problem and were quite content to follow behind the servicemen and arrest the often nude and bleeding Mexican-American youths (McWilliams 1968).

The Mexican government found it necessary to intervene (as it had several times previously) in an effort to obtain protection of the rights of Chicanos. Both the intervention of the Mexican government (our allies in World War II) and that of the U.S. federal government was needed to settle the Zoot Suit Riots. If nothing else was accomplished by this rioting, the U.S. government finally admitted that its citizens of Mexican descent were "Americans." In its communications with Mexico throughout the incident, the United States government stipulated that this was a matter which concerned and involved only "Americans."

The Chicano struggle following World War II was heightened by an awareness of rights—if one can fight and die for a country as a citizen, then one should share the rights of citizenship. The struggle was also fueled by changes brought about during and as a result of the war. Among those changes were greater urbanization of the Chicanos, a shift from agricultural to industrial employment, a greater opportunity for education (G.I. bill), and some degree of acculturation. The struggle after the war and up to the mid-1960s was a political one, which focused on efforts to effect change by working within the system. It was political in that it sought to confront issues within the political arena and through government intervention.

However, the fear of deportation during the 1950s and during Operation Wetback had been sufficient to silence a number of Chicano activists. After this period came the McCarran-Walter Act and the McCarran Internal Security Act, which threatened internment in camps, deportation, or denaturalization for such political acts as being members or affiliates of what were defined as subversive organizations, effecting an almost complete intimidation of Chicano leaders. During that era, aliens equaled radicals—who were, of course, assumed to be Communists. A good number of Chicanos, especially working-class union organizers, were deported for engaging in political activities, such as setting up ethnic units within the trade union locals, belonging to the workers' alliance, being members of relief organizations during the depression, or being members of the CIO. A considerable number of Chicanos were subjected to denaturalization proceedings (Acuna 1972).

  ¯ After approximately 115 years of struggle, Chicanos were still effectively subjugated by the dominant society. Critical changes in the characteristics of the Chicano populations, such as a high degree of urbanization, less migration, a steady decrease in the number of foreign-born Chicanos or of those born of foreign parents, a higher level of educational attainment, a degree of acculturation, and a developing lower-middle class, had little impact on the overall status of Chicanos as a group. By the mid-1960s many Chicanos were disillusioned and angered by their lack of progress—by the lack of real change—in their overall condition. They were critical of themselves for having thought that the sacrifice of their culture and values would obtain freedom and equality in the United States. Now they knew better.

  The political and social environment of the 1960s was conducive and supportive to the civil rights movement. The Chicanos said, "Ya basta," and their demands and struggle for equality and participation became known as the Chicano Movement during the mid-1960s and early 1970s. The Chicano Movement resulted in a number of procedural changes, which gave Chicanos the "right" (federal clout) to exercise their civil rights, and which also provided access to "equal opportunity." Among the changes were equal access to education, employment, political participation (voting), social and mental health services, and enforcement of the right to bilingual-bicultural education.

  However, lest we assume that procedural access to their rights meant viable access and a substantive improvement in the status of Chicanos, it is important to note that the socioeconomic and political status of Chicanos as a group has not been substantively changed. While there was a period of minor gains during the 1960s and early 1970s, various analyses of social indicators provide evidence that Chicanos are still on the lower rungs of the ladder relative to members of the dominant society.

CHICANOS TODAY AND TOMORROW

At the present time, Chicanos are the fastest growing minority in the United States. By the year 2000, Chicanos, combined with others of Latino descent, will be the largest minority population in the United States. After Mexico City, Los

Angeles has the largest urban population of persons of Mexican descent. But there are numerous misconceptions that have resulted in problems for Chicanos. Several of these problems center around the establishment and delivery of social and health services to Chicanos. One major misconception is that Chicanos are essentially a rural, migrant population of agricultural workers. Yet over 80 percent of Chicanos reside in urban areas, and continued urbanization is a consistent trend in the American Chicano population. Most urban Chicanos reside in high-density, central city areas, which evidence all the characteristics of poverty. At this time the major impact of urbanization on the Chicano family is one of the adaptation. In many instances families migrate to large urban areas in search of employment, only to find that they lack skills for any but the most demeaning jobs.

Another broadly held misconception is that the civil rights movement and subsequent legislation, combined with the War on Poverty, have taken care of the "Chicano problem." As noted above, the struggle of the mid-1960s and early 1970s provided procedural access for Chicanos and other minorities. It did not, however, result in changing structural inequalities. Symptoms and not causes were addressed, and, as a result, equal access has not meant viable access. In addition, the Chicanos' ability to utilize "equal access" to education, employment, and social and health services is circumscribed by a history of accumulated inequalities, as well as by linguistic and cultural differences. Therefore it is not surprising to find that as of 1978, 23 percent of the Chicano population over twenty-five years of age had completed less than five years of school, and less than half of that age group, as compared to the dominant population, had completed high school. Twice as many Chicano families as those of the dominant society are below the poverty level. Approximately two thirds of Chicano families have an income under $15,000, as compared to less than one half of majority families with incomes below $15,000. The median income for the white male is $10,123, as compared to $7,708 for the Chicano male (Gallegos and de Valdez 1979).

Thus, exclusion historically has been the operative variable in defining the boundaries between the Chicano and the Anglo. In recent years, promises of assimilation have been neglected or have been expounded under the guise of the melting-pot theory. But these ideas ask that the Chicano accept the blame for being excluded from the dominant society. The consequences of this exclusion have been two-fold. First, the Chicano has been forced to maintain a strong sense of cultural integrity, especially in the areas of values and language. Second, Chicanos as a group have been kept in a dependent poverty status. Chicanos and other minorities have had to depend on themselves for survival. Exclusion from the mainstream and from major culture organizations has resulted in the development of parellel organizations to meet the service and social needs of the Chicano community. Chicanos understand their powerlessness, and so have used or developed alternative organizations to increase their political power. Three of these are the Church, the service organization, and the political organization. We will describe each of these three organizations briefly.

THE CHURCH

The majority of Chicanos are nominal, if not practicing, Catholics, and the religious norms of the Church play an important role in daily life. The rites of entry, Baptism, Confirmation, and Holy Communion are highly valued and fully celebrated by the extended family and friends. Great care is given to the selection of the *padrino* and *madrina* (godparents) for the care of the child, because the *padrinos* become a part of the extended family. The Church attends at births, deaths, and marriages, but the Chicano customs that surround the sacraments are maintained and reinforced by the extended family and community, not by the Church.

It is important to note that the Church has not played a role in unifying religion and ethnicity for Chicanos, as it did for other immigrant groups. One recalls the Irish, Italian, or Polish Catholic Church. One does not speak, however, of the Chicano or Hispanic Catholic Church in this century, nor have the Chicanos developed their own parallel, as the blacks did with the Protestant denominations.

The Catholic Church took an essentially antagonistic stance with respect to Chicanos. This is explained in part by the subordinate status of Chicanos vis-à-vis the dominant society, but also by the Church's missionary stance with regard to Chicanos (Breely 1972, Grebler et al. 1970). This stance, combined with the lack of social involvement and advocacy, explains why the Church's impact has been limited to the religious life of the Chicano. The impact of the Church as an institution has occured only in areas such as villages, where Chicanos are the majority population and where the parish priest is a Chicano. Allegiance to the Church as an institution seems to vary in proportion to the degree to which the Church is perceived as reinforcing and maintaining ethnic identity.

The religious precepts of the Church, however, are in many ways a controlling factor in the lifestyle of Chicanos. They are especially controlling of the Chicano woman's life, for part of her traditional role is to reinforce the principles of the Church and to assure her family's salvation through her example and her prayers. Even nontraditional Chicanos who have been raised as Catholics feel the impact of the Church through this prescribed role. Nowhere is this more true than in issues of sex, birth control, and divorce. The woman is supposed to model herself after the Virgin Mary. Sex is strictly limited (on pain of mortal sin) to those who are married. Of course, a double standard exists. Maintaining the cult of virginity is the woman's responsibility. Men's sexual freedom is condoned, if not encouraged, within the culture.

The Church's stance on divorce has relaxed to the extent that a person is no longer automatically excommunicated if he or she divorces. However, the strong Church sanctions against divorce still keep people married longer than is tolerable in many instances and produces guilt about remarrying if either partner has had a divorce. Examples of the impact of the Church in this regard are plentiful, but the following case should suffice to make the point.

A Chicana in her late fifties, who had divorced the father of her eight children when he abandoned her, and remarried several years after, was stricken with cancer.

She was denied the sacraments, since she had been excommunicated. However, she had faithfully attended Mass all her life and had raised her children as Catholics. On her deathbed she asked for a priest and expressed a wish to receive the Eucharist and the last sacraments. The condition on which she was permitted to receive these sacraments was that she agree to forsake her husband of over twenty years—the partner of her second marriage—to renounce her marriage, and to ask God's forgiveness for this grave sin. Further, if through some miracle she should recover, she could no longer maintain the relationship with her husband. The second marriage was not recognized, and, as far as the Church was concerned, she was living in sin.

The Church's stance on birth control has unofficially wavered, but its stance on abortion has remained firm. This fact explains to some degree the large size of most Chicano families, for many Chicanos continue to have children when they cannot afford them economically, physically, or emotionally. It also explains the psychological trauma experienced by some younger Chicanas who elect to use birth control methods other than rhythm, since it is held that they are using unnatural methods to thwart God's intention of procreation, and that each "pill" represents accumulated loss of grace. While the Chicano family does not sanction an illegitimate birth, the chances of such a child being raised by the family are good.

Clearly, the impact of the Church's religious precepts are not felt equally in all segments of the Chicano community. A number of variables mitigate against this, including class, education, degree of acculturation, density of Chicano population, and rural-urban differences. General observation would suggest that the Church's impact is felt less among college-educated, middle-class, nontraditional Chicano families who are living in urban areas not significantly populated by Chicanos. The impact of the Church would be greater on those of lower socioeconomic status, who adhere to traditional cultural norms and customs, and who reside in areas where the majority population is Chicano, such as rural villages or urban barrios.

COMMUNITY SERVICE ORGANIZATIONS

Community service organizations and mutal aid societies perform many needed functions in the Chicano community. As a result of the Chicano movement, many of these parallel service organizations receive federal funds in order to expand services, and this number has been augmented by community-focused (and often controlled) subunits of social service agencies, particularly in organizations such as community mental health clinics, migrant education programs, and farmworkers' clinics.

Mutual aid societies continue to play a role in providing emergency assistance and various forms of burial insurance. They are essentially conservative organizations and are not known for social advocacy. Their existence and to some degree their efficacy are greatest in rural agricultural areas and in the barrios of the Southwest.

Community service organizations in the Chicano community are usually categorized according to the services they offer, the degree of Chicano control, and the political stance of the organization. The most prevalent Chicano community organization is the multiservice type. This does not necessarily mean that such organizations provide *all* services. Rather, they provide some services and provide referrals and/or advocacy in obtaining other services, especially from governmental entities, such as employment agencies or departments of social and health services.

These organizations vary in size from community to community, and also within communities. Northwest Rural Opportunities (NRO) is an example of one of the largest and most capable of these organizations. It developed from a volunteer, grass-roots organization into a multimillion-dollar operation, servicing the many and varied needs of the Pacific Northwest's migrant population. NRO is staffed primarily by Chicanos and is directed by a board of Chicanos. At the other extreme are the "shoestring organizations" that usually develop around a particular need or issue and are maintained by volunteers. Eventually these miniorganizations either are absorbed into larger organizations, expand, or die.

It is not unusual to find several organizations purporting to offer the same services to the Chicano community. Consequently, territorial or turf battles, while infrequent, nevertheless do occur. Another recurring phenomenon in Chicano communities is the purposeful establishing of organizations to provide services that are already being provided by an existing Chicano organization. This is often done for political reasons, that is, to cater to that portion of the constituency whose political stance is different from that of the existing organization.

Community service organizations and clinics have benefited the Chicano community in ways other than providing needed services. They have often given to the community both ownership and involvement in the administration and direction of program and services. Even the turf battles, while dysfunctional in that they sometimes factionalize the community, are useful in serving to politicize and increase public awareness.

Chicano allegiance and willingness to be served by these organizations are predicted on two factors. The strongest of these is the organization's record in helping individuals or families. The second factor is the political stance and advocacy strategies that are employed by the organization. If potential clients find that an organization's political stance is radically different (in most cases, too radical), they may select an alternate Chicano organization if there is one, or, if not, they may seek help from an organization in the dominant society. A high degree of acculturation (which usually coincides with higher socioeconomic status) sometimes mitigates against use of services offered by Chicano organizations. Strong cultural identity, on the other hand, is a motivation for exhausting all available Chicano sources for help before seeking direct assistance from the dominant society.

POLITICAL ORGANIZATIONS

Chicano political organizations have played primarily an educational role in the Chicano community. These organizations, with the exception of La Raza Unida (a third party founded in Texas and partially expanded to Colorado and California) are nonpartisan in nature. Their activities for the most part are local, and may consist of registration and getting-out-the-vote drives, forums, lobbying on issues of concern to Chicanos, and, occasionally, endorsing or running candidates and campaigning for them.

The effectiveness of these organizations is essentially local in nature. None have been effective when they have sought to expand outside of the originating state. The best known, La Raza Unida Party, had several electoral successes in rural areas of Texas. Others are MAPA (Mexican American Political Association), in California, and PASO (Political Association of Spanish Speaking Organizations), in Texas. Strictly speaking, there is no one Chicano political organization that can be said to represent all Chicanos. Politically, Chicanos are as diverse in their philosophies and allegiances as are members of the dominant society. The success of these political organizations at the local level speaks to the greater potential for homogeneity of issues and concerns in a smaller area, and does not, as some have noted, suggest that Chicanos are incapable of organizing nationally. Coalitions of local Chicano organizations service Chicano concerns at the national level.

It should also be noted that, due to costs in energy, time, and money, involvement in political organizations appeals primarily to the middle or upper classes. The Chicano community as a whole is of lower socioeconomic status. Consequently, the pool from which political organizations may draw is miniscule. The only exception has been La Raza Unida, which was able to draw a strong core of support from low-income Chicanos. A good deal of that support can be explained by the fact that the party could offer tangible results, as has been the case with the farmworkers' union in California.

Even though Chicanos do not have and probably would not want a national political organization, they have increased their potential for lobbying and applying political pressure at the national level in a number of ways. Among these have been the involvement of previously nonpolitical organizations such as LULAC (League of United Latin Citizens) and the G.I. Forum, both social and service organizations of long standing in the Chicano community. These two organizations (although considered ultraconservative in many quarters) are now illustrative of the very thin line between social service and political organizations in the Chicano community.

More recent political organizations operating at the national level include El Congreso (a lobbying organization for the Spanish-speaking), and IMAGE, an organization of Chicano federal employees. In addition, MALDEF is the national litigation and legal education arm of Chicanos. The fact that Chicanos are now involving themselves in attempts to coalesce for political purposes has been instrumental in bringing about some federal legislation addressed to the needs of Chicanos, including the Bilingual Education Act and the extension of the Voting Rights Act.

STATE OF THE RESEARCH:
IMPLICATIONS FOR DIRECT SERVICE
WITH INDIVIDUALS AND FAMILIES

The Chicano continues to be an enigma within American culture. The current status of research on Chicanos is inadequate. This status is largely due to institutional racism. Society has simply not been interested in a comprehensive understanding of this minority group. Until recent years, interest has been limited to that shown by cultural anthropologists and sociologists. But during the past ten years, there has been an increase of research generated by Chicanos themselves. This research has been predominantly of the theory development and descriptive type. The need continues for empirical testing of conclusions, hypotheses, and suggested approaches to culturally specific treatment. A number of factors contribute to this situation.

Beyond the obvious issues of racism, discrimination, and oppression, which tend to encourage and perpetuate ignorance about Chicanos, there are other factors that contribute to the difficulty of describing a distinctive Chicano culture. The Chicanos are a heterogeneous group. Regionality, degree of acculturation, socioeconomic status, and even color contribute to a diversity of notions about what it means to be Chicano.

In 1978 President Carter commissioned a report on mental health. A subpanel on the Mental Health of Hispanic Americans issued a report, which noted that:

> A recent positive development has been the accelerated growth of research activities focusing on the mental health of Hispanic Americans. The most comprehensive bibliography currently available indicates that the knowledge base of the subject consists of some 2,000 works. Of these, approximately 75 percent have been published since 1970. Unfortunately, however, quality has not kept pace with quantity and the research literature on Hispanic mental health has yet to attain the status of an integrated body of scientific knowledge. It remains plagued by stereotypic interpretations, weak methodological and data-analytic techniques, lack of replicability of findings and the absence of programmatic research. (President's Commission on Mental Health 1978)

The Commission goes on to identify four possible causes of this "fragmented and often contradictory" research. First, until recently, social science theories and models were based on white norms, which made generalization to Hispanics inappropriate. Secondly, the research has failed to account for the heterogeneity of Hispanics and Hispanic subgroups. Thirdly, there has been a failure to incorporate an interdisciplinary approach. Finally, there has been a failure to account for Chicanos in their contemporary circumstances.

In addition, ideology has had an effect on recent research. Traditional research had been stereotypic and pejorative, often fostering a negative culture view. In reaction, Chicano and Chicano-sympathetic researchers set out to destroy stereotypes and to argue the cultural strengths of "Chicanismo." In this regard, the literature of the early 1970s documented "traditional values" and "cultural strengths," rather than "cultural barriers" (Sotomayor and Torres-Gil, cited in Valle-Mendoza 1978: 5). There are, of course, strengths; however, it is possible that recent research has tended to overcompensate for the negative aspects of earlier researchers. For example, it has been posited that Chicanos utilize *curanderos* (folk healers) and that this explains in part their underutilization of traditional services. This notion has not been empirically verified, and its veracity is coming under increasing doubt among Chicano scholars.

The reader is cautioned to acknowledge, therefore, the limitations of the available research. However, research of sufficient quantity and quality is being generated to give the human service worker a general sense of direction. For the purposes of this text, it is useful to consider the implications of these findings within the framework of direct service to individuals and families.

We know that Chicanos constitute a high-risk population with regard to a number of social problems, including mental health. We also know that this situation is due to their marginal acculturation and their low socioeconomic status. These factors subject Chicanos to a number of high stress indicators (President's Commission on Mental Health 1978), including:

1. Poor communication skills in English. (Spanish is the language of preference in over 50 percent of all Hispanic households, according to Padilla and Padilla 1977.)
2. Cycle of poverty. One half of all Hispanic families subsist in urban poverty (President's Commission on Mental Heath 1978).
3. Survival of traditional culture coping mechanisms, which are routinely ineffectual in an urban technical society. Retention of family values and Spanish language remain in the most distinguishing charactertistics (President's Commission on Mental Health 1978; Acosta 1979).
4. High mobility. Almost 84 percent of Chicanos are urban dwellers (U.S. Census 1976).
5. Racism and discrimination.

Each of the above factors is known to correlate with psychosocial stress and the concomitant need for treatment intervention (Padilla et al. 1975). Yet in spite of overwhelming indicators of need, Chicanos continue to underutilize traditional helping services. Hispanic researchers conclude that service delivery must be reviewed with respect to the social status and cultural differences of Chicanos. Such research could well begin with the Chicano family.

FAMILY PATTERNS
AND ADAPTATIONS TO STRESS

Much has been written in recent years about the Chicano family, often typified as a natural support system, which buffers individual members from the stressfulness of being a minority in an Anglo society. It has also been depicted as a defensive adaptation—"they take care of their own"—and the underutilization of mental health services has been attributed to this pheonomenon. However, notions about the extended family have not received sufficient empirical verification to warrant very many conclusions about help-seeking behavior.

The difficulty of obtaining verification of family patterns as adaptations to stress is due in part to the great degree of heterogeneity among Chicanos. There are regional differences, generational differences, and even differences in language and customs. One study in Southern California noted that, generationally, immigrants from Mexico identified themselves as Mexicans; first-generation, U.S.-born respondents as Mexican-Americans; and second-generation, U.S.-born as Chicanos (Keefe et al. 1979). Many Mexican-Americans from New Mexico identify themselves as Spanish-American or Hispanic. Some New Mexicans retain an aristocratic ambiance, stemming from the long-ago Spanish land grants, which vastly differentiates them from the city slicker Chicano from Califas (California). This is again different from the rural simplicity of the *campesino* on the labor trail from southern Texas to the Pacific Northwest or the upper Midwest. There are subtle differences among these subgroups in language, customs, eating habits, and even physical stature that an observer can detect when comparing them. Given the limited interest and resources that are available for the study of the Chicano family, we are at best able to provide only a generalized view of this phenomenon, and we must caution the reader to acknowledge this limitation.

The symbolic manifestation of the Chicano "familia"affects every sphere of Chicano life. Despite factors of assimilation and acculturation, the family and, more broadly, the concept of familia continue to assert a primary socializing function. The implications are seen in the social structure, which reflects a historically adaptive system of interaction and role identification. Although assimilation and acculturation have some impact, the degree to which this family value is retained can be understood from a consideration of the traditional Mexican-American family.

The concept of familia refers to the notion of family and to all of the associated implications thereof. The concept has two manifestations, one real and one symbolic. Familia is for Chicanos a primary socializing force, based on traditionalism through language, custom, and social role. The traditional Chicano family structure is hierarchical, with ascribed sex and status roles. For example, children have primary value. Often it is heard of Chicano parents that "they live for their children." Chicanos often assume a stereotyped self-concept of martyrdom, as when a woman stays with an alcoholic and/or abusive husband "for the sake of the children." A man may combine an often conflicting role of economic responsibility with an often unrealistic vestige of power and dominance. The hierarchical structure is also apparent in sibling relationships. An eldest daughter is ushered quite early into the role of mothering younger siblings. The eldest male child is imbued with a sense of specialness and privilege and, at the same time, with familia responsibility—if the father is incapacitated, financial responsibility automatically goes to the eldest son. While these descriptions are highly generalized, they are meant to depict a hierarchical traditional family structure. The degrees to which this type of structure is maintained will, of course, depend greatly on the individual case and the degree to which cultural change has occured.

The apparent rigidity of a traditional family structure serves well to socialize individual members into a culture and into a sense of world order. Less emphasis is placed on what one does in life than on who one is. In turn, a sense of self is highly influenced by family relationships. One result is that less value is placed upon material acquisition than on spiritual presence. Personal courtesy and respect are values which develop from this family interaction. It is perhaps easy to see how attributes such as "fatalism" can be attributed to such a cultural perspective. Further, some research posits that the Chicano is more cooperation-oriented than competition-oriented. While these latter notions seem to be true and substantial when one considers the family as an affective and harmonic entity, as opposed to one which is individualistic, impersonal, and materialistic (as Anglo-American families are sometimes characterized), there is danger in overgeneralizing. For example, the notions of fatalism or lack of competitiveness have been used to justify the low economic status and apparent underachievement of Chicanos. Theories which conclude that the culture and values of Mexican-Americans are the ultimate and final causes of their low economic status, low academic achievement, and low utilization of mental health services—the damaged culture view—have been the framework within which many social scientists have written about Mexican-Americans (Montiel 1970). At best, these theories result in an argument for cultural deprivation, one which establishes a deficiency in an individual's culture and ultimately in the individual himself.

Family cohesion is a traditional value in Mexican-American culture (Ramirez and Castaneda 1974). The notion of family has broad implications in Chicano culture, for it transcends the commonly known concept of the extended-family system and generalizes toward communal awareness. It expands to include another value, identified by Ramirez and Castaneda (1974) as the personalization of interpersonal relationships. This value is commonly known among Chicanos as *personalismo*. The notion of helping networks or natural systems aids in illustrating this broader conception. The eldest male was the patriarch, commanding authority and respect of all his sons, daughters, and grandchildren. His sons might marry, but it was assumed that brother, sister, father and son would always provide for one another. When grandparents became aged and disabled, their sons, daughters, and grandchildren know they should provide for them. Government played a minimal role in family security. (Tijerina 1978)

For Chicanos, the notion of familia extends beyond blood lines and effects a community spirit. The extended family (together with the helping network) is formalized through the religious ceremony of godparenting. Grandparents, uncles, aunts, and cousins are all members of an immediate support system. The role of *comadre* or *compadre* (friend and confident) further extends this network. As the network enlarges, it comes to mean affinity and comfort with other Chicanos and things culturally familiar. Therefore, the *cantina,* the Church, and the community center all serve as culturally appropriate sources for therapeutic consultation.

Yet the stress of racial discrimination, poverty, and substandard housing, which often result in cultural and personal identity conflicts, high rates of delinquency, and school dropouts, makes it clear that Latino community social service needs are great. It is also apparent that Latinos do not make extensive use of social service facilities. The most logical explanation for this may be the irrelevance of these current services to their needs (Padilla et al. 1975). Too often the services are not only irrelevant to the needs of the Chicano but are also in conflict with the social and cultural structures that govern the barrio life. "Many Mexicans continue to uphold the traditional family function of solving their own problems. They believe in protecting and caring for the troubled family member, rather than sending him to the Anglo clinic or hospital for treatment which may be interpreted as a form of rejection" (Burrel and Chavez 1971).

The burden of caring for needy family members falls on the shoulders of the overtaxed family and community. This culturally based helping network has an effect on social service delivery; for example, consider recent research in the area of mental health services utilization by Mexican-Americans. The Mexican-Americans make up the second largest minority group in the United, yet it is generally recognized and accepted that mental health services are underutilized by this population.

> In the United States, the Spanish speaking/surnamed population receives mental health care of a different kind, of lower quality and in lesser proportions than that of any other ethnically identifiable population. Demographers consistently agree that ethnic minority group members and particularly minority group members who are poor, receive less health care than the rest of the population. (Padilla and Ruiz 1973)

In the city of San Jose, California, a survey of patient visits to the Central Center during 1968 showed only 4 percent to be Mexican-American. This is under half of what would be expected (Padillo and Ruiz 1973). Similar situations exist in other areas as well. In a recent study of the knowledge and use of public mental health clinics by Mexican-Americans in East Los Angeles, it was determined that 48 percent of the respondents knew about their neighborhood clinic, but only 2 percent used the mental health clinic (Torrey 1970).

It has been suggested that one of the reasons that human service workers do not see many Chicano clients is that the Chicano family provides emotional nurturance to such a degree that there is less incidence of emotional problems among Chicanos, as compared to other groups.

Some evidence exists for the point of view that certain aspects of the (Mexican American) culture provide protection against mental breakdown or continued familial support after a breakdown. The most influential proponents include Jaco (1959 and 1960) and Maden (1964). Both writers base their conclusions on Mexican American samples drawn from south Texas. Jaco, after finding that Mexican Americans are under-represented in residential care facilities for the mentally ill, argues that the extended family system of Mexican Americans provides warmth and support during periods of high emotional stress. Jaco concludes that this familial support system results in a reduced rate of mental breakdowns among Mexican Americans. (Padilla and Ruiz 1973: 12)

The reason for underutilization of services by Mexican Americans has been widely discussed, but little progress has been made in changing the utilization pattern. Torrey (1970) stated of the San Jose Community Mental Health Center, for instance, that "in terms of fulfilling the Mental Health Centers Act, it is well above average; in terms of fulfilling the needs of a significant minority of its constituents, it is hopelessly inadequate." Torrey further cited six reasons for this inadequacy, stating that services are irrelevant (1) because they are inaccessible; (2) because of language considerations; (3) because they are class-bound; (4) because they are culture-bound; (5) because they are caste-bound; and (6) because Mexican-Americans have their own system of mental health services.

In seemingly direct contrast to some of the notions about Chicano life as described above, a study by Keefe et al. (1979) discounts the idea that Chicano help-seeking practices are significantly different than those of their Anglo counterparts. Their study, conducted over a three-year period, contrasted Chicano and Anglo help-seeking patterns in three Southern California cities. These researchers concluded that Chicanos relied on family support mainly because this resource was readily available to them. Anglos would have used such a resource had they had an equally extensive network of family and friends. Their study further indicated that Chicanos did not make extensive use of extended family relations for emotional problems so much as they utilize one person in the immediate nuclear family. This behavior was not significantly different from their Anglo counterparts. There was very little use of *curanderos* or folk healers, and also little use of community organizations or clergy. There was, however, more resistance on the part of Chicanos to utilizing mental health professionals than there was for Anglos.

These findings give testimony to the need for further empirical investigation about Chicano behavior. We know that family life is a stabilizing and socializing force in all cultures and that within Chicano life the familia is a primary value. However, we cannot conclude that the family love and an extended kinship system, which are hallmarks of Chicano culture, are adequate substitutes for human services. The maintenance of such notions about Chicano preferences, and resources "has long permitted the Anglo culture to minimize the significance of underutilization of therapy services by Mexican Americans" (Acosta 1980). With such an attitude, human services could continue in good conscience to be oppressive and unresponsive to the social service needs of the Chicano.

MAJOR SOCIAL SERVICE NEEDS
AND IMPLICATIONS
FOR HUMAN SERVICES

For Chicanos, the overriding need in all social service areas is for the development and implementation of culture specific models of treatment. Such a need is evident in one-to-one therapy, in family treatment, in community services, and in social policy development. Acknowledgments must be made of the Chicano perspective in defining need. Chicanos do not see mental health services as different and separate from social service needs, such as housing, jobs, education, or child care.

Chicanos continue to be disproportionately represented among the nation's poor, unemployed and underemployed, and undereducated and they are underrepresented among recipients of health services. Since population characteristics of this group reflect that almost one half are presently children or adolescents, one can surmise that child welfare and education will be increasing areas of need. Drug abuse and alcoholism are prevalent in Chicano communities. The list of Chicano service needs includes all of the major social problems in America today. The alarming fact about these problems is not that they exist (and sometimes with greater incidence in the Chicano community than elsewhere), but that the mainstream approaches to their solution are inappropriate and inadequate.

The echoing demand from Chicanos is the need for culturally relevant services. At its least, this demand means a need for services delivered in a culturally responsive and supportive manner. What a need for culturally relevant services means operationally is less clearly developed, although a number of models and approaches have been suggested. Gaviria and Stern (1980) provide some useful comments regarding the problems of developing culturally relevant services.

These authors note that the three constituencies that have been active in planning and hence defining "culturally relevant" services for Chicanos have been (1) funding agencies (2) social scientists, and (3) Latino activists. Federal and state funding agencies consider the accessibility of services to be the key issue in fostering culturally relevant services. Although in its original implementation this notion included education-consultation, use of paraprofessional staff, and insuring community input, cultural relevance as a goal has been narrowed to geographic and physical location concerns. Social scientists, on the other hand, determine culturally relevant services to be those that acknowledge the importance of "indigenous healers, becoming aware of culturally defined systems of disease etiology and treatment, and evaluating behavior symptomatic of mental illness in a cultural as well as medical psychiatric content" (Gaviria and Stern 1980, p. 66).

The final group, the Chicano (Latino) activists, determined the key issue of cultural relevance to be the hiring of an indigenous staff. Professionally trained experts are perceived of as "too far removed from community problems." For this group, intuitive "street knowledge" is of most value in delivering culturally relevant services.

There has been a retreat from the culturally relevant social change approach by the community mental health movement. The social scientists have contributed little to defining culturally relevant services. Their research, however descriptive, has yet to be empirically validated and operationally applied to alternative models. The activists, on the other hand, do give some clues to the concept of culturally relevant services. Indigenous paraprofessionals identified six factors which they felt contributed to the relevance of their service:

1. Empathetic feelings for the patient's experience.
2. Feeling that they also had lived through the stresses experienced by patients.
3. A conviction that their past life experiences had trained them well for their work in mental health.
4. Sense of geographic continuity resulting from working and living in the community.
5. Greater flexibility and mobility in meeting with the patient than can be attributed to traditionally trained personnel.
6. Ease of verbal communication because of similar language use.

Hence, specific *skills* for culturally relevant treatment are identified: empathy, flexibility, and verbal facility. The authors note that language and class similarity are important variables in effective therapeutic communication. Such a match is not always possible, and therefore cultural awareness and sensitivity must bridge the differences.

The meaning of culturally relevant services lies in combination of the above perspectives. Culturally relevant services must include the social change commitment of funding agencies, the empirically tested knowledge of the social scientist, and the practicability of the indigenous experience. Unfortunately, these three constituencies often remain at odds, and the practitioner and client suffer the gap. Efforts to bring cultural awareness and sensitivity to policy makers, administrators, and other decision makers must be pursued. Research must be brought out of academia, and community-based utilization and testing must be encouraged. Finally, bilingual and bicultural staff members should be hired, and mechanisms for community input into service delivery programs insured. These actions would contribute to the development and implementation of culture-specific treatment in a responsive manner.

The cultural awareness approach acknowledges that ours is a pluralistic society. For the bicultural individual, it is also a constant stressor. Throughout his or her life, the Chicano is socialized by two sets of norms, a victim of sociocultural dissonance, as Fabrega and Wallace (1976: 253) point out:

> A current assumption in psychiatry is that individuals who live in areas that are undergoing cultural change experience psychological distress as a result of having to cope with the deprivation and social disorganization that often accompany this change. . . . The model assumes, first of all, that for an individual to develop high psychological organization and adaptive skills, attitudes, roles, and behavior patterns learned in the home should be internally consistent and similarly valued by the parents. Ideally, there should also be a high degree of correspondence between the sentiments learned in the home and those generally followed and socially sanctioned in the community.

━ The implication is that Chicano life is fraught with stress. While further research is needed before a conclusion is achieved, simple observation indicates that this premise is true enough for direct practice use: A practitioner must ascertain as soon as possible in the therapeutic process the stress level of the client. How does this particular client deal with stress? What are the immediate stressors in this individual's life? Is cultural conflict an immediate or overriding stressor in the presenting problem? The following list of intervention skills with Hispanic clients is extrapolated from the work of Ruiz and Padilla (1977: 401-8):

1. Respect the importance of *personalismo* to Latinos: that is, greeting clients as soon as they arrive at the agency, using first names rather than formal titles.

2. Small talk at the initial meeting and at the beginning of subsequent sessions is very important to establish and maintain rapport.

3. Because of possible differences in the perception of time, a social worker should make an appointment to meet with the prospective client immediately, and should schedule that meeting as soon as possible.

4. Latinos tend to perceive psychological problems as more similar to physical problems than do non-Latinos. Thus, nondirective approaches in requests for reviews of childhood history or instructions to introspect should be used judiciously.

5. Many Latino clients may have preconceptions of counseling interviews and sessions based on an analogue of a medical examination. Thus they may anticipate a more active approach from the counselor, for example, inquiry that is goal-oriented and leading to concrete solutions for identified problems.

6. The higher frequency of extended-family structure and the greater importance of family interaction indicate that family and other group approaches should be used more often. Family-oriented therapies would yield higher success rates among Latinos.

7. Sex roles are more rigidly defined. Sons have more and earlier independence, fathers have more prestige and authority, and the aged receive more respect.

8. Familial interdependence does not carry the connotation of pathological dependency such behavior might imply in other cultures.

9. Counseling centers should emphasize a "business model" approach and aggressively pursue clientele for their services.

10. Services should include written and oral translation, contact with government agencies, employment training, remedial education, and legal education (voting, etc.).

11. Members of the community should be active at all levels of the agency, so as to establish confidence and support of prospective clients.

━ While cultural conflict is a source of stress, this author wishes to note that it is also a vital source of growth and change (Gallegos 1978). This perspective is a positive view of culture, which acknowledges a variety of coping and survival skills, not the least of which is the natural support system. The application of the natural networks theory seems uniquely suited to Mexican-American populations. Padilla et al. (1975) felt that reliance on the extended family for support is the primary means of coping with emotional stress for Mexican-Americans. Friends and com-padres are extensions of this informal network of support.

It is likely that these friends and *compadres* are the central figures that Collins and Pancoast (n.d.) describe. In their view of Torrey's work, they have indi-cated that in addition to *curanderos,* there is another group in the Mexican-Ameri-can community.

> . . . of helping people who have no title and who serve as advisors on an en-tirely voluntary basis. They have no training as healers but have gained an informal reputation as problem solvers. . . . These people have regular jobs that they work at daily but they devote many evening and weekend hours to counseling those who ask them for help.

Padilla's study also bore this out. He found that of the mental health re-sources used by the respondents in their study during a one-year period prior to the research interview, 62 percent used either a relative, a *compadre,* or a friend for help with an emotional problem, while only 2 percent used a mental health clinic, and 2 percent used a *curandero.*

This suggests that a more productive approach would be to provide consulta-tion to the natural networks already in place. Collins and Pancoast (n.d.) indicated that the "goals of consultation with natural helpers are similar to those of consulta-tion with professionals," but there are some variations and additions. The major objectives remain the same: helping the consultees solve problems in their practice and increasing their ability to do so unassisted in the future. The range of problems that the consultees deal with may, however, be broader than that of the profes-sionals, and the problems may be more diffuse. Consultants may need to rely more heavily on their role as partners seeking answers than that of experts offering solu-tions. In conventional consultation settings, consultants confine their efforts to helping consultees, to improve problem solving within their assigned position. In working with natural neighbors, consultees have an additional goal—to enlarge their circles of influence, and at the same time to improve the quality of their interven-tions at every level.

Recent research has provided such recommendations for improvements in service delivery to Mexican-Americans, as making services more geographically accessible, solving transportation problems to the services, providing services in Spanish, and making mental health professionals more knowledgeable about the culture. Most studies have pointed to the need for continued research. The Council on Social Work Education, in its *Chicano Task Force Report* (Ruiz 1973: 4), recommended that:

> Research activity should be generated with significant Chicano input that concentrates on the positive rather than corrective aspects of the Chicano experience. Data is [sic] needed in areas of human behavior (aging, delin-quency, self image), sociology of the barrio, the psychology of Chicanismo, and creativeness which can lead to enriching curriculum. Basically, this in-

volves the funding of research projects that attempt to identify and build on the existing informal service delivery systems. This approach does not eliminate nor discredit the life experience of the Chicano community but rather builds on what already is there.

To neither discount nor discredit the life experience of the Chicanos and their community, bur rather to build upon what already is there, is the message to be conveyed as the beginning of cultural awareness. Such an attitude is to be a minimal expectation for Chicanos and their communities to have of human service workers. This minimal standard of service must begin with a sincere interest and investment. Such a beginning, couched in cultural awareness and sensitivity, would serve as a foundation from which to move toward real empowerment of Chicanos. Cultural awareness in human services work is a first step toward the ultimate goal of empowering Chicano individuals and communities toward self-determination, self-respect, self-esteem, and the eventual access to rightful resources.

EPILOGUE

An epilogue provides the opportunity for an author to stand back from what has been written and, in a more personal way, comment on what it all seems to mean. To fulfill that ceremonial function, I want to underscore several implications of the approach to social services that has been presented here.

First, it should be apparent that cultural awareness requires more than techniques or "skills" for handling specific kinds of clients with special kinds of problems. Much of social work training is skills oriented, as are portions of this book. But to leave the matter there is to suggest that cultural awareness and sensitivity are matters of technical competence, of "expertise." Cultural awareness for social workers should more correctly be viewed as a kind of outlook on the world, one which includes useful intervention skills with culturally distinctive clients, but one which is not limited to that. Philosophically, it is an outlook open to learning about others and a willingness to do so by utilizing their perceptual categories rather then formulas and points of view imposed from the outside. That is, it is an approach which seeks to limit and control ethnocentrism. Politcally, the approach suggests broad-based participation by people and communities in deciding what it is they really need and how it should be provided. Cultural traditions and resources and ways in which they can be used to resolve personal and community problems must take clear priority over agency agendas or the opinions of external experts in planning programs and delivering services.

Second, I am concerned with what will be required to establish cultural awareness among social workers as a matter of practice and of professional expectation.
Quite frankly, I am not impressed by one-shot workshops as a way of preparing
people to deal with their culturally distinctive clients. Such training techniques
trivialize the importance of the issue and too often make people feel they have
learned something when in fact they have not. At minimum, cultural awareness as
a way of carrying out professional responsibilities involves (a) continuous discussion
among workers of ways to design services so that they better match the backgrounds and expectations of clients; (b) opportunities to learn about ethnic and
minority clients and particularly the minority-directed agencies that serve those
clients; and (c) a long-term commitment to working with clients from particular
cultural groups and communities, with worker energy focused as much on the
ethnographic setting of the clients as on specific problem and service topics. Anything less would not be adequate.

Third, there is the question of who will be the beneficiary of cultural awareness training and research. Throughout this book, we have written of ethnic and
minority groups. And it is certainly clear, upon reading the chapters on specific
groups, that minority groups have deserved better than they have received from
established social services. It would be an error, however, to think that what we
have called cultural awareness is applicable *only* to recognized minorities. There is a
large and significant amount of cultural variation among people who have not been
discussed in this book. These would include the so-called "white ethnics," as well
as those who are distinctive in our society for reasons of religion, class, geographical
location, or lifestyle. The principles of cultural awareness obviously apply to them,
just as they apply whenever the worker and the client come from significantly
different cultural or community settings. The impulse to "ghettoize" cultural
awareness training by treating it as simply a minority issue must, therefore, be
resisted. Cultural awareness, as has been repeatedly stated, is a way of doing things
and of perceiving the world. It is not and cannot be narrowly circumscribed by the
interests or concerns of any particular ethnic or minority group. It is, rather, a
broadly humanistic way of approaching social services for all people.

Finally, the way in which we have used ideas such as cultural awareness,
ethnic competence, help-seeking behavior, and the like should suggest that these are
open-ended concepts. Our entire presentation is one large hypothesis, composed of
many smaller, supportive hypotheses. As such, the system as described is subject to
testing, critique, evaluation, restatement, and refinement. For it to be seen as anything other than that would be to misconstrue and misuse the approach that has
been presented. Our concern as authors has been to look at human services to see
what works, what might work, and how people's needs can be more equitably met.
We hope that is the concern of our readers as well.

APPENDIX:
CROSS-CULTURAL
LEARNING ACTIVITIES

INTRODUCTION

The field of social work is rich in training techniques and materials. Therefore, there is little point in attempting to replicate here the training procedures and exercises that have been developed by others. What has been provided is not a set of exercises in the usual sense, but a sample of activities that can be expanded, revised, or modified to suit the interests of differing kinds of learners. All the activities can be carried out by individuals working on their own or as part of class or term-paper projects.

These activities exemplify some of the themes presented in the book. They do so by emphasizing one or more of the basic tenets of an anthropological or a cross-cultural approach: the emic perspective, cross-cultural comparison, and the method of participant observation.

Two kinds of activities are listed, and the differences between them are important in terms of training goals and objectives. We have distinguished cultural awareness activities from those concerned with the acquisition of cultural knowledge. Cultural awareness refers to a kind of sensibility or frame of mind in regard to cross-cultural understanding. It has to do with qualities of openness, alertness, and, particularly, flexibility in relations with others. It focuses on attitudes and values. Cultural awareness activities tend to deal with the inner state of the learner.

But cultural awareness is not, and we emphasize this point, cross-cultural learning in the sense of acquisition of knowledge and information about distinctive client communities. Cultural awareness must be supplemented with ethnographic information if it is to become something other than a kind of self-indulgence in training exercises for their own sake. The cultural knowledge activities, therefore, emphasize learning about others within the comparative perspective. As learning devices, they are outwardly focused so that the student can begin to develop an information and knowledge base. Cultural knowledge is as important as cultural awareness if the learner is to gain a sense of what can and needs to be learned about ethnically distinctive clients.

There are many additional sources of training ideas that will be helpful to those seeking more detailed information. The field guides written by Johnson (1975), Bollens and Marshall (1973), Bogdan (1972), Lofland (1971), and Edgerton and Langness (1974) all contain valuable information on participant observation and on the mechanics as well as the philosophy of that type of research. Detailed studies on cross-cultural counseling and communication will be found in the excellent books of Ross (1978), Pedersen et al. (1976), and Brislin and Pedersen (1976). Cross-cultural research and training are discussed in relation to health services and nursing in Brownlee (1978) and in Leininger (1978). The East-West Center Culture Learning Institute in Hawaii has issued a series of monographs entitled *Topics in Culture Learning* (Brislin 1976), and these contain research and case studies. Finally, the Society for Intercultural Education, Training, and Research (SIETAR), at Georgetown University, regularly issues new volumes in its excellent series on cross-cultural learning. Past volumes have covered theory, education and training, and special topics in research (Hoopes et al. 1977, 1978a, 1978b). The Society has also issued a manual (Weeks et al. 1977) and a sourcebook (Hoopes and Ventura 1979) on cross-cultural training experiences. These references should be consulted to supplement the activities suggested below.

1. CULTURAL AWARENESS: SOCIAL WORK AND VALUES

The values that social workers learn are acquired during the socialization process, when the worker as student learns the skills and knowledge of the discipline and begins to develop a sense of professional attachment or identity (Levy 1976). The importance of these values in the socialization process has been described by Levy:

> Social work values constitute a basis for rational choices in professional situations. These are the values to which social workers are expected to be committed. They represent preferences with respect to ways of doing it; preferences with respect to how people are to be regarded who are directly or indirectly affected by what is done or not done; and preferences with respect to safeguards to be accorded such persons, because of the risks and entitlements to which they are subjected or exposed as a result or in the process of its being done. (Levy 1977: 7)

Now, what might these values which "represent preferences" be? While it is difficult to say that any particular listing of values would be typical of the profession, we can nevertheless select two instances which seem to summarize much that has been said on the topic. Pincus and Minahan (1973: 39) believe that social work's two principal values are (1) taking action to ensure that people have access to the resources, services, and opportunities needed to meet various life tasks, to alleviate distress, and to realize their aspirations; and (2) having respect for the dignity and individuality of the recipients of these services. McLeod and Meyer (1967) have been more specific in suggesting such principles as (1) belief in the worth and dignity of the individual human being and the importance of maximizing his or her potential; (2) belief in the right of every individual to exercise control over his or her own destiny, that is, self-determination; (3) belief that the group has responsibility for the welfare of its own members; (4) the assertion that individuals should have the security and satisfaction of meeting basic biological and culturally acquired needs in order to achieve self-realization; (5) the notion that scientific and pragmatic problem-solving approaches are optimal; (6) commitment to social reform, planned change, and progress; (7) acceptance of diversity and heterogeneity in ideas, values, and lifestyles; (8) belief that human nature is socially determined and that change often requires environmental alterations; (9) the view that the interdependence of all members of society (group responsibility) supersedes individual autonomy; and (10) the notion that all individuals are unique.

As an exercise in cross-cultural imagination, list each of these ten values on a sheet of paper. Then try to imagine an ethnographic example in which they would be inappropriate to the cultural background of the client. For instance, can you visualize an occurrence wherein the "right of every individual" to manage his or her own affairs might conflict with an obligation to others in a particular community? And what of the "commitment to social reform, planned change and progress"? What assumptions about the "needs" of others are contained in such a "commitment"? How are reforms translated into intervention with clients, and why? Each of these value statements should help the student better understand the difficulties in applying values uncritically to cross-cultural encounters.

2. CULTURAL AWARENESS: ETHNICITY AND IDENTITY

Ethnicity is a general human phenomenon and is not limited to such topics as "race relations" or "minority groups." There is no region of the world in which ethnicity is not an important issue in political and policy decision making, in the allocation of scarce resources, and in personal choices concerning friendship, marriage ties, and place of residence. For all of us, self-identity is in some sense "ethnic," in that we have diverse origins and loyalties, which are related to the kinds of status and privileges we may or may not enjoy. Among black or Hispanic students, for instance, ethnicity as a personal characteristic may be relatively easy to define. For whites or Anglos, however, defining one's ethnicity may be more difficult. Yet simply because most of us are immigrants or descended from immigrants, and because we implicity associate the lifestyle we enjoy with specific ethnic or national origins, we are all to some degree members of ethnic groups. The issue, then, is not who is ethnic and who is not. It is the relative importance given to ethnicity in personal identity and, beyond that, in access to social and economic privileges. The purpose of this exercise is to give each student an opportunity to confront and clarify the meaning of ethnicity in a personal way. It is a step toward defining ethnicity in terms of one's own life history, in order to understand the commonality of this process for all people. The exercise also suggests the intimate relationship between ethnic assignation and access to the privileges and benefits that are nominally available in the larger society.

In responding to the following statements and questions, it is important to be precise as possible, keeping in mind that your own intuitive sense of family history is as important as what you might be able to verify through old documents or from conversations with older family members. The goal of this exercise is to clarify your own perceptions of your ethnic background and how you relate them to your sense of personal identity.

(a)   Identify your family origins as far back as you can trace specific ancestors. Where possible, specify the earliest dates, names, and places of which you can be sure. If you are unsure, speculate about probable ancestors and how far back you might be able to trace them, as though you were planning to do genealogical research.

(b)   Why and how did your ancestors come to this country? Speculate on the conditions they left behind and on their possible motives for leaving these conditions.

(c)   When your ancestors arrived here, their ethnic background undoubtedly influenced how they were perceived and treated by others. Describe both a disadvantage and an advantage your ancestors may have experienced because of their ethnicity. Examples might include matters of religion, racial characteristics, economic background, language, family patterns, or political involvement.

(d)   Look at any of the ethnic advantages you have listed. These are often reflected in family strengths, the desirable things people do or experience because they are members of a particular family and a particular ethnic group. Can you name any specific privileges, advantages, or family strengths that you or your family members have enjoyed because of your family's ethnic background or identity? List these.

(e)   In one or two sentences, name your ethnic background, and describe one important personal benefit that you enjoy as a consequence of that ethnicity.

The exercise provides data from your own family background that illustrate a number of points concerning ethnicity. First, we are all "ethnic" in some way. Your information should assist you in identifying the source of your own ethnicity. Obviously some knowledge of national history is important to enable you to interpret family data. But if you have answered the question with as much detail as possible, some connections to a distinctive cultural background should be evident.

Second, the data you have listed for your family background on items 3 and 4 should make it clear that ethnicity is something more than old family portraits, heirlooms, or preparation of "ethnic" dishes based on old-country recipes. Ethnicity is a matter of how people define themselves, of how they are defined by others, and of the impact that those definitions have on what people aspire to become and what they are able to accomplish.

Finally, your personal and family data on items 4 and 5 should illustrate a fundamental social reality: there are no self-made men or women in this or any other country. What people possess in the way of positions, material goods, opportunities, and sense of place in the world relate in large part to their ethnic group membership. Certainly there are "rugged individuals" and high achievers and people who claim to have "pulled themselves up by their own bootstraps." But the fact is that we all started with something fundamental, our group membership. That gave each of us a position of relative advantage or disadvantage in relation to all others. Those advantages and disadvantages are often perpetuated over generations as part of each individual's ethnic identity. Ethnicity, therefore, is both a basis for establishing personal identity and social roles and also a criterion for group cohesion and loyalty.

3. CULTURAL AWARENESS:
WORKING WITH
MINORITY PROFESSIONALS

The chapter on ethnicity and social services dealt with the role of minority practitioners as brokers, advocates for their community, and mediators between their clients and other professionals. The aim of this activity is to clarify your own expectations for work with minority practitioners and clients—what you anticipate your major problems will be, and how you intend to resolve them as a practitioner yourself.

Each participant should respond to the statements below concerning the role of minority practitioners in social services. Responses can be written or verbal, but everyone should take a stand of some kind. A polite "pass" on a given question is not acceptable. These are controversial topics, and an informed, critical awareness is crucial to developing sensitive intervention skills. There are no right or wrong answers, and each statement is deserving of some discussion of its strengths and weaknesses.

(a)   It is best that clients and practitioners be of the same ethnic background if any successful counseling or therapy is to be transacted.

(b)   White practitioners experience fewer discontinuities between personal and professional values than do minority practitioners.

(c)   Learning the cultural values and norms of an ethnic minority client and having some facility in his or her language are absolutely necessary in providing services.

(d)   While cultural awareness training can provide important skills in dealing with a multiethnic client caseload, it is unrealistic to suppose that the white practitioner can replace the bicultural, bilingual practitioner.

(e)   Minority practitioners should place a higher priority on community advocacy roles and expectations than professional upward mobility.

(f)   Minority practitioners and nonminority professionals experience many dissimilarities in their career goals and can be expected to respond differently to the expectations of the job.

(g)   There are uniform, established procedures for acquiring counseling skills and for providing counseling services. These procedures should be taught and practiced without reference to the ethnicity of the worker or client.

(h)   Minority practitioners ought to assume primary responsibility for caseloads with ethnic minority clients, because they are better qualified to do so.

(i)   While it is important for nonminority practitioners to work cooperatively with their minority colleagues, they should avoid interethnic counseling where they feel a lack of cultural knowledge about prospective clients.

(j)   Ethnic minority content should be widely dispersed in the social work curriculum, rather than concentrated in a few specialized courses or training programs.

As a follow-up exercise, plan to visit a minority-staffed social service agency in your community. Participants should meet with minority practitioners and discuss the kinds of interventive strategies used in work with a particular ethnic and minority client population and the kinds of value dilemmas or cultural conflicts they encounter on their jobs relative to their agencies, professions, and ethnic backgrounds. These visits should be followed by discussions in which participants can compare notes about their interviews and discuss these in the context of the chapter on ethnicity and minority professionals.

4. CULTURAL AWARENESS
AND RACISM

Racism is an ugly topic and one that is insufficiently discussed by professionals in human service occupations. There are a number of reasons for this omission. First, the overt expression of racist sentiments is considered poor form in polite circles, although that does not usually prevent it in confidential or "locker-room" conversations. Most educated people know the etiquette of racial language, and it is the observance of that etiquette that accounts for some containment of bigoted expressions. Second, racism is often equated with prejudice and is assumed to represent an ignorant, uninformed, or unworthy attitude toward persons who are racially or ethnically different. Racism in this sense is viewed as a sickness of mind, readily attributable to the ill-mannered (and perhaps violent) among us. Identifying these individuals as the carriers of the disease pinpoints blame and relieves others of complicity in their actions. Third, racism is sometimes viewed as a holdover from our unfortunate past. Slavery, detention camps, and Indian hunting are fortunately

behind us, and it is therefore held that the task now is to eliminate their consequences through education, job training, service programs, and other efforts to
relieve the plight of those afflicted.

These views of racism, as impropriety, as ignorance, and as unfinished
national business, are what make racism so difficult to see and to change when it is
in our midst. These perceptions are, in fact, often part of the problem, not the solution.

According to black social worker Barbara E. Shannon, writing in *Social Casework* (1970), racism must be viewed instead as a value, like a political or a religious
belief, one that serves some purpose for the individual. The nature of that purpose
has been suggested by Wellman (1977), who regards racism as a means of protecting
privileges. Viewed in this way, racist terminology and jokes, displays of ill-con-
ceived attitudes, or overt acts of discrimination are not the only clues to the
presence of racism. How one rationalizes one's place in a system of institutions
and institutional practices, as well as the place of ethnically distinctive others, can
have important bearings on the perpetuation or resolution of racially based problems. Wellman describes five kinds of rationales by which inequality is explained
and ultimately explained away by people who normally do not consider themselves bigots. Each rationale is "reasonable," given a particular vantage point; that
is, each explanation justifies one's place in society and the benefits so received. It
also accounts for the failure of others to enjoy the same benefits and privileges.
Each rationale, then, is an expression of values in some sense. Wellman's description
of each rational comes from his sociological analysis of interviews with five different respondents. I have summarized these, and the listing below is my own adaptation. However, these examples are not dissimilar from explanations offered to me
by some social workers in the course of research for this book. The rationalizations
are as follows:

(a) Balance Sheet Justice

Resources are scarce, everyone has to struggle to get what they have, and
there is really not enough time, energy, or money to do everything that we would
really like to do. Priorities must be established and decisions made. It is too bad
that minorities sometimes get short-changed this way. Perhaps they should do what
others have done: get their act together and put pressure on the system to get their
fair share. They certainly deserve better than they have had. But things being as
they are, it seems inevitable that the gains of some will be the loss of others.

(b) Changing Others

We live with many contradictions, and it is hard to know what is right. It may
be true that in many ways this is a racist society, but there are many caring people
who wish it were otherwise. Discrimination in hiring is wrong but zealotry in affirm-
ative action just alienates people. Better education for minorities would help, but
at the same time there is a need to protect standards. Admittedly, service organiza-

tions are sometimes inefficient and unfeeling, but if you stop to give special attention to one, then others just pile up at the door waiting their turn. Many of these difficulties will probably be solved when there is better education for minorities and when ways are found to help them into the mainstream.

(c) Individualized Action

It is clear that there are inequalities. It is also clear that many people from disadvantaged groups make less use of what they do have, limited though it may be, than they might. There is a real need for these people to get on with the business of taking control of their lives, of owning their own experience. Ultimately, it all comes down to individual initiative, a little assertiveness, and that is the level at which it makes a difference. People need to learn how to clarify what it is they want and how to go after it. Then things will change, at least for them.

(d) Improving Communication

Basically, all people are the same and want the same things out of life. Color, class, and ethnic origins really make little difference except when people want them to. When individuals go into agencies, offices, even businesses, they are seeking specific solutions to specific problems. If difficulties and misunderstanding result, that is due to a failure of communication, not to bad intentions. If people could only communicate better, they would have fewer difficulties. We all need to work on that.

(e) Learning to Think Straight

Racism and tension make it impossible for people to really see what is happening to them. People get funny ideas, or they get paranoid and see things that aren't really there. We all have this problem, of having a limited perspective and not knowing the impact of your statement or mannerisms on others. But race and cultural differences only magnify what is already a complex situation. If people could only straighten out their thoughts and unravel all their feelings about this, it would help a lot.

As explanations of racial problems, these are, for the most part, liberal and polite accounts. They are not the statements of overt bigots. But they all have the function of separating the people who make them from the tragedy and misery they observe in others. They deny responsibility for problems and suggest that it is the victim alone who will have to make the changes that will result in some better state of affairs. No challenges to the status quo, nor to the privileged position of most whites in it, are contained here. Wellman notes the essence of racism cannot be simple bigotry or meanness. It must include attitudes and acts that have as their consequences the intended or unintended perpetuation of racially based limitations on other people's opportunities and achievements. Each statement above is an example of such an attitude.

What concerns us as a learning experience in all of this is that the learner explore each of these positions in terms of his or her own beliefs on race. Is there agreement or disagreement with some of these positions? Do any of the examples express a value system that sounds familiar? What does each example suggest about the causes of racism, the reasons it is perpetuated, and the kind of action that might be required to resolve it? Do any of these statements suggest anything about the value of the profession, or about workstyles in professional relationships? Do they reflect policy statements or guidelines that the learner has seen? Can similar examples be found in training materials used in classes or workshops? The task for the learner might be to take one of the statements above, one that approximates his or her own position, or one that does not, and pick it apart for its hidden assumptions and its implications for professional practice.

Having explored these issues, through discussion or reading, one must wonder at some point: what can anyone do about it? Shannon (1970) suggests, at least as a beginning, a number of steps. We suggest the learner examine these and attempt to formulate ways of implementing them without relying on the assumptions and rhetoric contained in the Wellman examples. According to Shannon:

(a)   White practitioners must examine more carefully the social context of client beliefs and behavior before concluding that anything in it is destructive or inappropriate. This issue, very simply, is one of ethnocentrism and of whether or not the worker is imposing on the client behavior or standards that are intended to enhance the worker's comfort.

(b)   White practitioners need to be aware of the adaptive patterns common to the client's own community and of how these can be adapted to a specific problem. This is a matter of having ethnographic information and a strong sense, derived from participant observation, of what that information means.

(c)   White practitioners should be aware that their own values and solutions are not the only ones, even within the white community. That community is a heterogeneous one, as are ethnic and minority communities. Recommendations to clients may or may not be helpful to them in other kinds of white-nonwhite relationships.

(d)   White practitioners need to be very critical of research, policy statements, program guidelines, and related information which assume the desirability of certain procedures or consequences in social service programs when these are based only on white models or on data from white communities and white clients. There is a tendency for whites to unthinkingly assume that what is acceptable to them is equally acceptable to others.

The problems posed by Wellman and Shannon are not small ones, and for that reason we have not tried to suggest simplistic exercises to be used in attacking them. What is required on this most difficult and (for some) awkward topic is discussion, critique, examination, and sensitization to all that is involved. That can be done individually, in groups, through reading, and by observation. In fact, these activities should be continuous ones. To treat the problem of racism otherwise is to trivialize its importance for too many people.

5. CULTURAL KNOWLEDGE:
SOCIAL MAPPING

In describing the concept of social mapping, Cochrane notes that "poverty is not merely a matter of not having things or access to them; it is also a matter of how people behave in particular cultural contexts" (Cochrane 1979: 37). This exercise concerns cultural contexts and ways the learner can become familiar with them. Without such background knowledge, it is virtually impossible to comprehend the sense of rationality and appropriateness that may underlie a client's responses to a problem.

The task for the learner is to identify a community for study and to become familiar with the cultural characteristics of that community. The community can be either a geographically coherent one or one which is dispersed but within which the members experience similar problems and have common concerns. An example of the former would be a slum neighborhood; of the latter, a group of single Indian parents in a large city. The exercise requires the collection and study of appropriate documents, including maps and census material; the analysis of sociological and anthropological studies of the community or of ones like it; and the development of a file of information that will be of use in informing other workers who may have clients from the community in question.

Following Cochrane's outline, and adapting it to the needs of social service workers, would require completion of the following steps:

(a) Define the community of interest and identify all relevant statistical and demographic information. On a map, identify the boundaries of the group and show any subdivisions that may be appropriate. Special attention should be given to subdivisions that are emically significant to members of the community. These would include the vernacular names they have for regions of the community and the significance of these designations.

(b) Describe the social organization of the community. Where are the resources located, and who controls them? What are the leadership roles, formal and informal, and who occupies them? What types of organizations are in the community, and what is the importance of each one? Certain values will probably attach to these organizations, and those values should be made as explicit as possible. Where there are important informal patterns, such as personal networks and cliques, these should be identified and their membership and activities described.

(c) Describe the prevailing belief system in the community. What are the predominant values? In what kinds of symbols and ceremonies are they expressed? What variations on prevailing values are permitted, tolerated, or disallowed? Where particular values seem important to the kinds of problems often handled by social workers, those values should be defined in detail. Their bearing on intervention activities and outcomes should be made explicit. The number of topics for values analysis is almost endless, but examples include male-female relations, parent-child relations, patterns of sharing and reciprocity, generational differences, the use of wealth, beliefs about the larger society, attitudes toward social services, and the like.

(d)   Patterns of change, historical and recent, should be described. How has the community in question experienced changes that have affected other communities? What shifts in wealth or political power have occurred? Can these be expected to continue, and what are their implications for social services?

(e)   How members of the community do, and do not, utilize social services should be described. Alternative sources of aid should be described, and community preferences as well as complaints made explicit. The relationship of wealth, values, and community organization to the use of services is always a complex matter.

The information collected on a community should be kept in one place and maintained. That way, current data are always available for training and consulting purposes. The file should be regularly reviewed by social service personnel most frequently in contact with members of the community. It can also serve as a basis for staff meetings and for planning new or revised services.

6. CULTURAL KNOWLEDGE: A FIELDWORK EXPERIENCE

The purpose of this exercise is to give participants a chance to meet the kinds of people that they may have known only through professional or institutional contacts. Both the chapter on ethnicity and that on language have stressed the need for a client- and community-based perspective on needs and on how social services fit into local ways of meeting those needs. It is assumed that most participants in this exercise will already have had some kind of field placement or work experience with ethnically distinctive clients. But to know clients in institutional or agency settings is to know them on the worker's turf. This exercise reverses that procedure. It requires the participant to leave the safety and emotional supports of the office and work routine and to enter the client's world. The participant should not view this as "slumming." Nor should he or she wear the "social work" or "researcher" label in approaching others. The success of the exercise depends on dropping those kinds of role identities and appearing simply as an interested onlooker who is seeking to understand what others are doing and thinking.

In addition to meeting clients in naturalistic settings, this exercise introduces an important technique for learning about culturally distinctive communities. A "key respondent" in participant observation research is an individual who acts as a guide to the group or culture the participant wishes to understand. A good key respondent is knowledgeable and articulate about his or her culture, is willing to share that knowledge, and has the time and interest to provide an introduction to a group or community. The key respondent is able to share his or her "cognitive map" of a distinctive social world with the learner. Finding and establishing a working relationship with a key respondent is a standard feature of all intensive cross-cultural work. Here that technique is applied to the needs of the social service practitioner.

Each participant should identify an agency in which he or she has previously been involved. List the kind of clients served: where they came from, what they wanted, how they acted, and how their problems were treated. Then describe in one paragraph how staff members (including the participant) felt about these clients: the kind of people they were, why they had the problems they had, and what would be best for them to do about their problems. If staff comments indicative of these points can be recalled, write them down in the paragraph. This should be a summarizing statement of staff beliefs and attitudes toward clients.

Identify an individual who can serve as a key respondent for several hours or for part of a day. That person may be another worker, but also could be an acquaintance or former client. The key respondent *must* be a member of the ethnic community in question; reliance on whites who claim to be knowledgeable (even when they are) will not do. Explain your purposes to the respondent: to learn something of the community as community members see it; to better understand why clients from the community have need of some services; to appreciate how people use community resources to deal with their problems; to discover how people feel about their relations with the larger society in general and with social service institutions and providers in particular.

You may want to meet several times with your key respondent. You should ask to be introduced to people in the community and to be taken to the kinds of places people in the community are likely to gather—perhaps to take part in some activity with others. During this exercise, ask your key respondent what things are going on and why. Inquire as to values, preferences, practices.

Act natural. If you present yourself as the cool scientific observer or as the enthusiastic, admiring devotee of the quaint and exotic, you will not only offend others and embarrass your respondent, but you will have failed the exercise completely. Becoming a learner of another culture is a humbling as well as a sensitizing experience. Approach it that way.

After your visit, write down the things you remember that were done or said. Then review the information from your first list. It is supported or refuted by what you saw or heard, or by what your key respondent described? Does it need to be modified or amplified in any way? If you were to report back to the staff about your experience, what would you want to tell them that would be useful in improving the delivery of services? If the exercise seems to confirm all the items in your original list, or if you learned nothing new, ask yourself what a minority social work student might have found in what you observed.

Share your list and observations in a group discussion. Discuss your findings in terms of possible discrepancies between the view of clients held by those who see them as "cases" and what you observed. Each participant in the exercise should make one specific suggestion for modifying services or training for agency staff in terms of what was discovered about clients during the community visit. List these and see if they could be developed into a general statement of service or training recommendations.

7. CULTURAL KNOWLEDGE:
MINORITY PROFESSIONALS

Most minority professionals have special insights into the needs of the communities they serve. But in addition, they are often particularly sensitive to the way social service organizations affect persons of minority background generally. What they know in this area is "insider information," the emic perspective. White social workers can learn much from their minority colleagues if they choose to do so. The questions listed below are examples of things that minority workers might be asked. Other questions can and should be added to the list.

(a) Relations with Clients
of Minority Groups

What are the distinctive problems of the minority clients whom you see?

Are there things that minority clients might say to a minority worker that they would probably not tell a white social worker?

How do they describe these things to you? Is there any special language or terms that they use?

What do clients expect you as a minority professional to understand intuitively about them and their problems?

What do you think clients look for in you that they would not expect in a white social worker?

Are there any distinctive advantages that you as a minority professional have with your clients?

(b) Relations with White Social Workers

In the relations of white social workers with minority clients, as you have seen them, is there anything that troubles you?

In your professional relations with white social workers, is there anything that troubles you? How could white social workers be more supportive of you as a minority professional?

What do you think white social workers could do or should know if they want to work more effectively with minority clients?

If a new social worker were assigned to your agency tomorrow, one who had never worked with minority clients before, and your task was to spend the day getting this worker started, specifically what would you do, and what would you want him or her to know by the end of the day?

(c) Role of Education

What in your formal or informal education best prepared you for working with minority clients?

What would have helped?

How do you keep up with research and other literature on minority communities and clients? What materials are important to you?

What advice would you give to a class of aspiring minority social work students?

(d) Agency and Policy

Can you describe instances where you felt the needs of your clients were in conflict with the type of service offered by your agency or the policies that prevailed?

Can you give an instance where you felt that your agency had failed a minority client? Why do you think that happened?

If you could restructure your office, program, or the personnel in it to better serve minority clients, what would you do?

8. CULTURAL KNOWLEDGE: PARTICIPANT OBSERVATION

There are many minority-oriented and -operated social service agencies, and their number is growing. They serve every ethnic group and deal with most of the problems handled by professionals in other agencies. But they often have a special tone which sets them apart from more established organizations. Part of that is due to the backgrounds of the clients and workers, and the distinctive ways in which they interact. Frequently, minority agencies work to emulate in their service activities some of the cultural characteristics of the communities they serve. They often do this under serious financial limitations, limitations which are often disruptive but which also increase the sense of urgency and importance about the work to be done.

A visit to a minority social service agency can be an illuminating experience, not only for social work students but also for established professionals. All the authors of this book have been involved with minority agencies in one way or another. The author has used the list of questions and statements below in a study involving white social workers who made visits to minority agencies. The list was used for training purposes, and it suggests some of the things that workers can ask about and look for as participant observers.

A word of caution: for an activity like this, the staff of a minority agency must be approached with all the sensitivity that would be involved in any effort to enter an unfamiliar community. Minority professionals are commonly overworked and underpaid, and they get more requests for "resource" assistance from whites than they can reasonably fulfill. White workers who are negotiating informational visits need to make clear what benefits, if any, are to accrue to minority agencies for the time and effort invested.

General Background

(a)   What is the recent history of minority social service organizations of this type in your area? How were they established, and what do they do?

(b)   What kind of training and experience is common for staff members in agencies of this type?

(c)   What are some of the common problems or complaints that are brought by ing, promotion and utilization of services, recruitment of staff, and the like?

(d)   What kinds of relationships do minority agencies have with other minority agencies, with large state organizations, and with county and city organizations? Do staff members have special feelings about these relationships?

Working with Clients in Minority and Ethnic Group Agencies

(a)   What are some of the common problems or complaints that are brought by clients to the agency?

(b)   In making an assessment or diagnosis of some of these problems, what kinds of questions do staff members ask of clients? Give some examples.

(c)   Do staff members feel that any of these problems are related to class or to the cultural characteristics of their clients? If so, describe what these problems might be.

(d)   What are some of the treatment plans or intervention strategies most commonly used by your staff? Describe how a plan is developed.

(e)   Are there any significant ways that these plans differ from those of other minority agencies or from those of agencies serving largely white clients?

(f)   Do the problems that clients bring to the agency and the ways staff deal with them suggest norms or values that are typical of the client community? Can these be defined?

Adjusting to a New Agency

(a)   Are there some common errors of assessment, diagnosis, or treatment that a visitor or worker unfamiliar with the agency or its clients might make? Can you describe an example?

(b)   Are there any special communication techniques or skills that a visitor or new worker should know about?

(c)   Are there any special words or phrases used by clients or staff members that might have a special meaning in the agency or the community? If so, list some of these and define them.

9. CULTURAL KNOWLEDGE: DESCRIBING CULTURAL SEQUENCES

One technique for acquiring ethnographic information is to record sequences of events which can later be analyzed for their cultural content and significance. Virtually anything can be a sequence in a given culture, provided it is repetitive and involves a number of members of the community. The possibilities are endless. At the macrolevel, the developmental cycle of the family is a common organizing device. The idea originally came from the work of Fortes (1958), in his studies of African family systems, and it has been widely extended since then. The career of the individual is a potential sequence. Life histories are collected by ethnographers in order to identify cultural themes as they are experienced by individuals (Langness 1965). Goffman (1961) has used the career concept in what he calls the "moral career" of the mental patient. Spradley (1970) has defined and described the career of inner-city tramps, whom he calls "urban nomads," particularly the parts of their careers involving police, jailers, and the courts. Each of these examples, as well as too many others to be cited, reveal rich insights into the life and culture of particular peoples or kinds of people. But despite the diversity of topic, setting, theoretical interest, or level of abstraction, most employ a common methodology. That methodology is adaptable to the needs of social work students' interest in acquiring ethnographic information. The steps involved in this methodology are as follows:

(a)   Establish a problem to be investigated. Write it down. Define all the terms as completely as possible. This sets the boundaries of the inquiry.

(b)   Examine the literature on the problem. Read across disciplines as appropriate. To limit the inquiry to the literature of a single discipline is the formula for parochialism. Read for data, methods, and general conclusions. Summarize these in writing.

(c)   Define hypotheses, specific problems, or issues to be examined. Be precise and write them down. This is a critical step, for it tells the observer what to look for at the field site. Without it, there can be no disciplined inquiry.

(d)   Determine appropriate recording techniques. Is the investigator going to take notes, use a tape recorder, or depend on memory? Whatever technique is used, it obviously should be practiced, so that it is not obtrusive.

(e)   Make repeated, detailed, and accurate observations of all the things relevant to the hypotheses or statements of problems. It will be apparent at this stage whether or not the hypotheses were sufficiently precise to allow identification of only those things that the observer wishes to record. Compile and index the results.

(f)   Analyze the data. What do they suggest about each of the hypotheses or problem statements? How do they bear on the discussion of the problem as represented in the research literature? How do they advance the learner's knowledge of the culture in question?

(g)   Draw your conclusions, and state them as new or revised hypotheses. Specify the population to which they apply and to what extent they can be generalized. Relate your findings to what you know about clients of this type generally and to how the information might be used in intervention, in training, and in further research.

These steps do not differ significantly from other forms of social inquiry. But their application to repetitive behavior among members of a single community can result in a surprising quantity of data in a short period of time.

10. CULTURAL KNOWLEDGE:
COVER TERMS AND ATTRIBUTES

Use of linguistic clues provided by respondents is one of the quickest, most efficient ways of acquiring ethnographic information. The technique, as we have outlined it here, is a simple one, although it has been developed by Spradley (1979) as part of a larger and much more complex investigative process, and his publications should be consulted for more details. All that is required by the learner is a linguistic sample from a respondent. For instance, consider the following conversation taken from the author's notes of an inerview with a child protective service worker:

> I see all kinds of clients. Just recently I worked with a woman who was very disturbed; I'd say she had severe depression. The child had a number of contusions on the head and arms and the X-rays showed subdural hematoma. I took that as evidence of the battered child syndrome and asked the judge for a preliminary hearing.

Just this snippet of conversation contains enough cover terms to keep an interview going for an hour or more. Remember that we described a cover term as a word or expression, sometimes in a vernacular, that may be unfamiliar to the interviewer but seems to have particular meaning or importance for the respondent. In this sample, there are at least seven cover terms of interest: clients, disturbed, depression, contusions, subdural hematoma, battered child syndrome, and preliminary hearing. Each stands for, or "covers," a block of information that is part of the shared subculture of protective service workers, the things they know as a kind of community, more or less specialized and unique to them. (Some of the terms, of course, are shared with other subcultures—other kinds of social workers, doctors, and lawyers—but it may be that meanings shift somewhat as we go from one professional culture to another. At least, we cannot assume that they do not.) These words are the emic labels of this category of practitioners.

Using the cover terms as guides, we can begin to elicit attributes which will help us define the cultural world of these workers. Attributes are identified by asking questions concerning kinds, qualities, descriptive characteristics, relationships, and the like. For instance, if this was our first of several interviews with this respondent, we might ask a global question: "How many kinds of *clients* are there? Can you list them for me?" In addition, the interviewee's comments suggest that there is a large category, *disturbed,* of which *depression* is a special case and *severe depression* an even finer division within the grouping. We might ask, therefore: "When you say *disturbed,* how many things does that include?" Or we could ask: "Can you tell me all the characteristics of *depression,* and how you distinguish *severe depression* from other kinds?" In short, we are asking: How do you know it when you see it? What to you are a thing's attributes? The same line of questioning can be pursued with each of the other cover terms. Some terms may be precise, such as the legal and medical ones; others may be generalized.

We do not demand full, exhaustive information from one respondent. Where the respondent's knowledge is unclear, that fact, too, provides important information. For instance, if the worker's knowledge of attributes for *battered child syndrome* is vague, contradictory, or shifting, that in itself would be important to know, since it would tell us that this particular worker may be making decisions about intervention without a clear, conceptual notion of what is involved. If interviews showed that to be true of a number of workers, we would have hard data for making a case for better training. Those data would have come to us from this ethnographic research style.

It is clear that even a tiny fragment of linguistic information is a clue to a great deal of cultural knowledge. The worker need only find the clues, the cover terms, and pursue them in a systematic way. The possibilities for doing this are endless. Spradley and McCurdy (1972) published examples of their students' interviews in a text for college freshmen. Those interviews ranged from subcultures as diverse as airline stewardesses to organized car thieves. Social workers who want to practice the technique can do so with other workers, focusing on the specialized tasks, skills, or client communities associated with their interview partners. Where willing clients are available, they might be interviewed on topics of interest to them. The author once interviewed a student volunteer in a class on social welfare research methods. There was no rehearsal or advance notice on the topic, and the student announced to the surprised class that he wanted to be interviewed about his year in the penitentiary. The author conducted the interview, and the class took notes. By the end of the hour, some of the rich vocabulary of the inmate subculture, as cover terms and attributes, was spread over two blackboards, and the students had an insider's glimpse of a world they had known only from their textbooks.

11. CODES OF ETHICS
IN SOCIAL WORK

Two codes of ethics that relate to the social work profession are presented below. Each views the discipline from a different perspective, and each emphasizes different concerns. Study and comparison of these codes will be useful in thinking about the issues raised in the book, particularly those sections on values and on ethnic group-social work relationships.

The learner might ask such questions as: What do these codes emphasize that distinguishes them from each other? What are their implications for practice and for policy? How would programs be changed if one or another of these codes were fully implemented? How would that influence relationships with clients whose ethnic background differed from your own? These are important concerns for social work, and the learner should examine the codes carefully with questions such as these in mind.

THE NASW CODE OF ETHICS

(Passed by the 1979 Delegate Assembly. Implementation set for July 1, 1980.)

I.   THE SOCIAL WORKER'S CONDUCT AND COMPORTMENT AS A SOCIAL WORKER
      A.   *Propriety.* The social worker should maintain high standards of personal conduct in the capacity or identity as social worker.
      B.   *Competence and Professional Development.* The social worker should strive to become and remain proficient in professional practice and the performance of professional functions.
      C.   *Service.* The social worker should regard as primary the service obligation of the social work profession.

D. *Integrity.* The social worker should act in accordance with the highest standards of professional integrity.

E. *Scholarship and Research.* The social worker engaged in study and research should be guided by the conventions of scholarly inquiry.

II.   THE SOCIAL WORKER'S ETHICAL RESPONSIBILITY TO CLIENTS

F. *Primacy of Clients' Interests.* The social worker's primary responsibility is to clients.

G. *Rights and Prerogatives of Clients.* The social worker should make every effort to foster maximum self-determination on the part of clients.

H. *Confidentiality and Privacy.* The social worker should respect the privacy of clients and hold in confidence all information obtained in the course of professional service.

I. *Fees.* When setting fees, the social worker should ensure that they are fair, reasonable, considerate, and commensurate with the service performed and with due regard for the clients' ability to pay.

III. THE SOCIAL WORKER'S ETHICAL RESPONSIBILITY TO COLLEAGUES

J. *Respect, Fairness, and Courtesy.* The social worker should treat colleagues with respect, courtesy, fairness, and good faith.

K. *Dealing with Colleagues' Clients.* The social worker has the responsibility to relate to the clients of colleagues with full professional consideration.

IV.   THE SOCIAL WORKER'S ETHICAL RESPONSIBILITY TO EMPLOYERS AND EMPLOYING ORGANIZATIONS

L. *Commitments to Employing Organizations.* The social worker should adhere to commitments made to the employing organizations.

V.   THE SOCIAL WORKER'S ETHICAL RESPONSIBILITY TO THE SOCIAL WORK PROFESSION

M. *Maintaining the Integrity of the Profession.* The social worker should uphold and advance the values, ethics, knowledge, and mission of the profession.

N. *Community Service.* The social worker should assist the profession in making social services available to the general public.

O. *Development of Knowledge.* The social worker should take responsibility for identifying, developing, and fully utilizing knowledge for professional practice.

VI.   THE SOCIAL WORKER'S ETHICAL RESPONSIBILITY TO SOCIETY

P. *Promoting the General Welfare.* The social worker should promote the general welfare of society.

A CODE OF ETHICS FOR
RADICAL SOCIAL SERVICE WORKERS

From Jeffry Galper, *The Politics of Social Services*
(Englewood Cliffs, NJ: Prentice-Hall, 1975).

As an effort to contribute to the development of a radical ideology and commitment capable of informing radical practice, we close by returning to the Code of Ethics of the professional social work association, the National Association of

Social Workers. In an earlier chapter we argued, point by point, that this Code contains a conservative bias that serves the best interests of neither client, worker, nor social well-being in general. We will consider each item of this Code, therefore, and suggest how it might be revised were it organized in service of the development of the kind of society we hope to build. In a sense, the following point-by-point comparison summarizes this book. As the existing Code encapsulates the analysis and goals of conventional practice, so our modifications encapsulate the analysis and goals of the radical social service worker. Our Code will have fourteen planks.

1.   I regard as my primary obligation the welfare of all human kind.

The existing Code suggests that the social welfare worker regards as a primary obligation the welfare of the individual or group served. The limiting and destructive nature of the individualistic and pluralistic strategies that follow from this obligation have been documented numerous times in this book. The well-being of any one of us is inseparable from the well-being of all of us, and this awareness must be reflected in radical practice.

2.   I will work toward the development of a society that is committed to the dictum, "From each according to his or her ability, to each according to his or her need."

The existing Code is concerned with nondiscrimination, in the civil libertarian sense, and commits the worker to serving all persons without bias. We have described the limitations inherent in the notion of equality of opportunity, which this plank reflects, and have suggested that our focus must be on outcomes as well as processes.

3.   I will struggle for the realization of a society in which my personal interests and my personal actions are consistent with my interests and actions as a worker.

At present, the Code suggests that personal interests be subordinated to professional responsibility and that statements and actions as a professional be kept apart from statements and actions as a private person. The personal fragmentation and politically conservative implications of this arrangement received attention elsewhere in this book. Our work and our lives must become increasingly integrated.

4.   I will consider myself accountable to all who join in the struggle for social change and will consider them accountable to me for the quality and extent of the work we perform and the society we create.

The current Code commits the worker to be responsible to himself or herself for this work. The need for collective accountability and struggle, however, is paramount. While personal standards are always desirable, we must add to them the critical collective concern.

5. I will work to achieve the kind of world in which all people can be free and open with one another in all matters.

The existing Code's commitment is to respect the privacy of all persons served. Without suggesting that one violate the trust of others, the emphasis on privacy must be counteracted inasmuch as our society is adept at using privacy to control us by keeping us apart. Openness is critical to the development of a society organized around positive mutual commitments.

6. I will use information gained from my work to facilitate humanistic, revolutionary change in the society.

The Code's commitment to the responsible use of information gained in professional work on the one hand implies a desirable concern for integrity. On the other hand, it suggests commitment to professional practice above a commitment to radical social change. This is not acceptable in radical practice.

7. I will treat the findings, views, and actions of colleagues with the respect due them. This respect is conditioned by their demonstrated concern for revolutionary values and radical social change.

This plank in the old Code argues for respect of colleagues per se. No commitment can be made to professional colleagues that is not in the context of a commitment to larger social values. Inasmuch as they do not have such a commitment, their findings, views, and actions must be rejected and challenged, though their humanity must always be acknowledged.

8. I will use all the knowledge and skill available to me in bringing about a radically transformed society.

The old Code's concern is that practice be conducted within the recognized knowledge and competence of the profession. This does not facilitate the kind of total engagement and total use of all resources which is required in the struggle for radical change.

9. I recognize my responsibility to add my ideas and findings to our society's knowledge and practice.

The existing Code's concern for adding such ideas and findings to social welfare knowledge and practice is worthy but limiting. Social work is a vehicle and servant. It is neither the temple nor the master.

10. I accept my responsibility to help protect the community against unethical practice by any individuals or organizations in the society.

The present Code asks for protection against such practices in the social welfare field. This is not enough. Our commitment is to struggle against the destructive elements of the whole.

11. I commit myself to use myself fully in the struggle for revolutionary change.

The existing Code urges readiness to provide services in public emergencies. Our society, at this time, is experiencing an emergency in an ongoing way. There is no more appropriate time for us to engage. Earthquakes, floods, and fires are minor happenings compared to the daily destruction wreaked by our institutions in the normal course of events.

12. I support the principle that all persons can and must contribute to the realization of a humanized society.

The old Code stresses the need for professional education for professional practice. Inasmuch as radical work is concerned with the fundamental reorganization of our society, at this time, is experiencing an emergency in an ongoing way. There is no participants.

13. I accept responsibility for working toward the creation and maintenance of conditions in society that enable all people to live by this Code.

The present Code's stress on enabling social workers in agencies to live by that code is isolating and limiting in view of the tasks before us.

14. I contribute my knowledge, skills, and support to the accomplishment of a humanistic, democratic, communal socialist society.

The Code's suggestion that we contribute knowledge, skills, and support to programs of human welfare is desirable but limited. We must be clear about our goals and courageous in putting the notion of a radically altered society on the agenda.

It seems likely that, for any one of us, if there is a will, there is not necessarily a way. Acting collectively, however, the possibilities of what we can create are very exciting. While radicals are more given to manifestos than Codes of Ethics, we need to find ways to think together about how we can proceed. If this Code, and this book serve any useful political purpose, it will be to facilitate that thinking.

BIBLIOGRAPHY

ABBOTT, KENNETH A., and ELIZABETH LEE ABBOTT
    1973   "Juvenile Delinquency in San Francisco's Chinese-American Community: 1961-1966," in Stanley Sue and Nathaniel N. Wagner, eds., *Asian-Americans: Psychological Perspectives* (Palo Alto: Science and Behavior Books): 171-80.

ACOSTA, FRANK X.
    1979   "Barriers between Mental Health Services and Mexican Americans: An Examination of a Paradox," *American Journal of Community Psychology* 7: 503-20.
    1980   "Research Priorities in Mental Health Service Delivery for Hispanics," in Joseph Gallegos, ed., *Research Priorities in Hispanic Mental Health Service Delivery: A Workshop Report* (Seattle: Western Research Associates): 16-27.

ACUNA, RODOLFO
    1972   *Occupied America: The Chicano Struggle toward Liberation* (San Francisco: Canfield Press).

ANGROSINO, MICHAEL V.
    1978   "Applied Anthropology and the Concept of the Underdog: Implications for Community Mental Health Planning and Evaluation," *Community Mental Health Journal* 14: 291-99.

ARVIZU, STEVEN F., and WARREN SNYDER
    1977   *Demystifying the Concept of Culture: Conceptual Tools* (Sacramento: Sacramento State University).

BARAKA, IMANU AMIRI
    1973   "A Black Value System, in *Contemporary Black Thought: The Best from the Black Scholar* (Indianapolis: Bobbs Merrill): 54-60.

BARNOW, VICTOR
    1963   *Culture and Personality* (Homewood, Ill.: The Dorsey Press).

BARRERA, MANUEL
    1978   "Mexican-American Mental Health Service Utilization: A Critical Examination of Some Proposed Variables," *Community Mental Health Journal* 14: 35-45.

233

BARTH, FREDERIK
    1969   *Ethnic Groups and Boundaries* (Boston: Little, Brown).
BAUWENS, ELEANOR
    1977   "Medical Beliefs and Practices among Lower Income Anglos," in Edward H.
            Spicer, ed., *Ethnic Medicine in the Southwest* (Tucson: University of Arizona
            Press): 241-70.
BEARDSLEY, R. K.
    1965   "Personality Psychology," in R. K. Beardsley and J. W. Hall, eds., *Twelve
            Doors to Japan* (New York: McGraw-Hill): 350-82.
BECKER, HOWARD S., and JAMES W. CARPER
    1956   "The Development of Identification with an Occupation," *American Journal
            of Sociology* 61: 289-98.
BENEDICT, RUTH
    1934   *Patterns of Culture* (New York: New American Library).
BENJAMIN, ALFRED
    1969   *The Helping Interview* (Boston: Houghton Mifflin).
BENNETT, JOHN W., ed.
    1975   *The New Ethnicity: Perspectives from Ethnology* (St. Paul: West Publishing
            Co.).
BILLINGSLEY, ANDREW
    1968   *Black Families in White America* (Englewood Cliffs, N.J.: Prentice-Hall).
    1969   "Family Functioning in the Low Income Black Community," *Social Casework*
            50: 563-72.
BLANCHARD, EVELYN
    1979   "Social Work Practice with American Indians," in James W. Green and Collin
            Tong, eds., *Cultural Awareness in the Human Services, A Training Manual*
            (Seattle: University of Washington Center for Social Welfare Research): 169-209.
BLANCHARD, EVELYN, and STEVEN UNGER
    1977   "Destruction of American Indian Families," *Social Casework* 58: 312-14.
BLOCH, JULIA B.
    1968   "The White Worker and the Negro Client in Psychotherapy," *Social Work* 13:
            36-42.
BOAS, FRANZ
    1943   "Recent Anthropology," *Science* 98: 311-14.
BOGDAN, ROBERT
    1972   *Participant Observation in Organizational Settings* (Syracuse, N.Y.: Syracuse
            University Press).
BOISSEVAIN, JEREMY
    1968   "The Place of Non-Groups in the Social Sciences," *Man* 3: 542-55.
BOLLENS, JOHN C., and DALE R. MARSHALL
    1973   *A Guide to Participation* (Englewood Cliffs, N.Y.: Prentice-Hall).
BOTT, ELIZABETH
    1957   *Family and Social Network* (London: Tavistock).
BOWMAN, B., W. CARLIN, A. GARCIA, C. MAYBEE, D. MILLER, and P. SIERRAS
    1975   *Native American Families in the City: American Indian Socialization to Urban
            Life* (San Francisco: Institute for Scientific Analysis).
BREELY, ANDREW
    1972   *The Denominational Society: A Sociological Approach to Religion in America*
            (Glenview, Ill.: Scott Foresman).
BRIM, JOHN, and DAVID SPAIN
    1974   *Research Design in Anthropology* (New York: Holt, Rinehart and Winston).
BRISLIN, RICHARD W., ed.
    1976   *Topics in Culture Learning* (Honolulu: East-West Center).
BRISLIN, RICHARD W., and PAUL PEDERSEN
    1976   *Cross-Cultural Orientation Programs* (New York: Gardner Press).
BRITAN, GERALD
    1978   "The Place of Anthropology in Program Evaluation," *Anthropological Quarterly*
            5: 119-28.

BROWNLEE, ANN TEMPLETON
    1978   *Community, Culture, and Care* (St. Louis: C. V. Mosby).
BROWNLEE, ANN, and MAUREEN J. GIOVANNINI
    1978   "The Role of the University in Sociocultural Training for International Health Careers," in William T. Vickers and Glenn R. Howze, eds., *Social Science Education for Development* (Tuskegee, Al.: Tuskegee Institute): 35-59.
BULATAO, J. C.
    1962   "Philippine Values: The Manilenos Mainsprings," *Philippine Studies* 10: 51-86.
BURREL, GRACE, and NELBA CHAVEZ
    1971   *The Community Mental Health Concept: Relevant and Irrelevant to Mexican American Community* (Denver: University of Denver).
CARROLL, JOHN B.
    1956   "Introduction" to John B. Carroll, ed., *Language, Thought, and Reality, Selected Writings of Benjamin Lee Whorf* (Cambridge: M.I.T. Press): 1-34.
CHADWICK, B., and J. STRAUSS
    1975   "The Assimilation of American Indians into Urban Society: The Seattle Case," *Human Organization* 34: 4.
CHANG, S. C.
    1965   "The Cultural Context of Japanese Psychiatry and Psychotherapy," *American Journal of Psychotherapy* 19: 593-606.
CHAVEZ, NELBA
    1980   "Hispanic Expectations of Mental Health Services," in Joseph Gallegos, ed., *Research Priorities in Hispanic Mental Health Service Delivery: A Work Shop Report* (Seattle: Western Research Associates): 28-34.
CHEN, P.
    1973   "Samoans in California," *Social Work* 18: 41-49.
CHENG, EVA
    1978   *The Elder Chinese* (San Diego: Center on Aging, San Diego State University).
CLARK, MARGARET
    1959   *Health in the Mexican-American Culture: A Community Study* (Berkeley: University of California Press).
CLOWARD, RICHARD A., and FRANCES FOX PIVEN
    1975   "Notes toward a Radical Social Work," in Roy Bailey and Mike Brake, eds., *Radical Social Work* (New York: Random House): vii-xlvii.
COCHRANE, GLYNN
    1979   *The Cultural Appraisal of Development Projects* (New York: Praeger).
COGAN, MORRIS L.
    1953   "Toward a Definition of Profession," *Harvard Educational Review* 23: 33-50.
COLLINS, ALICE H., and DIANE L. PANCOAST
    n.d.   *Natural Helping Networks: A Strategy for Prevention* (Washington, D.C.: National Association of Social Workers).
CORDOVA, F.
    1973   "The Filipino American: There's Always an Identity Crisis," in S. Sue and N. Wagner, eds., *Asian-Americans: Psychological Perspectives* (Palo Alto: Science and Behavior Books): 136-39.
COWGER, CHARLES D.
    1977   "Alternative Stances in the Relationship of Social Work to Society," *Journal of Education for Social Work* 13: 25-29.
CRUSE, HAROLD
    1967   *The Crisis of the Negro Intellectual* (New York: William Morrow).
CURRY, ANDREW E.
    1964   "The Negro Worker and the White Client: A Commentary on the Treatment Relationship," *Social Casework* 45: 131-36.
DANISH, STEVEN J., and ALLEN L. HAUER
    1973   *Helping Skills: A Basic Training Program* (New York: Behavioral Publications).
DAVIS, FRED, and PATRICK BIERNACKI
    n.d.   "Ex-Marijuana Users Interview Guide," unpublished manuscript quoted in John Lofland 1971: 79.

DAVIS, OSSIE
    1969   "The Language of Racism: the English Language Is My Enemy," in Neal Post-
            man, Charles Weingartner, and Terence P. Moran, eds., *Language in America*
            (New York: Pegasus): 73-9.
DELANEY, ANITA J.
    1979   *Black Task Force Report: Project on Ethnicity* (New York: Family Service
            Association of America).
DELORIA, V.
    1969   *Custer Died for Your Sins* (New York: Avon Books).
de VALDEZ, THERESA ARAGON
    1978   *The Nature of Chicano Political Powerlessness* (Ann Arbor: University Micro-
            films).
DOI, T.
    1962   "Amae: A Key Concept for Understanding Japanese Personality Structure,"
            Psychology 5: 1-7.
DOUGLAS, MARY
    1966   *Purity and Danger* (Baltimore: Penguin Books).
DURAN, L. I., and H. R. BERNARD, eds.
    1973   *Introduction to Chicano Studies* (New York: Macmillan).
EDGERTON, ROBERT B.
    1976   *Deviance: A Cross-Cultural Perspective* (Menlo Park, CA: Cummings).
EDGERTON, ROBERT B., and L. L. LANGNESS
    1974   *Methods and Styles in the Study of Cultures* (San Francisco: Chandler and
            Sharp Publishers).
ENDO, RUSSELL
    1974   "Japanese Americans: The 'Model Minority' in Perspective," in Rudolph Gomez,
            Clement Cottingham, Jr., Russell Endo, and Kathleen Jackson, eds., *The Social
            Reality of Ethnic America* (Lexington, MA: D. C. Heath): 189-213.
EVERETT, MICHAEL W., JACK O. WADDELL, and DWIGHT B. HEATH
    1976   *Cross-Cultural Approaches to the Study of Alcohol* (The Hague: Mouton).
FABREGA, HORACIO, JR.
    1974   *Disease and Social Behavior* (Cambridge: MIT Press).
FABREGA, H., and CAROLE WALLACE
    1976   "Value Identification and Psychiatric Disability: An Analysis Involving Ameri-
            cans of Mexican Descent," in Carole Hernandez et al., eds., *Chicanos: Social
            and Psychological Perspectives* (St. Louis: C. V. Mosby): 253-62.
FARRIS, C.
    1973   "A White House Conference on the American Indian," *Social Work* 18: 80-86.
    1975   "The American Indian: Social Work Education's Neglected Minority," *Journal
            of Education for Social Work* 11: 137-43.
FERGUSON, FRANCES N.
    1976   "Stake Theory as an Explanatory Device in Navajo Alcoholism Treatment
            Response," *Human Organization* 35: 65-78.
FIBUSH, ESTHER
    1965   "The White Worker and the Negro Client," *Social Casework* 46: 271-77.
FIBUSH, ESTHER, and BeALVA TURNQUEST
    1970   "A Black and White Approach to the Problem of Racism," *Social Casework*
            51: 459-66.
FITZPATRICK, J. P.
    1971   *Puerto Rican Americans* (Englewood Cliffs, N.J.: Prentice-Hall).
FOGLEMAN, B.
    1972   *Adaptive Mechanisms of the North American Indian to an Urban Setting* (Ann
            Arbor: University Microfilms).
FORTES, M.
    1958   "Introduction," in J. R. Goody, ed., *The Developmental Cycle in Domestic
            Groups* (Cambridge: Cambridge University Press): 1-14.
FOSTER, GEORGE
    1965   "Peasant Society and the Image of Limited Good," *American Anthropologist*
            67: 293-315.
    1967   *Tzintzuntzan: Mexican Peasants in a Changing World* (Boston: Little, Brown).

FOSTER, GEORGE M., and BARBARA GALLATIN ANDERSON
    1978   *Medical Anthropology* (New York: John Wiley and Sons).
FUJII, SHARON M.
    1976   "Elderly Asian Americans and Use of Public Services," *Social Casework* 57: 202-07.
GAINES, ATWOOD D.
    1979   "Definitions and Diagnosis: Cultural Implications of Psychiatric Help-Seeking and Psychiatrists' Definitions of the Situation in Psychiatric Emergencies," *Culture, Medicine and Psychiatry* 3: 381-418.
GALARZA, ERNESTO
    1969   *Merchants of Labor: The Mexican Bracero Story* (Santa Barbara: McNally and Loftin).
GALLEGOS, JOSEPH
    1978   *A Reconceptualization of Pluralism for Social Work Education* (Denver: University of Denver).
GALLEGOS, JOSEPH, and THERESA ARAGON de VALDEZ
    1979   "The Chicano Familia," in James W. Green and Collin Tong, eds., *Cultural Awareness in the Human Services: A Training Manual* (Seattle: University of Washington): 277-340.
GAMIO, MANUEL
    1930   *Mexican Immigration to the United States* (Chicago: University of Chicago Press).
    1931   *The Mexican Immigrant: His Life Story* (Chicago: University of Chicago Press).
GAVIRIA, M., and G. STERN
    1980   "Problems in Designing and Implementing Culturally Relevant Mental Health Services for Latinos in the U.S.," *Social Science and Medicine* 14: 65-71.
GEERTZ, CLIFFORD
    1976   "From the Native's Point of View: On the Nature of Anthropological Understanding," in Keith Basso and Henry A. Shelby, eds., *Meaning in Anthropology* (Albuquerque: University of New Mexico Press): 221-37.
GELMAN, SHELDON R.
    1980   "Esoterica: A Zero Sum Game in the Helping Professions," *Social Casework* 61: 48-53.
GHALI, SONIA BADILLO
    1977   "Cultural Sensitivity and the Puerto Rican Client," *Social Casework* 58: 459-68.
GIBSON, MARGARET, and STEVEN F. ARVIZU
    1977   *Demystifying the Concept of Culture: Methodological Tools* (Sacramento: Sacramento State University).
GLAZER, NATHAN, and DANIEL PATRICK MOYNIHAN
    1963   *Beyond the Melting Pot* (Cambridge: MIT Press).
GOFFMAN, ERVING
    1959   *The Presentation of Self in Everyday Life* (Garden City, N.Y.: Doubleday).
    1961   *Asylums* (Garden City, N.Y.: Doubleday).
GOODE, WILLIAM J.
    1957   "Community Within a Community: The Professions," *American Sociological Review* 22: 194-200.
GOODENOUGH, WARD H.
    1957   "Cultural Anthropology and Linguistics," in P. L. Garvin, ed., *Report of the Seventh Annual Round Table Meeting on Linguistics and Language Study* (Washington, D.C.: Georgetown University): 1-4.
GOODMAN, MARY ELLEN
    1970   *The Culture of Childhood* (New York: Columbia University Press).
GOOD TRACKS, JIMM G.
    1973   "Native American Non-Interference," *Social Work* 18: 30-34.
GORDON, RAYMOND L.
    1969   *Interviewing* (Homewood, IL: The Dorsey Press).
GRAVES, THEODORE D.
    1967   "Acculturation, Access and Alcohol in a Tri-Ethnic Community," *American Anthropologist* 69: 306-21.

1970   "The Personal Adjustment of Navajo Indian Migrants to Denver, Colorado," *American Anthropologist* 72: 35-54.
GREBLER, LEO, JOAN MOORE, and R. GUZMAN
1970   *The Mexican American People* (New York: The Free Press).
GREEN, JAMES W.
1973   "The British West Indian Alien Labor Problem in the Virgin Islands," *Caribbean Studies* 12: 56-75.
1978   "The Role of Cultural Anthropology in the Education of Social Service Personnel," *Journal of Sociology and Social Welfare* 5: 214-29.
1980   "A Cultural Approach to Understanding Child Abuse" (manuscript).
GREEN, VERA
1970   "The Confrontation of Diversity within the Black Community," *Human Organization* 29: 267-72.
GREENWOOD, ERNEST
1957   "Attributes of a Profession," *Social Work* 2: 45-55.
GUMPERZ, JOHN J., and DELL HYMES, eds.
1972   *Directions in Sociolinguistics* (New York: Holt, Rinehart and Winston).
HALL, J. W.
1965   "Education and Modern National Development," in R. K. Beardsley and J. W. Hall, eds., *Twelve Doors to Japan* (New York: McGraw-Hill): 384-426.
HANDELMAN, DON
1976   "Bureaucratic Transactions: The Development of Official-Client Relationships in Israel," in Bruce Kapferer, ed., *Transaction and Meaning* (Philadelphia: Institute for the Study of Human Issues): 223-75.
HANNERZ, ULF
1969   *Soulside: Inquiries into Ghetto Culture and Community* (New York: Columbia University Press).
HARRINGTON, MICHAEL
1962   *The Other America* (New York: Macmillan).
HARRIS, MARVIN
1968   *The Rise of Anthropological Theory* (New York: Crowell).
HAWKINS, HOMER C.
1973   "Trends in Black Migration in 1863 to 1960," *Phylon* 34: 140-52.
HAYES-BAUTISTA, DAVID E.
1978   "Chicano Patients and Medical Practitioners: A Sociology of Knowledge Paradigm of Lay-Professional Interaction," *Social Science and Medicine* 12: 83-90.
HEISS, JEROLD
1975   *The Case of the Black Family* (New York: Columbia University Press).
HENDERSON, GEORGE P.
1979   *Understanding and Counseling Ethnic Minorities* (Springfield, IL: Charles C. Thomas).
HERSKOVITS, MELVILLE J.
1936   "Applied Anthropology and the American Anthropologist," *Science* 83: 215-22.
1947   *Man and His Works* (New York: Alfred A. Knopf).
HICKS, GEORGE L.
1975   "The Same North and South: Ethnicity and Change in Two American Indian Groups," in John Bennett, ed., *The New Ethnicity* (St. Paul: West Publishing Co.).
HILL, ROBERT B.
1971   *The Strengths of Black Families* (New York: National Urban League).
HILL, THOMAS W.
1978   "Drunken Comportment of Urban Indians: 'Time-Out' Behavior?" *Journal of Anthropological Research* 34: 442-67.
HO, M. K.
1976   "Social Work with Asian Americans," *Social Casework* 57: 195-201.
HOMMA-TRUE, R., S. CHEN, S. OW-LING, and W. LOUIE
1976   "Exploration of Mental Health Needs in an Asian American Community: Review of Oakland's Asian Community Mental Health Services" (manuscript).

HOOPES, DAVID S., PAUL B. PEDERSEN, and GEORGE W. RENWICK, eds.
    1977   *Overview of Intercultural Education, Training and Research, Volume I: Theory* (Washington, D.C.: Society for Intercultural Education, Training and Research).
    1978a   *Overview of Intercultural Education, Training and Research, Volume II: Education and Training* (Washington, D.C.: Society for Intercultural Education, Training and Research).
    1978b   *Overview of Intercultural Education, Training and Research, Volume III: Special Research Areas* (Washington, D.C.: Society for Intercultural Education, Training and Research).

HOOPES, DAVID S., and PAUL VENTURA, eds.
    1979   *Intercultural Sourcebook, Cross-Cultural Training Methodologies* (Washington, D.C.: Society for Intercultural Education, Training and Research).

HSU, F. L. K.
    1971   *The Challenge of the American Dream: The Chinese in the United States* (Belmont, CA: Wadsworth).

INDIAN FREE CLINIC
    1978   "Final Report of Developmental Disabilities Project, California Department of Health Contract #75-54405" (Huntington Park, CA: Indian Free Clinic).

ISHIKAWA, WESLEY H.
    1978   *The Elder Guamanian* (San Diego: Center on Aging, San Diego State University).
    1978   *The Elder Samoan* (San Diego: Center on Aging, San Diego State University).

ISHISAKA, HIDEKI, et al.
    1977   "Family Structure and Marital Treatment" (Seattle: Asian Counseling and Referral Service) (manuscript).

IVEY, A.
    1971   *Microcounseling* (Springfield, IL: Charles C. Thomas).

IWATA, M.
    1962   "The Japanese Immigrants in California Agriculture," *Agricultural History* 36: 35-37.

JACO, G. E.
    1959   "Mental Health of Spanish Americans in Texas," in M. K. Opler, ed., *Culture and Mental Health* (New York: Macmillan): 467-85.

JACOBS, SUE-ELLEN
    1974a   "Action and Advocacy Anthropology," *Human Organization* 33: 209-14.
    1974b   "Doing It Our Way and Mostly for Our Own," *Human Organization* 33: 380-82.
    1979   "Our Babies Shall Not Die: A Community's Response to Medical Neglect," *Human Organization* 38: 120-33.

JENKINS, SHIRLEY
    1975   "Collecting Data by Questionnaire and Interview," in Norman Polansky, ed., *Social Work Research* (Chicago: University of Chicago Press): 131-53.

JOHNSON, C. L.
    1973   "Gift Giving and Reciprocity among the Japanese Americans of Honolulu," *American Ethnologist* 1: 295-307.

JOHNSON, F. A., A. J. MARSELLA, and C. L. JOHNSON
    1974   "Social and Psychological Aspects of Verbal Behavior in Japanese Americans," *American Journal of Psychiatry* 131: 580-83.

JOHNSON, JOHN M.
    1975   *Doing Field Research* (New York: The Free Press).

JONES, DOROTHY M.
    1974   *The Urban Native Encounters the Social Service System* (Fairbanks: University of Alaska).
    1976   "The Mystique of Expertise in the Social Services," *Journal of Sociology and Social Welfare* 3: 332-46.

JORGENSEN, JOSEPH G.
    1977   "Poverty and Work among American Indians," in H. Roy Kaplan, ed., *American Minorities and Economic Opportunity* (Itasca, IL: F. E. Peacock Publishers): 170-97.

JUNG, M.
   1976   "Characteristics of Contrasting Chinatowns," *Social Casework* 57: 149-54.
KADUSHIN, ALFRED
   1972   *The Social Work Interview* (New York: Columbia University Press).
KANESHIGE, EDWARD
   1973   "Cultural Factors in Group Counseling and Interaction," *Personnel and Guidance Journal* 51: 407-12.
KAPFERER, BRUCE, ed.
   1976   *Transaction and Meaning, Directions in the Anthropology of Exchange and Symbolic Behavior* (Philadelphia: Institute for the Study of Human Issues).
KARDINER, ABRAM
   1945   *The Psychological Frontiers of Society* (New York: Columbia University Press).
KARNO, MARVIN, and ROBERT B. EDGERTON
   1969   "Perceptions of Mental Illness in a Mexican-American Community," *Archives of General Psychiatry* 20: 233-38.
KEARNEY, MICHAEL
   1975   "World View Theory and Study," in Bernard J. Siegel, Alan R. Beals, and Stephen A. Tyler, eds., *Annual Review of Anthropology* (Palo Alto: Annual Reviews) 4: 247-70.
KEEFE, S., A. PADILLA, and M. CARLOS
   1979   "The Mexican-American Extended Family as an Emotional Support System," *Human Organization* 38: 144-52.
KEIL, CHARLES
   1966   *Urban Blues* (Chicago: University of Chicago Press).
KELLY, G. P.
   1977   *From Vietnam to America: A Chronicle of Vietnamese Immigration to the United States* (Boulder, CO: Westview Press).
KEYES, CHARLES F.
   1977   *The Golden Peninsula* (New York: Macmillan).
KIEFER, C. W.
   1974   *Changing Cultures, Changing Lives* (San Francisco: Jossey-Bass).
KIM, BOK-LIM C.
   1972   "Casework with Japanese and Korean Wives of Americans," *Social Casework* 53: 273-79.
   1973   "Asian-Americans: No Model Minority," *Social Work* 18: 44-53.
   1978   *The Asian Americans: Changing Patterns, Changing Needs* (Montclair, N.J.: Association of Korean Christian Scholars in North America).
KITANO, H. L.
   1969   *Japanese Americans: The Evolution of a Subculture* (Englewood Cliffs, NJ: Prentice-Hall).
KLEINMAN, ARTHUR M.
   1973   "Medicine's Symbolic Reality, On a Central Problem in the Philosophy of Medicine," *Inquiry* 16: 206-13.
   1974   "Social, Cultural and Historical Themes in the Study of Medicine in Chinese Societies: Problems and Prospects for the Comparative Study of Medicine and Psychiatry," in Arthur Kleinman, Peter Kunstadter, E. Russel Alexander, and James L. Gale, eds., *Medicine in Chinese Cultures* (Washington, D.C.: Department of Health, Education and Welfare): 589-643.
   1977   "Lessons from a Clinical Approach to Medical Anthropology Research," *Medical Anthropology Newsletter* 8: 11-16.
   1978a   "Concepts and a Model for the Comparison of Medical Systems as Cultural Systems," *Social Science and Medicine* 12: 85-93.
   1978b   "International Health Care Planning from an Ethnomedical Perspective: Critique and Recommendations for Change," *Medical Anthropology* 2: 71-94.
   1978c   "Rethinking the Social and Cultural Context of Psychopathology and Psychiatric Care," in Theo C. Manschreck and Arthur M. Kleinman, eds., *Renewal in Psychiatry* (New York: John Wiley and Sons): 97-138.
KLUCKHOHN, CLYDE, and HENRY A. MURRAY, eds.
   1948   *Personality in Nature, Society and Culture* (New York: Knopf).

KOHUT, HEINZ
  1971   *Analysis of Self: A Systematic Approach to the Psychoanalytic Treatment of Narcissistic Personality Disorders* (New York: International Universities Press).
KORBIN, JILL
  1976   "Anthropological Contributions to the Study of Child Abuse," (manuscript).
KROEBER, A. L., and C. KLUCKHOHN
  1952   *Culture: A Critical Review of Concepts and Definitions* (Cambridge, MA: Papers of the Peabody Museum No. 47).
KULP, D. H., II
  1925   *Country Life in South China: The Sociology of Familism: Volume I. Phenix Village, Kwantung, China* (New York: Columbia University Teachers College, Bureau of Publications).
KUNG, S. W.
  1962   *Chinese in American Life* (Seattle: University of Washington Press).
KUNKEL, PETER, and SARA SUE KENNARD
  1971   *Spout Spring: A Black Community* (New York: Random House).
KUPFERER, HARRIET J.
  1979   "A Case of Sanctioned Drinking: The Rupert's House Cree," *Anthropological Quarterly* 52: 198-203.
LANDES, RUTH
  1965   *Culture in American Education: Anthropological Approaches to Minority and Dominant Groups in the Schools* (New York: John Wiley and Sons).
LANGNESS, L. L.
  1965   *The Life History in Anthropological Science* (New York: Holt).
LAPUZ, L. V.
  1973   *A Study of Psychopathology* (Quezon City: University of the Philippines Press).
LEACH, EDMUND
  1968   *A Runaway World?* (New York: Oxford University Press).
LEE, JUDITH A. B.
  1980   "The Helping Professional's Use of Language in Describing the Poor," *American Journal of Orthopsychiatry* 50: 580-84.
LEE, R. H.
  1960   *The Chinese in the United States of America* (New York: Oxford University Press).
LEININGER, MADELEINE
  1973   "Witchcraft Practices and Psychocultural Therapy with Urban U.S. Families," *Human Organization* 32: 73-83.
  1978   *Transcultural Nursing: Concepts, Theories, and Practices* (New York: John Wiley and Sons).
LEMERT, E. M.
  1954   *Alcohol and the Northwest Coast Indians* (Berkeley: University of California Press).
LEVINE, LAWRENCE W.
  1977   *Black Culture and Black Consciousness* (Oxford: Oxford University Press).
LeVINE, ROBERT A.
  1973   *Culture, Behavior, and Personality* (Chicago: Aldine).
LEVITAN, SAR, WILLIAM B. JOHNSTON, and ROBERT TAGGART
  1975   *Minorities in the United States: Problems, Progress, and Prospects* (Washington, D.C.: Public Affairs Press).
LEVY, CHARLES C.
  1976   *Social Work Ethics* (New York: Human Sciences Press).
  1977   "Values in Social Work Education," in Boyd E. Oviatt, ed., *Values in Social Work Education: Cliché or Reality?* (University of Utah: Graduate School of Social Work): 1-9.
LEVY, JERROLD E., and STEPHEN J. KUNITZ
  1974   *Indian Drinking, Navajo Practices and Anglo-American Theories* (New York: John Wiley and Sons).

LEWIN, ELLEN
    1979   "The Nobility of Suffering: Illness and Misfortune among Latin American Immigrant Women," *Anthropological Quarterly* 52: 152-58.
LEWIS, DAVID LEVERING
    1981   *When Harlem was in Vogue* (New York: Alfred A. Knopf).
LEWIS, DIANE K.
    1975   "The Black Family: Socialization and Sex Roles," *Phylon* 36: 221-37.
LEWIS, OSCAR
    1965   *La Vida: A Puerto Rican Family in the Culture of Poverty/San Juan and New York* (New York: Random House).
LIDE, PAULINE D.
    1971   "Dialogue on Racism, A Prologue to Action?" *Social Casework* 52: 432-37.
LIEBOW, ELLIOT
    1967   *Tally's Corner* (Boston: Little, Brown).
LIN, T., and M. C. LIN
    1978   "Service Delivery Issues in Asian North American Communities," *American Journal of Psychiatry* 135: 454-56.
LIN, T., K. TARDIFF, G. DONETZ, and W. GORESKY
    1978   "Ethnicity and Patterns of Help Seeking," *Culture, Medicine and Psychiatry* 2: 3-13.
LINTON, R.
    1972   "The Distinctive Aspects of Acculturation," in D. Walker, ed., *The Emergent Native Americans: A Reader in Culture Contact* (Boston: Little, Brown): 6-19.
LOCKLEAR, HERBERT H.
    1977   "American Indian Alcoholism: Program for Treatment," *Social Work* 22: 202-07.
LOFLAND, JOHN
    1971   *Analyzing Social Settings* (Belmont, CA: Wadsworth).
LOTT, J. T.
    1976   "Migration of a Mentality: The Philipino Community," *Social Casework* 57: 165-72.
LUBOVE, ROY
    1969   *The Professional Altruist: The Emergence of Social Work as a Career, 1880-1930* (New York: Atheneum).
LYMAN, STANFORD M.
    1970   *The Asian in the West* (Desert Research Institute, University of Nevada System, Social Science and Humanities Publication No. 4).
    1974   *Chinese Americans* (New York: Random House).
LYNCH, F., ed.
    1964   *Four Readings on Philippine Values* (Quezon City: Ateneo de Manila University Press).
MacANDREW, CRAIG, and ROBERT B. EDGERTON
    1969   *Drunken Comportment* (Chicago: Aldine).
MADSEN, WILLIAM
    1964   *Mexican-Americans of South Texas* (New York: Holt, Rinehart and Winston).
MALUCCIO, ANTHONY N.
    1979   *Learning from Clients, Interpersonal Helping as Viewed by Clients and Social Workers* (New York: The Free Press).
MANDELBAUM, DAVID G., ed.
    1949   *Language, Culture and Personality, Selected Writings of Edward Sapir* (Berkeley: University of California Press).
    1965   "Alcohol and Culture," *Current Anthropology* 6: 281-94.
MARCOS, L. R., M. ALPERT, L. URCUYO, and M. KESSELMAN
    1976   "The Effect of Interview Language on the Evaluation of Psychopathology in Spanish-American Schizophrenic Patients," *Journal of Psychiatry* 133: 1275-78.
MARTIN, ELMER P., and JOANNE MITCHELL MARTIN
    1978   *The Black Extended Family* (Chicago: University of Chicago Press).
MARTINEZ, CERVANDO, and HARRY W. MARTIN
    1966   "Folk Diseases among Urban Mexican-Americans: Etiology, Symptoms and Treatment," *Journal of the American Medical Association* 196: 147-50.

MASS, A. I.
    1976   "Asians as Individuals: The Japanese Community," *Social Casework* 57: 160-64.
MASUDA, R. N.
    1937   "The Japanese Tanomoshi," *Social Processes in Hawaii* 3: 16-19.
MAYES, NATHANIEL H.
    1978   "Teacher Training for Cultural Awareness," in David S. Hoopes, Paul B. Peder-
            sen, and George Renwick, eds., *Overview of Intercultural Education, Training
            and Research, Volume II: Education and Training* (Washington, D.C.: Society
            for Intercultural Education, Training and Research): 35-44.
McADOO, HARRIETTE
    1977   "Family Therapy in the Black Community," *American Journal of Orthopsy-
            chiatry* 47: 75-79.
    1979   "Black Kinship," *Psychology Today* (May), 12: 64ff.
McFEE, MALCOLM
    1968   "The 150% Man, a Product of Blackfeet Acculturation," *American Anthro-
            pologist* 70: 1096-1103.
McLEOD, DONNA L., and HENRY J. MEYER
    1967   "A Study of the Values of Social Workers," in E. J. Thomas, ed., *Behavioral
            Science for Social Workers* (New York: Collier-Macmillan): 401-16.
McWILLIAMS, CAREY
    1968   *North from Mexico: The Spanish Speaking People of the United States* (New
            York: Green Wood Press).
MEAD, MARGARET
    1978   *Letters from the Field: 1925-1975* (New York: Harper and Row).
MEIER, M. S., and F. RIVERA
    1972   *The Chicanos: A History of Mexican Americans* (New York: Hill and Wang).
MELENDY, H. B.
    1972   *The Oriental Americans* (New York: Hippocrene Books).
MILLER, N.
    1978   *Utilization of Services for the Developmentally Disabled by American Indian
            Families in Los Angeles* (Ann Arbor: University Microfilms #7820261).
    1980   "Cultural Beliefs and Institutional Barriers: Issues in Service Utilization among
            Urban Indians," in J. Karkalits, ed., *Proceedings, Health and Education Systems:
            Coordinating Social Work Services for Handicapped Children* (Washington, D.C.:
            MCH Training Project #2031, PHS/HSA, Department of Health and Human
            Resources): 47-60.
MITCHELL, J. CLYDE, ed.
    1969   *Social Networks in Urban Situations* (Manchester: Manchester University Press).
MONTERO, DARRELL
    1979   "Vietnamese Refugees in America: Toward a Theory of Spontaneous Inter-
            national Migration," *International Migration Review* 13: 624-48.
MONTIEL, MIGUEL
    1970   "The Social Science Myth of the Mexican American," *El Grito* 3: 56-63.
MOORE, JOAN W., and ALFREDO CUELLAR
    1970   *Mexican Americans* (Englewood Cliffs, NJ: Prentice-Hall).
MORALES, A.
    1971   "Distinguishing Psychodynamic Factors from Cultural Factors in the Treatment
            of the Spanish-Speaking Patient," in N. Wagner and M. Haug, eds., *Chicanos:
            Social and Psychological Perspectives* (St. Louis: Mosby): 279-80.
MORALES, ROYAL F.
    1976   *Asian and Pacific American Curriculum on Social Work Education* (Los Angeles:
            Asian American Community Mental Health Training Center).
MOYNIHAN, DANIEL P.
    1965   *The Negro Family: The Case for National Action* (Washington, D.C.: Depart-
            ment of Labor).
MUNOZ, RICARDO F., LONNIE R. SNOWDEN, and JAMES G. KELLY
    1979   "The Process of Implementing Community Based Research," in Ricardo F.
            Munoz, Lonnie R. Snowden, and James G. Kelly, eds., *Social and Psychological
            Research in Community Settings* (San Francisco: Jossey-Bass Publishers): 14-29.

MURASE, KENJI
    1977   "Minorities: Asian Americans," in *Encyclopedia of Social Work* (Washington, D.C.: National Association of Social Workers): 953-60.
MURASE, T., and F. JOHNSON
    1974   "Naikan, Morita and Western Psychotherapy," *Archives of General Psychiatry* 31: 121-28.
NALL, FRANK C., and JOSEPH SPEILBERG
    1967   "Social and Cultural Factors in the Responses of Mexican-Americans to Medical Treatment," *Journal of Health and Social Behavior* 8: 299-308.
NATIONAL ASSOCIATION OF SOCIAL WORKERS
    1980   Code of Ethics (New York: National Association of Social Workers).
NEE, VICTOR G., and BRETT de BARY NEE
    1974   *Longtime Californ': A Documentary Study of American Chinatown* (Boston: Houghton Mifflin).
NELSON, B.
    1965   "The Psychoanalyst as Mediator and Double Agent," *Psychoanalysis Review* 53: 375-90.
NEUTRA, R., J. LEVY, and D. PARKER
    1977   "Cultural Expectations versus Reality in Navaho Seizure Patterns and Sick Roles," *Culture, Medicine and Psychiatry* 1: 225-75.
NORBECK, E., and G. A. DeVOS
    1972   "Culture and Personality: The Japanese," in F. L. K. Hsu, ed., *Psychological Anthropology in the Behavioral Sciences* (Cambridge, MA: Schenkman): 21-70.
NORTON, DOLORES G., et al.
    1978   *The Dual Perspective* (New York: Council on Social Work Education).
NYDEGGER, W., and C. NYDEGGER
    1966   *Tarong: An Ilocos Barrio in the Philippines* (New York: John Wiley and Sons).
O'NELL, CARL W.
    1976   "An Investigation of Reported "Fright" as a Factor in the Etiology of Susto, 'Magical Fright'," *Ethos* 3: 41-63.
ONODA, L.
    1977   "Neurotic-Stable Tendencies among Japanese-American Sansei and Caucasian Students," *Journal of Non-White Concerns in Personnel and Guidance* 5: 180-85.
OPLER, MORRIS E.
    1945   "Themes as Dynamic Forces in Culture," *American Journal of Sociology* 51: 198-206.
OWAN, TOM
    1975   "Asian Americans: A Case of Benighted Neglect and the Bilingual-Bicultural Service Delivery Implications to the Spanish Speaking Americans and Native Americans" (paper presented at the National Conference of Social Welfare, San Francisco).
PADILLA, E. R., and A. M. PADILLA, eds.
    1977   *Transcultural Psychiatry: An Hispanic Perspective* (Los Angeles: University of California, Spanish Speaking Mental Health Research Center).
PADILLA, A. M., and R. A. RUIZ
    1973   *Latino Mental Health: A Review of the Literature* (Washington, D.C.: Government Printing Office).
PADILLA, A. M., R. A. RUIZ, and A. ALVAREZ
    1975   "Community Mental Health Services for the Spanish Speaking/Surnamed Population," *American Psychologist* 30: 892-905.
PARKE, ROSS D., and CANDACE WHITMER COLLMER
    1975   *Child Abuse: An Interdisciplinary Analysis* (Chicago: University of Chicago Press).
PEDERSEN, PAUL
    1976   "The Field of Intercultural Counseling," in Paul Pedersen, Walter J. Lonner, and Juris G. Draguns, eds., *Counseling across Cultures* (Honolulu: University of Hawaii Press): 17-41.
PEDERSEN, PAUL, WALTER J. LONNER, and JURIS G. DRAGUNS, eds.
    1976   *Counseling across Cultures* (Honolulu: University Press of Hawaii).

PELTO, PERTTI J., and GRETEL H. PELTO
  1970   *Anthropological Research: The Structure of Inquiry* (New York: Harper and Row).
  1973   "Ethnography: The Fieldwork Enterprise," in John J. Honigmann, ed., *Handbook of Social and Cultural Anthropology* (Chicago: Rand McNally and Company): 241-88.
  1975   "Intra-Cultural Diversity: Some Theoretical Issues," *American Ethnologist* 2: 1-18.
  1978   *Anthropological Research: The Structure of Inquiry*, 2d ed. (Cambridge: Cambridge University Press).
PETERSEN, WILLIAM
  1971   *Japanese Americans* (New York: Random House).
PETERSON, ROBERTA
  1978   *The Elder Philipino* (San Diego: Center on Aging, San Diego State University).
PHILIPS, SUSAN V.
  1974   "Warm Springs 'Indian Time'," in Richard Bauman and Joel Sherzer, eds., *Explorations in the Ethnography of Speaking* (New York: Cambridge University Press): 92-109.
PIKE, KENNETH
  1954   *Language in Relation to a Unified Theory of the Structure of Human Behavior* (Glendale, CA: Summer Institute of Linguistics).
PINCUS, ALLEN, and ANNE MINAHAN
  1973   *Social Work Practice: Model and Method* (Itasca, IL: F. E. Peacock Publishers).
PITTMAN, D. J., and C. R. SNYDER, eds.
  1962   *Society, Culture and Drinking Patterns* (New York: John Wiley and Sons).
PRESIDENT'S COMMISSION ON MENTAL HEALTH
  1978   *Report on Mental Health of Hispanic Americans* (Washington, D.C.: Government Printing Office).
PRICE, JOHN A.
  1972   "The Migration and Adaptation of American Indians to Los Angeles," in H. Bahr, B. Chadwick, and R. Day, eds., *Native Americans Today: Sociological Perspectives* (New York: Harper and Row): 428-39.
  1975   "An Applied Analysis of North American Indian Drinking Patterns," *Human Organization* 34: 17-26.
RAHE, R. H., et al.
  1976   "Psychiatric Consultation in a Vietnamese Refugee Camp," *American Journal of Psychiatry* 135: 185-90.
RAINWATER, LEE
  1970   *Behind Ghetto Walls* (Chicago: Aldine).
RAINWATER, LEE, and WILLIAM YANCEY, eds.
  1967   *The Moynihan Report and the Politics of Controversy* (Cambridge: MIT Press).
RAMIREZ, MANUEL, and ALFREDO CASTANEDA
  1974   *Cultural Democracy: Bicognitive Development, and Education* (New York: Academic Press).
RED HORSE, JOHN, et al.
  1978   "Family Behavior of Urban American Indians," *Social Casework* 59: 67-72.
RICHAN, WILLIAM C., and ALLEN R. MENDELSOHN
  1973   *Social Work: The Unloved Profession* (New York: New View Points).
RITTER, E., H. RITTER, and S. SPECTOR
  1965   *Our Oriental Americans* (New York: McGraw-Hill).
RODRIGUEZ, RICHARD
  1974   "Going Home: The New American Scholarship Boy," *American Scholar* 44: 15-28.
ROMANO, OCTAVIO
  1968   "The Anthropology and Sociology of Mexican Americans," *El Grito* 2: 13-26.
ROSS, E. LAMAR, ed.
  1978   *Interethnic Communication* (Athens: University of Georgia Press).
RUBEL, ARTHUR J.
  1960   "Concepts of Disease in Mexican-American Culture," *American Anthropologist* 62: 795-814.

1964   "The Epidemiology of a Folk Illness: Susto in Hispanic America," *Ethnology* 3: 268-83.

1966   *Across the Tracks: Mexican-Americans in a Texas City* (Austin: University of Texas Press).

RUIZ, JULIETTE, ed.
1973   *Chicano Task Force Report* (New York: Council on Social Work Education).

RUIZ, RAMON E., ed.
1963   *The Mexican War: Was It Manifest Destiny?* (New York: Holt, Rinehart and Winston).

RULE, JAMES B.
1978   *Insight and Social Betterment, A Preface to Applied Social Science* (New York: Oxford University Press).

RYAN, WILLIAM
1969   *Blaming the Victim* (New York: Pantheon Press).

SANDAY, PEGGY REEVES, ed.
1976   *Anthropology and the Public Interest* (New York: Academic Press).

SARANA, GOPALA
1975   *The Methodology of Anthropological Comparisons,* Viking Fund Publications in Anthropology #53 (Tucson: University of Arizona Press).

SAUNDERS, LYLE
1954   *Cultural Difference and Medical Care: The Case of the Spanish Speaking People of the Southwest* (New York: Russell Sage Foundation).

1972   "Healing Ways in the Spanish Southwest," in Gartly Jaco, ed., *Patients, Physicians and Illness* (Glencoe, IL: The Free Press): 189-206.

SCANZONI, JOHN N.
1977   *The Black Family in Modern Society* (Chicago: University of Chicago Press).

SCHENSUL, STEPHEN L., and JEAN J. SCHENSUL
1978   "Advocacy and Applied Anthropology," in George H. Weber and George J. McCall, eds., *Social Scientists as Advocates* (Beverly Hills, CA: Sage): 121-66.

SCHMIDT, STEFFEN W., LAURA GUASTI, CARL H. LANDE, and JAMES C. SCOTT, eds.
1977   *Friends, Followers, and Factions: A Reader in Political Clientelism* (Berkeley: University of California Press).

SCHULMAN, SAM, and ANNE M. SMITH
1963   "The Concept of 'Health' among Spanish Speaking Villagers of New Mexico," *Journal of Health and Human Behavior* 4: 226-34.

SENATE IMMIGRATION COMMISSION
1911   "Report," (Washington, D.C.) 23: 151-60.

SHANNON, BARBARA E.
1970   "Implications of White Racism for Social Work Practice," *Social Casework* 51: 270-76.

SHORE, JAMES H., and WILLIAM M. NICHOLLS
1975   "Indian Children and Tribal Group Homes: A New Interpretation of the Whipper Man," *American Journal of Psychology* 132: 454-56.

SHORE, JAMES H., and BILLIE VON FUMETTI
1972   "Three Alcohol Programs for American Indians," *American Journal of Psychiatry* 128: 134-38.

SIMMONS, LEONARD C.
1963   " 'Jim Crow': Implications for Social Work," *Social Work* 8: 24-30.

SINGLETON, JOHN
1977   "Education and Ethnicity," *Comparative Education Review* 21: 329-44.

SNOW, LOUDELL F.
1973   " 'I Was Born Just Exactly with the Gift,' an Interview with a Voodo Practitioner," *Journal of American Folklore* 86: 272-81.

1974   "Folk Medical Beliefs and Their Implications for Care of Patients," *Annals of Internal Medicine* 81: 82-96.

1977   "Popular Medicine in a Black Neighborhood," in Edward H. Spicer, ed., *Ethnic Medicine in the Southwest* (Tucson: University of Arizona Press): 19-95.

1978   "Sorcerers, Saints, and Charlatans: Black Folk Healers in Urban America," *Culture, Medicine and Psychiatry* 2: 69-106.

SOCIAL CASEWORK
    1964   "Editorial Notes: Race Relations in Social Work," *Social Casework* 45: 155.
SOLOMON, BARBARA B.
    1976   *Black Empowerment: Social Work in Oppressed Communities* (New York: Columbia University Press).
SOTOMAYOR, MARTA
    1977   "Language, Culture and Ethnicity in Developing Self-Concept," *Social Casework* 58: 195-203.
SOUFLEE, FREDERICO
    1977   "Social Work: The Acquiescing Profession," *Social Work* 22: 419-21.
SPANG, ALONZO
    1970   "Eight Problems in Indian Education," *Journal of American-Indian Education* 10: 1-4.
SPRADLEY, JAMES P.
    1970   *You Owe Yourself a Drunk: An Ethnography of Urban Nomads* (Boston: Little, Brown).
    1972   *Culture and Cognition* (San Francisco: Chandler Publishing Co.).
    1979   *The Ethnographic Interview* (New York: Holt, Rinehart and Winston).
SPRADLEY, JAMES P., and DAVID W. McCURDY
    1972   *The Cultural Experience* (Chicago: Science Research Associates).
    1975   *Anthropology: The Cultural Perspective* (New York: John Wiley and Sons).
STACK, CAROL B.
    1970   "The Kindred of Viola Jackson: Residence and Family Organization of an Urban Black Family," in N. E. Whitten and John F. Szwed, eds., *Afro-American Anthropology: Contemporary Perspectives* (New York: The Free Press): 303-12.
    1975   *All Our Kin: Strategies for Survival in the Black Community* (New York: Harper and Row).
STAPLES, ROBERT
    1971   "Toward a Sociology of the Black Family: A Theoretical and Methodological Assessment," *Journal of Marriage and the Family* 33: 119-35.
    1976   *Introduction to Black Sociology* (New York: McGraw-Hill).
STATHAM, DAPHNE
    1978   *Radicals in Social Work* (London: Routledge and Kegan Paul).
STEELE, CHARLES
    1973   *American Indians and Urban Life: A Community Study* (Ann Arbor, MI: University Microfilms #7311959).
STEWARD, JULIAN H., et al.
    1956   *The People of Puerto Rico* (Urbana: University of Illinois Press).
STEWART, E. C., J. DANIELIAN, and R. J. FESTES
    1969   *Simulating Intercultural Communication through Role Playing* (Alexandria, VA: Human Resources Research Organization).
SUE, D. W., and KIRK, B. A.
    1972   "Psychological Characteristics of Chinese American Students," *Journal of Counseling Psychology* 19: 471-78.
SUE, STANLEY, and HERMAN McKINNEY
    1975   "Asian Americans in the Community Mental Health Care System," *American Journal of Orthopsychiatry* 45: 111-18.
SUNDBERG, NORMAN D.
    1976   "Toward Research Evaluating Intercultural Counseling," in Paul Pedersen, Walter J. Lonner, and Juris G. Draguns, eds., *Counseling across Cultures* (Honolulu: University of Hawaii Press): 139-69.
SUNG, B. L.
    1967   *Mountain of Gold: The Study of the Chinese in America* (New York: Macmillan).
TAFT, RONALD
    1977   "Coping with Unfamiliar Cultures," in N. Warren, ed., *Studies in Cross-Cultural Psychology* (New York: Academic Press): 121-53.
TAUEBER, I.
    1958   *The Population of Japan* (Princeton: Princeton University Press).

TenHOUTON, WARREN D.
    1970   "The Black Family: Myth and Reality," *Psychiatry* 33: 145-73.
THOMAS, ALEXANDER, and SAMUEL SILLEN
    1972   *Racism and Psychiatry* (New York: Brunner-Mazel).
TIJERINA, ANDRES, ed.
    1978   *Human Services for Mexican American Children* (Austin: University of Texas Center for Social Work Research).
TORRES-GIL, F. M.
    1972   "Los Ancianos de la Raza: A Beginning Framework for Research Analysis and Policy" (Masters thesis, Brandeis University).
    1978   "Age, Health, and Culture: An Examination of Health among Spanish Speaking Elderly," in Miguel Montiel, ed., *Hispanic Families* (Washington, D.C.: National Coalition of Hispanic Mental Health Organizations): 83-102.
TORREY, E. F.
    1970   "The Irrelevancy of Traditional Mental Health Services for Urban Mexican Americans" (paper presented at the American Orthopsychiatry Association, San Francisco).
TOWNSEND, JOHN MARSHALL
    1978   *Cultural Conceptions and Mental Illness* (Chicago: University of Chicago Press).
TRIANDIS, HARRY C.
    1972   "An Approach to the Analysis of Subjective Culture," in William P. Lebra, ed., *Transcultural Research in Mental Health* (Honolulu: University of Hawaii Press): 248-49.
TRUAX, CHARLES B., and KEVIN M. MITCHELL
    1971   "Research on Certain Therapist Interpersonal Skills in Relation to Process and Outcome," in Allen Bergin and Sol Garfield, eds., *Handbook of Psychotherapy and Behavior Change* (New York: John Wiley and Son): 299-344.
TSENG, W. S., and J. F. McDERMOTT
    1975   "Psychotherapy: Historical Roots, Universal Elements and Cultural Variations," *American Journal of Psychiatry* 132: 378-84.
TUCK, RUTH D.
    1943   "Behind the Zoot-Suit Riots," *Survey Graphics* (August), 32: 313-16.
TURNER, R. H., and SAMUEL SURACE
    1956   "Zoot-Suiters and Mexicans: Symbols in Crowd Behavior," *American Journal of Sociology* 62: 14-20.
VALLE, RAMON, and LYDIA MENDOZA
    1978   *The Elder Latino* (San Diego: Center on Aging, San Diego State University).
VAN WILLIGEN, JOHN
    1979   *Anthropology in Use* (Pleasantville, NY: Redgrave Publishing Co.).
VONTRESS, CLEMMONT E.
    1976   "Racial and Ethnic Barriers in Counseling," in Paul Pedersen, Walter J. Lonner, and Juris G. Draguns, eds., *Counseling across Cultures* (Honolulu: University of Hawaii Press): 42-64.
VUONG, THUY G.
    1976   *Getting to Know the Vietnamese and Their Culture* (New York: Frederick Ungar).
WALLACE, ANTHONY F. C.
    1970   *Culture and Personality* (New York: Random House).
WATANABE, T. M.
    1977   *The Japanese American Community Study* (Seattle: University of Washington Department of Anthropology).
WAX, ROSALIE H., and ROBERT K. THOMAS
    1961   "American Indians and White People," *Phylon* 22: 305-17.
WEAVER, JERRY L.
    1977   *National Health Policy and the Underserved* (St. Louis: C. V. Mosby).
WEEKS, WILLIAM H., PAUL B. PEDERSEN, and RICHARD W. BRISLIN, eds.
    1977   *A Manual of Structured Experiences for Cross-Cultural Learning* (Washington, D.C.: Society for Intercultural Education, Training and Research).

WELLMAN, DAVID T.
    1977   *Portraits of White Racism* (London: Cambridge University Press).
WHITE, L., and B. CHADWICK
    1972   "Urban Residence, Assimilation and Identity of the Spokane Indian," in H. Bahr, B. Chadwick, and R. Day, eds., *Native Americans Today: Sociological Perspectives* (New York: Harper and Row): 239-49.
WHITTEN, NORMAN E.
    1962   "Contemporary Patterns of Malign Occultism among Negroes in North Carolina," *Journal of American Folklore* 75: 311-25.
WILSON, PETER J.
    1974   *Oscar, an Inquiry into the Nature of Sanity* (New York: Random House).
WINTROB, R. M.
    1973   "The Influence of Others: Witchcraft and Rootwork as Explanations of Behavior Disturbances," *Journal of Nervous and Mental Disorders* 156: 318-26.
    1977   "Belief and Behavior: Cultural Factors in the Recognition and Treatment of Mental Illness," in Edward F. Foulks et al., eds., *Current Perspectives in Cultural Psychiatry* (New York: John Wiley and Sons): 103-12.
WISE, F., and N. MILLER
    1981   "The Mental Health of the American Indian Child," in G. Powell, A. Morales, and J. Yamamoto, eds., *The Psycho-Social Development of Minority Group Children* (New York: Brunner-Mazel): 47-59.
WOLCOTT, HARRY
    1975   "Criteria for an Ethnographic Approach to Research in Schools," *Human Organization* 34: 111-27.
WOLF, ERIC R.
    1966a   "Kinship, Friendship and Patron-Client Relations in Complex Societies," in Michael Banton, ed., *The Social Anthropology of Complex Societies* (New York: Praeger): 1-22.
    1966b   *Peasants* (Englewood Cliffs, NJ: Prentice-Hall).
YAMIGIWA, J.
    1965   "Language as an Expression of Japanese Culture," in R. K. Beardsley and J. W. Hall, eds., *Twelve Doors to Japan* (New York: McGraw-Hill): 186-221.
YANAGISAKO, S. J.
    1975   "Two Processes of Change in Japanese-American Kinship," *Journal of Anthropological Research* 31: 196-224.
YETMAN, NORMAN, and C. HOY STEELE
    1971   *Majority and Minority: The Dynamics of Racial and Ethnic Relations* (Boston: Allyn and Bacon).
YOUNGMAN, GERALDINE, and MARGARET SADONGEI
    1974   "Counseling the American Indian Child," *Elementary School Guidance and Counseling* 8: 272-77.
ZOLA, I. K.
    1972   "The Concept of Trouble and Sources of Medical Assistance," *Social Science and Medicine* 6: 673-80.

INDEX